THE EXPULSION OF JEWS FROM COMMUNIST POLAND

THE MODERN JEWISH EXPERIENCE

Deborah Dash Moore and Marsha L. Rozenblit, *editors*
Paula Hyman, *founding coeditor*

THE EXPULSION OF JEWS FROM COMMUNIST POLAND

Memory Wars and Homeland Anxieties

Anat Plocker

INDIANA UNIVERSITY PRESS

This book is a publication of

Indiana University Press
Office of Scholarly Publishing
Herman B Wells Library 350
1320 East 10th Street
Bloomington, Indiana 47405 USA

iupress.org

Manufactured in the United States of America

First printing 2022

Library of Congress Cataloging-in-Publication Data

Names: Plocker, Anat, author.
Title: The expulsion of Jews from communist Poland : memory wars and
homeland anxieties / Anat Plocker.
Description: Bloomington : Indiana University Press, 2022. | Series: Modern
Jewish experience | Includes bibliographical references and index.
Identifiers: LCCN 2021028665 (print) | LCCN 2021028666 (ebook) | ISBN
9780253058652 (paperback) | ISBN 9780253058669 (hardback) | ISBN
9780253058645 (ebook)
Subjects: LCSH: Jews—Poland—History—20th century. |
Poland—History—March Events, 1968. |
Antisemitism—Poland—History—20th century. | Poland—Politics and
government—1945-1980. | Communism—Poland—History—20th century.
Classification: LCC DS134.55 .P57 2022 (print) | LCC DS134.55 (ebook) |
DDC 943.8/004924—dc23
LC record available at https://lccn.loc.gov/2021028665
LC ebook record available at https://lccn.loc.gov/2021028666

I dedicate this book to the memory of my grandparents,
Mania and Józef (Harry) Goldkorn and
Renia and Józef Plocker.

CONTENTS

Preface ix

List of Abbreviations xv

Introduction *1*

1 From Inclusion to Exclusion *19*

2 Not to Be Trusted *36*

3 The Encyclopedia and "The Falsification of History" *65*

4 We, the Students *93*

5 "To Warsaw Students" *122*

6 "Zionism Is Not a Danger to Poland" *160*

Conclusion *197*

Index 209

PREFACE

MICHAEL SFARD, A WELL-KNOWN ISRAELI HUMAN RIGHTS LAWYER, and his law firm have litigated in the last fifteen years hundreds of cases pertaining to the everyday lives of Palestinians living in the territories occupied by Israel. Michael is the grandson of the Polish Jewish poet David Sfard and the film scholar Regina Dreyer-Sfard, on his father's side, and of the author Janina Bauman and the renowned sociologist Zygmunt Bauman, on his mother's, all of whom the Polish state forced out of Poland following the March 1968 events, along with Michael's parents, Anna and Leon. Their family story is told in Janina Bauman's memoir of the period, *A Dream of Belonging* (1988). In 1968, Leon Sfard, a political activist at Warsaw University, was jailed for a few weeks for his involvement in the dissident student movement. Fifty years later, in 2018, Michael said in an interview for a British website, "It [his father's involvement in March 1968] undoubtedly had a very big impact on me. Our home was very political, and I grew up with the principle that you should do the moral thing, even at a cost."[1] In a 2009 article for the Israeli daily *Haaretz* entitled "Back to Warsaw 1968," Michael wrote:

> I saw the military prosecutor speaking with pathos about the need to keep him [Mohammed Khatib, one of the Palestinian leaders of the Bil'in protests] in custody, about his being a 'security risk.' Just like my father and his friends in Warsaw in 1968, when they organized demonstrations against the regime and for democracy. There, too, the authorities arrested the leaders of the protest in an effort to make them disappear. There, too, the arrests were made in the pre-dawn hours. There, too, there were police officers who made the arrests, secret service agents who carried out the interrogations, prosecutors who prosecuted and judges who judged. And there, too, each one was a small but essential cog in a huge machine whose purpose was the control and oppression of millions."

Michael concluded, "Warsaw 1968 is not like Bil'in in 2009, the conflict is different, the world is different, but there is something similar in all

---

1. *Fathom*, "'A Liberal Society and Respect for Human Rights Are Critically Important for the Well-Being of the Individual': An Interview with Michael Sfard," September 2018, http://fathomjournal .org/a-liberal-society-and-respect-for-human-rights-are-critically-important-for-the-well-being -of-the-individual-an-interview-with-michael-sfard/.

attempts to oppress human beings."[2] In his book *The Wall and the Gate*, Michael explains that he has taken up the Palestinian cause because Palestinians in the Israeli occupied territories have no citizenship status. In 1968, his parents and grandparents, for a short period, had no passports and no citizenship; the Polish communist government had issued them one-way travel documents and illegally stripped them of their citizenship. In many ways, this book explores the story of the Sfard/Bauman family, as they played important roles in the history of both the Jewish community and the Polish dissidents. It analyzes the process by which state authorities deprive citizens of their citizenship, how the "cogs in the machine" turn a minority into a "security threat" and force people out of their homeland. And it traces a story of the triumph of nationalism over citizenship rights and equality. Unlike Adam Michnik's assertion that the March events were a "dry pogrom," a story typical and at the same time unique to Jews, this book shows that the anti-Jewish campaign in 1968 is an integral part of the modern history of Europe and of nationalism.

The study of the March Events in Poland has been, for me, a personal and academic exploration, a family history as well as an intellectual journey. My family was also forced to leave in 1968: my mother, then a student at Warsaw University, my grandparents, and my teenage uncle all immigrated to Israel in 1968; my father and his family moved to Israel from Poland in 1957. My maternal grandparents, Józef and Mania, had been prewar communists who, according to family myth, met at a party function. They escaped to the Soviet Union in 1939, fleeing the German invasion, and as communists, they returned to Poland when the war ended. My grandfather, Józef Goldkorn, worked for the TSKŻ, the Social Cultural Association of Jews in Poland. He had risen to prominence in the Upper Silesia section, where he became head of the local TSKŻ. When they moved to Katowice in 1946, the Polish authorities in Upper Silesia were busy expelling ethnic Germans from the region, as part of the ongoing mass deportation of millions of Germans out of the newly acquired western territories of the state. Anti-Jewish violence also swept Poland at the time, as the state aimed for a "homogenous" Poland within its new borders. Twenty years later, my grandparents and their children moved to Warsaw, where my grandfather wrote for *Folks Sztyme*, the Yiddish-language daily, until the state forced him out of his job and his country as well.

---

2. Michael Sfard, "Back to Warsaw 1968," *Haaretz*, September 4, 2009, https://www.haaretz.com/1.546912.

A few years after I had begun working on this project, my uncle, Włodek Goldkorn, published in Italian (and later in Polish) a "literary memoir" of his childhood in Poland entitled *A Child in the Snow*. In it, he describes my grandparents' attachment to communist Poland: "Now . . . we are at home [u siebie]."[3] They felt that way despite the attacks on Jews in Poland after World War II. The new Poland, the socialist one, was nevertheless supposed to fulfill their "Dream of Belonging"; as Janina Bauman explained years later, she had indeed felt that she belonged to Polish culture as the daughter of acculturated and secular Polish Jews.[4] Her son-in-law, Leon Sfard, saw his identity differently: "I was a Jew and a Pole . . . both things, not one before the other."[5] In a world that places ethnic-national identity above all others, however, such dreams of belonging have little chance of coming true. Their Poland showed them the door.

I owe my existence perhaps to Władysław Gomułka, the first secretary of the Polish communist party (the Polish United Workers' Party), since he encouraged Jewish immigration to Israel throughout his reign and my parents met in a circle of Polish-speaking friends in Bat Yam, a city just south of Tel Aviv, in the late 1960s. In 1967, Gomułka went as far as to urge Jews to choose a homeland, rejecting the idea that Polish Jews could be just that, Poles and Jews, "not one before the other." For some, like Leon Sfard, this led to immigration to Israel, for "living in Sweden or America, or somewhere like that, would be like being a tourist for your entire life."[6] Israel made similar demands of Polish Jews, to be one or the other. Though Israel highly desired the arrival of the new immigrants, they received a rather cold welcome in their new homeland. Some Israelis wondered why they had stayed in Poland for so many years after the Holocaust, failing to shift their loyalty to Zionism until 1968. Several 1968 immigrants, including Janina and Zygmunt Bauman, Michael's grandparents, therefore left Israel within a few years. His parents, Anna and Leon, and his paternal grandparents chose to stay in Israel, as did my family. My parents built their lives in Israel, striving to become part of Israeli society, and my father, the Polish-speaking refugee, became a prominent journalist while my mother worked

3. Włodek Goldkorn, *Dziecko w śniegu* (Wołowiec: Wydawnictwo Czarne, 2018), 58.
4. Janina Bauman, "Living with Anti-Semitism," in *Imaginary Neighbors: Mediating Polish-Jewish Relations after the Holocaust*, ed. Dorota Glowacka and Joanna Zylinska (Lincoln: University of Nebraska Press, 2007), 64.
5. Piotr Osęka, *My Ludzie z Marca: Autoportret pokolenia '68* (Warsaw: ISP-PAN, Wydawnictwo Czarne, 2015), 325.
6. Osęka, *My Ludzie z Marca*, 327.

in the civil service. My uncle, Włodek Goldkorn, went on his own path, immigrating to Italy where he, too, became a journalist and an award-winning writer, publishing in Italian and Polish. Tragically, Janina Bauman could not belong in Israel either. In her words, "I left that country [Poland] in the distant past abandoning all my young hopes and passion. Now I belong nowhere. But perhaps to belong means to love and to be loved and this is all that truly matters."[7] After the fall of communism, when it became possible to go back to Poland, Janina Bauman still felt that she could not live in Poland. She feared that history would repeat itself and chose to continue her life of "not-belonging" in England: "That's why I can't return. Because I would have nowhere to run to if I ever heard that I was a stranger, that I was unwanted in my native country. And that is something I wouldn't be able to live with from day to day."[8]

This project has led me to live in a number of countries where I have experienced some of that feeling of "not belonging." I would like to thank family, friends, and colleagues who have helped me along the journey of this book. First, I thank my PhD adviser at Stanford University, Norman Naimark, who encouraged me to follow my intellectual curiosity and challenge received wisdom in the field. His support, trust, and guidance have been irreplaceable on the winding road to this book. At Stanford, I also wish to thank Katherine Jolluck, James Sheehan, and Steven Zipperstein for comments and suggestions at early stages of this project. My wonderful friends from my graduate school days at Stanford provided companionship, conversation, and support throughout those challenging years. They are Jelena Batinic, Kathryn Ciancia, James Ward, Tamara Venit-Shelton, and Daniel Halliday. Daniela Blei once called me her "academic spouse," and I could not thank her enough for years of brainstorming, discussion, and kvetching, as we have moved from graduate school into careers and parenthood. Her friendship has been invaluable to me. Dina Moyal is a dear friend and supportive colleague: together we went through two graduate programs and countless years of debate and late-night conversations on Eastern Europe and Soviet history. Special thanks also to Peder Roberts for the laughter, the fun, and the wonderful time spent together. Tamar Saguy, Anna Reiman (formerly Newheiser), and Anette Seidel Arpaci, excellent scholars and terrific friends, made my year of writing at Yale so much more enjoyable.

---

7. Janina Bauman, *A Dream of Belonging: My Years in Postwar Poland* (London: Virgo, 1988) 202.
8. Bauman, "Living with Anti-Semitism," 65.

Many friends and colleagues provided crucial help and support in Poland, where I conducted much of the archival research for this book. First, I thank Dariusz Stola for the many productive discussions and debates on March 1968 and for his careful reading of and suggestions on the manuscript. I am grateful to Jerzy Eisler and Paweł Ceranka for their generous help with archival research. I also thank the knowledgeable staff at the Archiwum Akt Nowych in Warsaw and at the Otwock branch of the Archiwum Państwowe. In Warsaw, I was fortunate to enjoy the friendship of Nili Amit and Maciej Kozłowski, Audrey Kichelewski, Michael Meng, and Marta Wróbel.

In Israel, Marcus Silber from the University of Haifa provided me an academic home for a few years, and I am grateful for his efforts and for our many conversations on Polish history. Arieh Kochavi and Yael Granot-Bein, also at the University of Haifa, created a welcome environment for me as well. A special thanks to Dan Diner, who started me on the long road from undergraduate student to published scholar and gave me a chance to publish my first article on 1968. I also owe a debt of gratitude to Igal Halfin, my first teacher on the history of communism and my adviser for my master's thesis, which dealt with the memory of the Holocaust in Stalinist Poland.

Krista Hegburg from the USHMM invited me to participate in two engaging and productive workshops, where I got to present and discuss my work at length in Washington, DC, and Shanghai. Jan Láníček, Hana Kubatova, and Jacob Labendz, whom I met in DC, provided valuable feedback on my project. A special thanks to Malgorzata Fidelis for her insightful comments on a late version of the manuscript and for her encouragement. I also thank Bożena Szaynok for her detailed and thoughtful notes on the text. The comments of the anonymous readers of the manuscript have also helped me improve it. I am very grateful to my editor at Indiana University Press, Dee Mortensen, for her relentless support, patience, and productive comments and for a wonderful and fruitful time presenting the manuscript together in Poland in 2019.

I am grateful to the Stanford University History Department for funding through the James Birdsall Weter Memorial Fund. The Center for Russian, East European & Eurasian Studies (CREEES) and the Taube Center for Jewish Studies at Stanford helped fund archival research in Poland. The Israeli Inter-University Academic Partnership in Russian and East European Studies and the Israeli Council for Higher Education funded further research in Poland and Israel, and the Adjunct Faculty Opportunity Fund at Stockton University provided funds for the completion of the manuscript. I would also like to thank the organizers of the conference, "Recovering Forgotten History: The Image of East-Central Europe in English-Language Academic and Text Books," for the opportunity to present and discuss the manuscript with scholars in Poland.

I thank my parents, Nelly and Sever Plocker, for their faith in me and in my work and for their unwavering support every step of the way and in every way. They pushed me to begin this project, curious about what I would find, and without their crucial help and insights through some of the more challenging times of research, moving, and writing, I could not have brought it to completion. I also thank my brother, Daniel, his wife, Lilach, and my dear nephews Shira and Alon for tolerating me through the more frustrating days of writing. My uncle Włodek Goldkorn also deserves my gratitude, as his work and our discussions on family history have inspired the more personal aspects of my project. On the long road to this book, I met Raz Segal, with whom I now share my life. His love, support, and constant encouragement have sustained me throughout. This work would not have seen the light of day without him. I hope that one day our daughter, Ella, would read this book and learn about her family, about their experiences and resilience as refugees and survivors, and about their search for belonging. Ella's endless curiosity, love, and light shine on my life every day.

ABBREVIATIONS

AAN—Archiwum Akt Nowych, Archives of New Records

AIPN—Archiwum Instytut Pamięci Narodowej, Archive of the Institute of National Remembrance

AK—Armia Krajow, Home Army

AL—Armia Ludowa, People's Army

CKŻP—Centralny Komitet Żydów w Polsce, the Central Committee of Jews in Poland

CPSSM—Commission for the Protection of Sites of Suffering and Martyrdom

FRG—Federal Republic of Germany

GDR—German Democratic Republic

JAC—Jewish Antifascist Committee

JDC—American Joint Distribution Committee

KPP—Komunistyczna Partia Polski, Communist Party of Poland

ORT—Organization for Rehabilitation through Training

PAP—Polish News Agency

PeKaO—Polska Kasa Opieki, Polish Aid Bank

PRL—Polska Rzeczpospolita Ludowa, People's Republic of Poland

PUWP—The Polish United Workers' Party, Polska Zjednoczona Partia Robotnicza

PWN—Państwowe Wydawnictwo Naukowe, National Scientific Publishers

TASS—Telegraph Agency of the Soviet Union

TSKŻ—Towarzystwo Społeczno-Kulturalne Żydów w Polsce, Social Cultural Association of Jews in Poland

WZO—World Zionist Organization

ZBoWiD—Związek Bojowników o Wolność i Demokrację, Society of Fighters for Freedom and Democracy

ZRWM—Związek Religijny Wyznania Mojżeszowego, Religious Union of the Jewish Faith

ŻTK—Żydowskie Towarzystwo Kultury w Polsce, Jewish Cultural Society

THE EXPULSION OF JEWS
FROM COMMUNIST POLAND

INTRODUCTION

IN JANUARY 2018, AN INTERNATIONAL SCANDAL ERUPTED AS the Polish parliament passed new legislation regulating the memory of World War II: publicly stating that Poles collaborated with German occupiers in the persecution and mass murder of Jews may lead to three years in jail or a fine. The law excludes academic and artistic contexts from retaliation. The Polish prime minister, Mateusz Morawiecki, defended the law, saying that it "protects the good name of Poland from slander" and that "the truth about World War II" must be safeguarded.[1] Similar memory laws have been passed in some of Poland's neighbors—Ukraine, Lithuania, and Latvia—in a bid to control the narrative of the war and to present the citizens of these countries as victims and rescuers who bravely resisted the Nazi occupation, silencing historical debates on questions of collaboration. The Polish prime minister held a press conference on the matter at the Ulma Family Museum of Poles Saving Jews in World War II in the small town of Markowa. The Ulmas, a Polish family, had hidden Jews during the war, and the Germans murdered them in March 1944 alongside the Jews they hid. The museum opened in March 2016 as part of the government's efforts to emphasize the role of Polish rescuers while rejecting new studies that drew attention to Polish participation in the persecution of Jews. The main exhibition in the museum presents the story of the Ulma family and the stories of other rescuers in the area. It does not, however, address the complexities of life in the Polish countryside during the German occupation, where Poles were victims, rescuers, and perpetrators all at the same time.[2] The museum's website explains, "The primary goal of the Museum is to show [the] heroic stance of the Poles who helped the Jews during German occupation, risking their

---

1. Anna Gorczyca, "Premier Mateusz Morawiecki w Markowej przekonywał zagranicznych dziennikarzy, że Polacy nie odpowiadają za Holocaust," in *Wyborcza Rzeszów*, 02.02.2008, https://rzeszow.wyborcza.pl/rzeszow/7,34962,22976085,premier-mateusz-morawiecki-w-markowej -przekonywal-zagranicznych.html.

2. Zofia Wóycicka, "Global Patterns, Local Interpretations: New Polish Museums Dedicated to the Rescue of Jews during the Holocaust," *Holocaust Studies: A Journal of Culture and History* 25, no. 3 (2019): 248–72. On the complexities, see, for example, Tomasz Frydel, "The Devil in Microhistory: The 'Hunt for Jews' as a Social Process, 1942–1945," in *Microhistories of the Holocaust*, ed. Claire Zalc and Tal Bruttmann (New York: Berghahn Books, 2016).

own lives and the lives of their families."[3] The choice of this location for the press conference on the memory legislation speaks for itself: the contemporary Polish government stresses the role of Poles as rescuers and victims and refuses to join the conversation on Polish collaboration, which it considers anti-Polish slander.

After some negotiations with the Israeli government, in late June 2018, the Polish prime minister announced that the law, despite being "just," would be amended because of pressure from "international interests." In return for amending the law, the Israeli prime minister, Benjamin Netanyahu, along with his Polish counterpart, Morawiecki, issued a joined statement. The declaration accepts the Polish narrative on the murder and rescue of Jews, highlighting Polish saviors and the Polish underground state's role in hiding Jews, and rejects "the actions aimed at blaming Poland or the Polish nation as a whole for the atrocities committed by the Nazis and their collaborators of different nations." It ends with a "rejection of anti-Polonism and other negative national stereotypes."[4]

This statement fulfills the aspirations of the very politicians who fifty years earlier, in 1968, succeeded in driving fifteen thousand Jews out of Poland.[5] They too rallied against "anti-Polonism" and sought to protect the good name of the nation. The rhetoric sounded by PiS, Prawo i Sprawiedliwość (Law and Justice), Morawiecki's party, and other right-wing figures during this affair is astoundingly similar to the rhetoric the communist government used against protesting students in March 1968. The language of contemporary Polish nationalism and its focus on the memory of World War II is closely related to the language of their predecessors, Polish nationalists who operated within the communist framework in the 1960s and 1970s. For instance, Polish rescue of Jews and the Righteous among the Nations are central themes in much of the 1967–68 propaganda. One of the key journalists of the 1968 press campaign, Ryszard Gontarz, claimed in a

3. Ulma Family Museum of Poles Saving Jews in World War II, accessed February 1, 2018, http://muzeumulmow.pl/en/museum/history-of-the-ulma-family/.
4. Official website of the prime minister of Poland, "Joint Declaration of Prime Ministers of the State of Israel and the Republic of Poland," June 27, 2018, https://www.premier.gov.pl/en/news/news/joint-declaration-of-prime-ministers-of-the-state-of-israel-and-the-republic-of-poland.html.
5. The number of emigrants is disputed. According to Dariusz Stola, who worked in the archives of the passport office, 15,000 Jews emigrated. According to others, the number is closer to 13,500. See Dariusz Stola, *Kraj bez wyjścia? Migracje z Polski, 1949–1989* (Warsaw: IPN & ISP PAN, 2010); Albert Stankowski, "Nowe spojrzenie na statystyki dotyczące emigracji Żydów z Polski po 1944 roku," in *Studia z historii Żydów w Polsce po 1945 roku*, ed. G. Berendt, A. Grabski, and A. Stankowski (Warsaw: Żydowski Instytut Historyczny, 2000), 139–51.

televised interview that millions rather than just thousands of Poles helped Jews during the Holocaust.[6] In one of his famous speeches from the time, First Secretary Władysław Gomułka, the head of the communist party from 1956, claimed that Jewish survivors from Poland owed their lives to Poles. In another striking example, in a January 2018 broadcast, a Polish radio right-wing personality called on those who object to the new memory legislation to pursue "Israeli citizenship,"[7] echoing very similar statements Gomułka made in 1967. In the words of the historian Brian Porter-Szűcs, First Secretary Gomułka "was grounded in the nationalist right."[8]

As this book shows, at the center of the battle between the communist government and the students in the late 1960s stood not only the issue of reforming communism and the generational struggle but also the question of the memory of World War II and the narration of the history of the war, with the communist party taking a Polish nationalist stance. In 1967–68, as today, the media focused on debates about concentration camps and the rescue of Jews during the Holocaust. During that period, the communist party aimed to make a Poland for Poles, defined in ethnic terms—a Poland where there would be only one point of view on the past. Today, the Polish government again rejects academic freedom and historical complexities, safeguarding instead a nationalist narrative of the past. On the eve of the fiftieth anniversary of the events described in this book, Prime Minister Morawiecki claimed that Poles and Poland were not responsible for the events because "Poland was under Russian control."[9] This book shows, by contrast, the extent to which the March 1968 anti-Zionist campaign was a Polish project carried out in the name of Poland's future.

This book tells the story of how, over the span of a year, from summer 1967, the communist party in Poland, which had maintained power since the end of World War II, persecuted and alienated its Jewish members, leading to their emigration. Key party members, acting out of a sense of insult to the Polish nation and demanding loyalty to the nation and its embodiment in the communist regime, worked successfully to eliminate Jewish

6. https://youtu.be/f11EqKmwWu4.
7. "Rafał Ziemkiewicz i Marcin Wolski żartują na antenie z „żydowskich obozów" 01.30.2018, in *Newsweek Polska*, https://www.newsweek.pl/polska/spoleczenstwo/ziemkiewicz-i-wolski-zartowali-o-zydowskich-obozow-smierci/mj8m463.
8. Brian Porter-Szűcs, *Poland in the Modern World: Beyond Martyrdom* (Wiley-Blackwell, 2014), 243.
9. The speech is available on YouTube: Mateusz Morawiecki podczas obchodów 50. rocznicy Marca '68 na Uniwersytecie Warszawskim, https://youtu.be/eDklsByZcQU.

presence in party and state institutions. Through the prism of the "anti-Zionist campaign," as the drive against the Jews is known in Poland, this book examines the relationship between ethnonational identity, communist ideology, and the memory of the Holocaust. I consider why in June 1967 the party turned against Polish Jews and why Poland's communist leader, Władysław Gomułka, following student unrest, chose to heed the call of certain party members to purge the Jews in the name of national security. I explore the mechanisms of "othering" in a national communist context and probe the meanings of anti-Jewish sentiments in the post-Holocaust period. National communism both emerged out of the official communist narrative of World War II and transformed it. The "ethnic turn" the communist party took in the 1960s—the growing importance of Polish national symbols and Polish ethnic identity—had not just influenced commemoration of the war but had stemmed from a key element in the identity of Poles as the primary victims of World War II. The communist party waged the campaign against Zionists in the name of Poles martyred in the war and forgotten because of a "Zionist plot" to raise awareness of the Holocaust and erase the memory of Polish heroism.

This is the first English-language book on the "anti-Zionist campaign" and the "March events" (Wydarzenia marcowe), as they are termed in Polish historiography, and the first to put their anti-Jewish character at the center of its analysis.[10] In March 1968, tens of thousands of students across Poland left their classrooms to protest against the communist regime and demand democratic reforms. The Polish United Workers' Party (Polska Zjednoczona Partia Robotnicza, or PUWP), responded by publicly accusing the student leadership of serving a "Zionist conspiracy" aimed at destabilizing the regime and destroying the country. These allegations continued the official condemnations that had rained down on Polish Jews nine months earlier for appearing to support Israel during and after the June 1967 War, in contrast to the official position of the Polish government. An anti-Zionist media campaign that blamed Polish Jews for political disorder and a massive purge of Jews from state institutions and party organs lasted until late summer 1968. In less than a year, the Polish communist regime curtailed

---

10. Dariusz Stola's work *Kampania antysyjonistyczna w Polsce 1967–1968* (Warsaw: Instytut Studiów Politycznych Polskiej Akademii Nauk, 2000) focuses on the anti-Zionist aspect of the propaganda and the subsequent Jewish emigration, while repeating the claim that antisemitism was merely a tool that the party used against the dissidents.

the reform movement and drove out of Poland about fifteen thousand Jews. This episode, seemingly a footnote in Polish history—short in heroism and suffering in comparison with preceding and subsequent events—is framed by World War II and the rise of the anticommunist movement Solidarity. Yet focusing on it contributes, on the one hand, to scholarship on the aftermath of World War II and its memory and, on the other hand, to the study of the opposition to communism in Eastern Europe, as well as bringing into relief the inner workings of regimes in the People's Republics.

The memory of the Holocaust in Poland has received growing scholarly attention and has been at the center of heated and emotionally charged disputes in Poland. Two opposite historiographical positions have emerged: one that stresses the impact of outside forces, German and Soviet, and presents Poles and Jews as the victims of external interventions, and another that focuses on relations between Jews and Poles and on Polish collaboration with the German occupiers and active participation in the murder and plunder of their Jewish neighbors.[11] This book demonstrates that the current narratives and positions on the Holocaust in Poland originated in the 1960s and were shaped after 1968. The period of discursive change that decade also gave birth to a myth of silence about the Holocaust in Poland: the belief that the particular fate of Polish Jews during World War II had not been discussed at all in public before the 1980s. The silence, however, resulted from the rise of a new generation in the party in the 1960s that followed a socialist-nationalist ideological path and objected to the upsurge in Holocaust commemoration in Poland and in the West. In their Poland, there was no room for anything "Jewish" that challenged Polish national myths, and they feared that Jews would obliterate the memory of Polish suffering during World War II.

Contrary to previous studies and accounts that portray the anti-Zionist campaign as a political device that party leaders use to mobilize the Polish street against the would-be reformers, I have found that a deeply rooted fear of a Jewish conspiracy set the tone for the regime's reaction to student unrest. Following the model set out by feminist scholar Sara Ahmed,[12] this analysis

11. For those who focus on external forces, see Halik Kochanski, *The Eagle Unbowed: Poland and the Poles in the Second World War* (Cambridge, MA: Harvard University Press, 2014); Timothy Snyder, *Bloodlands: Europe between Hitler and Stalin* (New York: Basic Books, 2012). For focus on Polish antisemitism, see Jan T Gross, *Neighbors: The Destruction of the Jewish Community in Jedwabne* (Princeton, NJ: Princeton University Press, 2001); Jan Grabowski, *Hunt for the Jews: Betrayal and Murder in German-Occupied Poland* (Bloomington: Indiana University Press, 2013); Barbara Engelking, *Jest Piękny Słoneczny Dzień: Losy Żydów Szukających Ratunku Na Wsi Polskiej 1942–1945* (Warsaw: Centrum Badan nad Zagłada Zydów, 2011).

focuses on fear as the key emotion, since it is through fearing others that a community of those "under threat" is created and separated from the "threatening others."[13] In the late 1960s, party members and Security Services officers constructed narratives of fear of Jews; they construed Jewish behavior as a threat to the existence of the Polish socialist nation. I do not view fear as a political tool in the hands of cynical politicians but rather as an emotion that stemmed from identification with the nation and from a perception of threat to the future of the collective.[14] Chief party members, rank-and-file activists, and state officials came to fear a Jewish threat, personified in "Zionist imperialist-nationalism." The Zionist enemy was an internal enemy, working from within the party and state, but also an external enemy operating internationally against Poland. This was similar to the image of the Jew in interwar Poland, when Polish nationalists perceived Jews as able to "move back and forth between the 'outside' and the 'inside' of a state, undermining the power of authorities to control their own territory," as historian Paul Hanebrink has recently described it.[15] Party members feared that Jews would undermine the current regime and take over the country in the guise of reforming socialism. Jews would do so as supporters of Zionism, which stressed the ethnonational aspect of Jewish identity and served as the guiding ideology of a state that allied with the Western powers, Poland's enemies. It is not that the word Zionist came to signify Jew, but rather that any Jew could now be a Zionist, a sliding between signs: if previously a Polish Jew could be either a communist or a Zionist, now "Jew" and "Zionist" became strongly linked in Polish political discourse and some in the party used them interchangeably.

A fear of Jews was not new in European or Polish political culture.[16] In the aftermath of World War II, despite the murder of most of Poland's Jews,

---

12. Sara Ahmed, "Collective Feelings: Or, the Impressions Left by Others," *Theory, Culture & Society* 21 (2004): 25–42. Ahmed stresses that emotions are relational and stem from contact with others, contact that in turn forms borders. I consider how an emotion such as fear delineated the boundaries of the nation since "how we feel about others is what aligns us with a collective."

13. Sara Ahmed, *The Cultural Politics of Emotions* (Edinburgh, UK: Edinburgh University Press, 2004), 72. In Ahmed's words, "Through the generation of 'the threat', fear works to align bodies with and against others."

14. To paraphrase Alon Confino, I aim at a "history of political communication" that includes emotional language, since "how can we explain politics with emotions left out?" Alon Confino, "Forum: History of Emotions," *German History* 28, no. 1 (2010): 67–80.

15. Paul Hanebrink, *A Specter Haunting Europe: The Myth of Judeo-Bolshevism* (Cambridge, MA: Harvard University Press, 2018) Kindle, location 1061.

16. Emotions are culturally conditioned and codified. Ahmed, *Cultural Politics of Emotions*, 69. For Poland, see Jan T. Gross, *Fear: Anti-Semitism in Poland after Auschwitz; An Essay in Historical Interpretation* (New York: Random House, 2006).

Poles feared more than ever the *Żydokomuna* (Judeo-communism), a myth according to which Jews controlled communism and sought to export it from the Soviet Union to Poland. The idea of *Żydokomuna* emerged during World War I and gained popularity in Poland when the young Polish state found itself bordering on the burgeoning Soviet empire and Poles worried that the Bolsheviks would try to expand their reign westward. Across Eastern Europe, fear of Jews became intertwined with fear of communism and with anxiety about retaining state sovereignty in the postimperial world.[17] At the end of World War II, after years of Nazi propaganda that equated Jews with communism and with the Soviet Army occupying Poland, dread of Jews taking over the country only grew. In the period after Stalin's death in 1953 and with the changes to the party's leadership, many in the party and state came to see Jews as responsible for the crimes of Stalinism, and they feared that Jews would once more take control of the party. Yet "the enemies" in 1968 were not simply Jews but nationalist Jews (i.e., Zionists), working in the name of a foreign country, Israel—a significant change from the cosmopolitan nature of prewar "Jewish threats." This change stemmed not only from an internal Polish process but also from a transformation in the situation of Diaspora Jews after the establishment of Israel: they came to be seen as the Diaspora of the Jewish state, and the actions of that state thus shaped the lives of Jews in other countries.[18]

What kind of enemy were the Zionists? Zionism, like other nationalisms, was anathema to communism's universalism and class-based ideology. In the interwar period, communist and socialist Jews across Eastern Europe fought against Zionist parties. Immediately after World War II, the communist regime in Poland concentrated on finding and eradicating Polish nationalists rather than Zionists. Across the border, in Czechoslovakia, Zionism was one of the charges leveled against the defendants in the Prague show trials of 1952; two Israeli citizens were among the accused.[19] In the Soviet Union, the 1950s were also a time of persecution of Jews and Zionism, culminating in the "doctors' plot," the allegation that Jewish doctors conspired to murder the heads of the communist regime. In Poland, the

---

17. See Hanebrink, *Specter Haunting Europe*. Hanebrink deals not with the question of whether Jews were really Bolsheviks but with the emergence of a new form of anti-Jewish prejudice.

18. See, for instance, Eli Lederhendler, ed., *The Six-Day War and World Jewry* (Bethesda: University Press of Maryland, 2000).

19. Karl Kaplan, *Report on the Murder of the General Secretary* (Columbus: Ohio State University Press, 1990).

communists shied away from Jewish topics, including Zionism, though the Jewish cultural association often criticized Zionism and Israel in its publications. The Polish government's attitude toward Zionism evolved in the 1960s. The communist regime under Gomułka's leadership after 1956 reembarked on the national path to socialism, which the party had abandoned in 1948, and sought to define itself in contrast to the Jews, the symbols of Stalinism in the eyes of many Poles. By 1967, Gomułka and the post-Stalinist communist leadership not only considered Zionism an enemy but also started searching for Polish Jewish Zionists who might have infiltrated the party; the Security Services increasingly presented Jews as taking part in a Zionist plot against the Polish government. Zionism became a real and present threat, and for at least a year, some party members feared that the small Jewish minority living in Poland would succeed in manipulating the reformist student movement to such an extent that it would turn Poland into a state ruled by Zionists and serving Jewish and American interests. Gomułka's March 19, 1968, speech demonstrated this approach: the first secretary claimed that disloyal "Zionist Jews" in Poland jeopardized the country's stability. The heads of the party believed that the Zionists were at the gate and that the anti-Zionist campaign was an act of self-defense by the Polish socialist homeland.

The use of terms in this book to refer to Jews requires explanation. In Polish nationalist discourse, a Jew could not be a Pole, often even in cases of conversion to Catholicism. Jews were treated as a national minority; the most liberal definition presented Poland as a "republic of many nations" (*rzeczpospolita wielu narodów*). Attempts by Jews to present themselves as an integral part of the Polish nation were often met with discomfort and contempt. The best Jews could hope for was full Polish citizenship, minimal discrimination, and inclusion in "the peoples of Poland."[20] Aware of this problem, the communist regime refrained from a uniform definition of Jew. Each department in the Ministry of Internal Affairs, and sometimes groups inside the same department, seemed to settle on a different device: *persons of Jewish descent* (*osoby pochodzenia żydowskiego*), *persons of Jewish*

---

20. For an extensive discussion, see Joanna Beata Michlic, *Poland's Threatening Other: The Image of the Jew from 1880 to the Present* (Lincoln: University of Nebraska Press, 2006); John Connelly, *From Enemy to Brother: The Revolution in Catholic Teaching on the Jews* (Cambridge, MA: Harvard University Press, 2012).

nationality (osoby narodowości żydowskiej), Polish Jews (Polscy Żydzi), or simply *Jews (Żydzi). Person of Jewish descent* was considered the most neutral and politically acceptable, similar to *Germans of Mosaic faith,* while *person of Jewish nationality* accentuated the difference between Poles and Jews. *Polish Jew* or *Jew* seemed also neutral, but often these terms were used to describe those who did not define themselves as Jews, imposing a certain identity on them. Party reports usually avoided the term *Jew* and seldom used *citizens of Jewish descent.* Instead, to denote Jews they used family names, which to the Polish ear, after centuries of training, sounded Jewish. The press, where there was more consistency, almost always used the terms *persons of Jewish descent* or *citizens of Jewish descent.* In both party and state official documents, the word *Zionist* did not replace the word *Jew;* rather, as noted above, any Jew after 1967 was a potential Zionist.

Jews in Poland after World War II usually chose one of three paths. Some (their number is unknown) decided to fully assimilate: they changed their names to Catholic-sounding ones and attempted to disappear into Polish society. Of the rest, a minority defined themselves as Polish Jews: they continued to speak some Yiddish, sent their children to Jewish schools and Jewish summer camps, and belonged to either the secular TSKŻ or to the smaller Jewish religious organization. The third group—and probably the largest—tried to pursue a middle road of sorts. These men and women saw themselves as "Polish citizens of Jewish descent," adopting the common communist phrase. They did not speak Yiddish at home or participate regularly in Jewish communal activity, but they also did not conceal their ancestry. By choice or by force, they came into close personal contact with one another and formed a social network of secularized Jews. In this book, I have followed self-definitions, using *Polish Jews* (or sometimes just *Jews*) when discussing those who identified themselves as such and who were involved with the TSKŻ or other Jewish activities, and using the term *of Jewish descent* to refer to students and intellectuals in the reform movement. As for non-Jewish Poles, I use *Poles* and not *Catholic Poles* to simplify the text and to avoid the use of religious definitions (for there are Poles who are neither Catholic nor Jews).

Research on the post-Stalinist era in Eastern Europe generally tends to overlook the Polish March. Overshadowed by the Prague spring—the formation of a reformist government in Prague and the subsequent Warsaw Pact invasion of Czechoslovakia in the summer of 1968—the March events aroused little interest outside Poland. Paul Lendvai's 1971 work, *Anti-Semitism without Jews*, still remains one of the more detailed references.[21] To the English reader, the events are made accessible mainly through textbooks on Poland and studies on dissidents in Eastern Europe.[22] They present March 1968 as the turning point in the history of the reformist-democratic movement: the moment when dissidents, in Poland and elsewhere in the Soviet bloc, turned from reform to outright opposition to the communist regime. After 1968, they no longer sought to improve communism but to topple it.[23] Timothy Snyder included the March events in his book on the "Bloodlands," dubbing this brand of anti-Jewish attitude "Stalinist anti-Semitism," a hatred of Jews that stemmed from the radicalization and racialization of the war years and from the establishment of Israel, which turned Jews into potential spies for an enemy state and its nationalist ideology. "Stalinist anti-Semitism" outlasted Stalin himself, reappearing in March 1968 in Poland. Snyder sees the anti-Zionist campaign as originating from inner-party struggles and antisemitic views of party leaders, a reflection of Gomułka's desire to take "revenge on Polish-Jewish communists," who had pushed him out of office in 1948.[24]

In Poland, the story of March 1968 began to be told in the midst of the events and immediately thereafter. Immigrants to the West and former student protestors and intellectuals who remained in Poland recounted their stories and analyzed the regime's motivations for launching the anti-Zionist campaign. This dissident narrative set the tone for how the campaign of 1967–68 was, and still is, portrayed in Polish: as the communist regime's canny response to intellectual unrest, intended to spark patriotic support for the party in its fight against a Zionist conspiracy. According to this

21. Paul Lendvai, *Anti-Semitism without Jews; Communist Eastern Europe* (Garden City, NY: Doubleday, 1971).

22. Norman Davies, *God's Playground: A History of Poland* (Oxford: Clarendon, 1981); Norman Davies, *Heart of Europe: The Past in Poland's Present* (Oxford: Oxford University Press, 2001); A. Kemp-Welch, *Poland under Communism: A Cold War History* (Cambridge: Cambridge University Press, 2008); Anita J. Prazmowska, *History of Poland* (Houndmills, Basingstoke, Hampshire: Palgrave Macmillan, 2004); Andrzej Paczkowski, *Spring Will Be Ours: Poland and the Poles from Occupation to Freedom*, trans. Jane Cave (University Park: Pennsylvania State University Press, 2003); Porter-Szűcs, *Poland in the Modern World*, chap. 9.

23. Peter Raina, *Political Opposition in Poland, 1954–1977* (London: Arlington Books, 1978); Robert Zuzowski, *Political Dissent and Opposition in Poland: The Workers' Defense Committee "KOR"* (Westport, CT: Praeger, 1992); Michael H. Bernhard, *The Origins of Democratization in Poland: Workers, Intellectuals, and Oppositional Politics, 1976–1980* (New York: Columbia University Press, 1993); Grzegorz Ekiert, *The State against Society: Political Crises and Their Aftermath in East Central Europe* (Princeton, NJ: Princeton University Press, 1996); Timothy Garton Ash, *Polish Revolution: Solidarity* (New Haven, CT: Yale University Press, 2002).

24. Timothy Snyder, *Bloodlands: Europe between Hitler and Stalin* (New York: Basic Books, 2010), 372.

interpretation, the rulers of communist Poland used antisemitism to divert attention from the reformist message the protesting students presented and to delegitimize the demonstrators in the eyes of the masses.[25] During the communist era, without accessible archives and local free press, contemporary Western analysts, experts on Eastern Europe, and the Polish émigré community could not understand the 1968 events without the mediation of immigrant and dissident accounts smuggled from Poland.

Inevitably, the dissidents' accounts and interpretation became the only reliable narrative. They stressed the regime's repression of the reform movement and largely disregarded the anti-Jewish dimension of the campaign. In 1968, the sociologist Zygmunt Bauman, one of the most prominent intellectuals pushed out of Poland and the in-law of David Sfard, former head of the TSKŻ, wrote in a widely cited text in *Kultura* (Paris), "The logic of the March events does not leave any doubts: it was a well-prepared, well-realized plan of provocation, directed from behind the scenes by a faction in the Polish United Workers' Party; its primary aim was the liquidation of remaining academic freedoms in Poland."[26] The communists in power were, in the words of Adam Michnik, the student leader turned prominent dissident, "boors and cretins" ("chamy i ciemniaki").[27] Their language was that of primitive propaganda, and they used antisemitism as part of internal party struggles for political power; the Jewish issue in itself had little meaning for the regime. As Irena Grudzińska Gross has argued, "I did not consider the anti-Jewish part of party propaganda as anything other than propaganda and manipulation, as empty as anything else the party said or used. Again, I was not the only one who thought in this way."[28] The dissidents strongly believed that by ignoring the anti-Jewish aspect of March 1968 they were refusing to accept the regime's labeling of them as Zionists and as Jews and retaining their agency and subjective definitions of identity.[29]

---

25. January Grzędziński, "Zwierzęta Patrzą na Nas," *Kultura* (Paris) 6/248-7 -7/249 (1968): 79–87; Władsław Bieńkowski, *Motoryi Hamulce Socjalizmu* (Paris: Instytut Literacki, 1969); Alina Grabowska, "Łódzki marzec," *Kultura* (Paris), 4 (1969): 75–77; Apolinar Kamiński, "Gomułka i Moczar," *Kultura* (Paris) 9 (1969); Marek Tarniewski [Jakub Karpiński], *Ewolucja czy rewolucja* (Paris: Instytut Literacki, 1975).

26. Zygmunt Bauman, "O frustracji i kuglarzach," *Kultura* (Paris), no.12 (1968).

27. Adam Michnik, "Dziady z dynamitu," *Gazeta*, January 31, 2008, http://wyborcza.pl /1,76842,4885182.html.

28. Irena Grudzińska Gross, "1968 in Poland: Spoiled Children, Marxists, and Jews," in *Promises of 1968: Crisis, Illusion, and Utopia*, ed. Vladimir Tismaneanu (Budapest: Central European University Press, 2011), 43–53, here 51.

29. Adam Michnik, *Letters from Prison and Other Essays*, trans. Maya Latynski (Berkeley: California University Press, 1985); Teresa Torańska, *Jesteśmy: Rozstania '68* (Warsaw: świat książki, 2008).

Contemporary Polish historiography tends to follow the dissident position and perceives the use of anti-Jewish and anti-Zionist language as marginal to the story of the student movement. Polish historians have predominantly examined personal and internal party struggles or concentrated on analyzing the emergence of opposition to communism. Of particular importance for the prominence of the "opposition to communism" narrative is Jerzy Eisler's work on March 1968. As the first book on the topic to be published in postcommunist Poland, Eisler's *Marzec 1968*, with its slant toward the dissident narrative, shaped the historiography that followed. Basing his work on interviews and memoirs, Eisler delved into the world of the students and intellectuals and produced a narrative about resistance to communism and the birth of the antiregime opposition. For him, March 1968 was a turning point for the opposition, and the propaganda campaign was mainly anti-intellectual and only marginally anti-Jewish.[30] Dariusz Stola, the Polish historian who published in 2000 the first and only book dedicated solely to the anti-Zionist campaign, labeled the campaign an "effective policy instrument" with roots in anti-Jewish resentment long established in the Ministry of Internal Affairs. By carefully analyzing the main themes of the Ministry of Internal Affairs' propaganda, Stola concluded that the ministry apparatus indeed saw Zionists as a real threat to the party, but he still wrote off the "crushing of Zionists" as the least important aspect of March 1968.[31] In a 2009 article in the journal *Polin*, Stola described the anti-Zionist campaign as "a tool for fighting the youth rebellion, through compromising its alleged instigators, leaders and goals as alien and perverse,"[32] yet he also conceded that for some elements in the party, fighting the Jews was the primary goal, but these members had, he posited, "irrational impulses."[33]

---

30. Jerzy Eisler, *Marzec 1968: Geneza, Przebieg, Konsekwencje* (Warsaw: PWN, 1991). Eisler's second book on March, *Polski Rok 1968*, broadly follows the same line. A well-researched eight-hundred-page monograph, *Polski Rok 1968* (The Polish year 1968) includes one chapter of fifty pages devoted to "Jews, Anti-Semitism, and Emigration." Eisler presents the history of 1968 as the eruption and subsequent crushing of opposition to the communist regime, mentioning the Jewish aspects only in passing. In his interpretation, the antisemitic propaganda the party used against the students was just a technique, interchangeable with any other that the regime could have chosen. Jerzy Eisler, *Polski Rok 1968* (Warsaw: Instytut Pamięci Narodowej, 2006), 88–140.

31. Dariusz Stola, "Anti-Zionism as a Multipurpose Policy Instrument: The Anti-Zionist Campaign in Poland, 1967–1968," *Journal of Israeli History* 25, no. 1 (March 2006): 175–201, quote from page 175; Dariusz Stola, *Kampania antysyjonistyczna w Polsce 1967–1968* (Warsaw: Instytut Studiów Politycznych Polskiej Akademii Nauk, 2000).

32. Dariusz Stola, "The Hate Campaign of March 1968: How Did It Become Anti-Jewish" *1968: Forty Years After, Polin* 21 (2009): 34.

33. Stola, "Hate Campaign of March 1968," 36.

Other historians have focused much attention on the personal and factional aspect of March and have portrayed the anti-Zionist campaign as a struggle for power and position in the regime.[34] They claim that the Ministry of Internal Affairs planned the campaign with the intent of purging state and party administration of senior and older party members.[35] According to Piotr Osęka, "A battle cry rose from all the anti-Zionist press articles, resolutions, speeches and denunciations: 'At last!' 'Now we have done it!' . . . The March propagandists cunningly and with a clear understanding of the public atmosphere played an emotional game. . . . The leading theme of the campaign was spreading hate against the privileged intelligentsia. The enemy, as portrayed in the propaganda, was a person of higher social standing. . . . Analyzed from this point of view, the 1968 propaganda seemed to serve as the reason for and instrument of a purge inside the party establishment."[36] More recent work on 1967–68 points to the "nationalist turn" the communist party took and to the importance of the anti-Zionist campaign to defining the boundaries of the national-communist discourse. This work by gender and cultural studies scholars, anthropologists, and art historians challenges the historiography and offers new interpretations of the communist period, including Holocaust commemoration and the rise of the opposition.[37]

Historians who insist on the pure instrumentality of the anti-Zionist campaign presuppose the effectiveness of antisemitism as a political tool in Poland. According to this view, the communist regime could use it to smother the opposition because Poles were predisposed to see Jews as menacing traitors. Yet even if the antisemitism of March 1968 was only an instrument in an inner-party political conflict, the question remains: Why did the quarreling factions use antisemitism "disguised" as anti-Zionism? Some historians trivialize this question and claim that antisemitism has been used as a tactical political tool throughout history. This kind of

---

34. Andrzej Friszke, *Opozycja Polityczna w PRL, 1945–1980* (London: Aneks, 2004); Marcin Zaremba, *Komunizm, legitymizacja, nacjonalizm: Nacjonalistyczna legitymizacja władzy komunistycznej w Polsce* (Warsaw: TRIO, 2001); Paweł Machcewicz, *Władysław Gomułka* (Warsaw: Wydawnictwa Szkolne i Pedagogiczne 1995); Piotr Osęka, *Syjoniści, inspiratorzy, wichrzyciele: Obraz wroga w propagandzie marca 1968* (Warsaw: Znak, 1999); Andrzej Fiszke, "Miejsce Marca 1968 wśród innych 'polskich miesięcy,'" in *Oblicza Marca 1968* (Warsaw: IPN Press, 2004), 19.

35. Piotr Osęka, *Marzec '68* (Krakow: Wydawnictwo Znak, 2008), 228, 232–35.

36. Osęka, *Marzec '68*, 232–35.

37. See: Katarzyna Chmielewska, Grzegorz Wołowiec, and Tomasz Żukowski, eds., *Rok 1966: PRL na zakręcie, Idee-Dyskursy-Praktyki* (Warsaw: Instytut Badań Literackich PAN Wydawnictwo, 2014); Katarzyna Chmielewska, Agnieszka Mrozik, and Grzgorz Wołowiec, eds., *Komunizm. Idee i praktyki w Polsce, 1944–1989* (Warsaw: IBL, 2018).

argument dismisses the need to understand why anti-Jewish violence burst at that specific moment in socialist Poland, and it is condescending toward Poles, portraying them as easily manipulated and naturally antisemitic. An answer that Polish historians sometimes offer to the question of why anti-semitism was used in March 1968 is that former fascists and ultranational-ist right-wingers infiltrated the communist party and hijacked the party's agenda; those who subscribed to antisemitism came to the left from the right. These scholars see the anti-Zionist propaganda of the party as the work of specific men who succeeded in imposing their nationalist agenda on the leadership of the Polish communist party.[38] Finding it difficult to resolve communist ideology with the anti-Jewish nature of the March 1968 propaganda, the researchers propose the "infiltration theory." This theory also presents antisemitism as the standard political tool of past Polish regimes, a propaganda provocation meant to distract the masses from the real troubles of the socialist economy.[39]

Polish scholars use terms such as *emotional game, spreading hate,* and *irrational impulses* to describe the anti-Zionist campaign, hinting that the March events could be understood by thinking about emotions and urges, but at the same time, the idea of using emotions as an analytical lens is dismissed as irrelevant to the historian trying to uncover the truth of the events and the interests behind them. This is another central assumption that Polish historians researching the 1967–68 period make: when party and government officials used highly charged racist language against the Jewish minority, they utilized typical communist "doublespeak." Accord-ing to this supposition, serious scholars should seek out the "true" inten-tions and interests of the regime, ignoring its open discourse. This work makes no such assumptions as it shows how emotions and words led to actions and to the formation of an apparatus for seeking, finding, and purg-ing Zionists. It answers a series of questions: How was a crisis created and controlled? How did information flow in the system? What was the rela-tionship between the heads of the regime and the low-level administration? Was fear of Jews merely a tool, a ruse to distract the masses, or an emotion with specific meanings in a particular time and place that motivated the rank and file of the party to action?

---

38. Michlic, *Poland's Threatening Other*, 230–61.

39. One of the first to present this theory was Kazimierz Jeleński, "Hańba czy wstyd," *Kultura* (Paris), no. 5/247 (1968): 55. Krystyna Kersten, *Polacy, Żydzi, komunizm: anatomia półprawd, 1939–68* (Warsaw: Niezależna Oficyna Wydawnicza, 1992).

In 1968, most Poles left the protesting students to struggle alone against the communist regime. Though some young workers joined the protests, a large-scale rebellion, as in neighboring Czechoslovakia, did not occur. The reform movement made little headway in Poland at the time, not only because of the perception that its leadership was predominantly Jewish but mainly because communism had not enjoyed great popular support in Poland and therefore reform, as part of the socialist project, seemed pointless. Many Poles felt that the system was imposed on their homeland, and they had little interest in discussions about the future of communist ideology. Moreover, by constantly seeking an authentic Polish communism, the promoters of the anti-Zionist campaign actually strengthened the myth of *Żydokomuna*. After all, the party proved that Jews in powerful positions had run Poland for quite a long time and had maintained their influence at least until 1968. To this day various Polish academic works, popular histories, and websites portray the communist regime in Poland as essentially Jewish and foreign.[40]

By the end, the anti-Zionist campaign had also alienated the stoutest pillar of socialism in Polish society: the secular leftist intelligentsia, many of them of Jewish descent. Without their support, communism in Poland weakened considerably. Yuri Slezkine wrote of Soviet Jewish elites: "The children of the most loyal of all Soviet citizens had become the most alienated of all anti-regime intellectuals."[41] So felt the sons and daughters of the most loyal Polish communists—party activists since the interwar period—when they suddenly found themselves accused of serving Zionist interests and involvement in a "Zionist-Jewish conspiracy." Unlike Soviet Jews, who could not emigrate from the Soviet Union and who belonged to a wide spectrum of sociopolitical classes, the Jews who had chosen to stay in Poland after 1956 and who participated in the March events were often members of the socialist elite. After March 1968, beaten and arrested, persecuted and discriminated against, they understood that Jews could not realize their dream of fully belonging to the Polish socialist nation.[42]

---

40. Marek Jan Chodakiewicz, *After the Holocaust: Polish-Jewish Conflict in the Wake of World War II* (Boulder: East European Monographs; New York: Distributed by Columbia University Press, 2003).

41. Yuri Slezkine, *The Jewish Century* (Princeton, NJ: Princeton University Press, 2004), 353.

42. I borrow the formulation "dream of belonging" from the memoir of the 1968 émigré Janina Bauman. See Janina Bauman, *A Dream of Belonging: My Years in Postwar Poland* (London: Virago, 1988).

The first chapter of this book discusses in brief the history of the relationship between communism and Jews in Poland, emphasizing the shift to a national form of communism in the 1950s and 1960s and placing changes in the situation of Jews in a larger context of recent Polish history. The second chapter analyzes the early phase of the anti-Zionist campaign, explaining how the communist government moved from condemnation of Israel as the aggressor to a struggle against "Zionist infiltrators" when in his famous speech Gomułka declared Polish Jews disloyal. Since the mid-1960s, Mieczysław Moczar and his appointees in the Ministry of the Interior promoted the idea that Jews had no place in the higher echelons of the Polish socialist nation and that their connections to communities outside Poland made them highly dangerous to the regime. In 1967, those views came to the fore, as Polish Jews met the ministry's expectations, exposing "true loyalties." Gomułka's decision to launch a public campaign against Polish Jews stemmed from his belief that Jews threatened his authority and from his fears that they were working against the interests of the Polish nation and might attempt to oust him again.

The third chapter centers on a dramatic political-historical dispute that highlights the similarities between 1968 and today and focuses on one of the major concerns of the "partisans": the memorialization of World War II. The little-studied event revolved around an entry in *Wielka Encyklopedia Powszechna* (The great general encyclopedia), published in 1966. The entry, devoted to Nazi concentration camps, maintained that the vast majority of the victims in *death camps* were Jews, not Poles. In July 1967, powerful hard-line circles in the party, and especially in the Ministry of Internal Affairs, expressed outrage that the censors had approved such an affront to the Polish people. The growing worldwide awareness of the genocidal nature of the persecution of Jews during World War II outraged and scared the politicians behind the anti-Zionist campaign: they feared that Polish heroism and suffering would be forgotten. This was the starting point for a campaign against the "falsification of history by world Zionism," with the encyclopedia and its Jewish editors singled out for shrill criticism.[43] The rhetoric of this campaign still echoes in Poland today.

Chapter four chronicles the growth of a reformist movement opposed to Gomułka's policies. It focuses on events leading to the student demonstrations of March 1968 and on the growing disenchantment

---

43. AIPN BU MSW II 51, 7.

of Polish intellectuals with Gomułka. From the center of the communist elite emerged a group of reformists ready to fight for greater freedoms. The regime responded to mounting unrest with even greater repression, in no way heeding the call for reform. The young intellectuals then went to battle against censorship.

Chapter five closely follows the spread of protests throughout Poland and analyzes the regime's violent reactions. The communist party apparatus and leadership, including Gomułka, intensified its attacks on Jews, presenting student leaders as Zionist Jews whose activities threatened Poland's stability, security, and unity. The protesting students, fascinated by the remarkable changes taking place in Czechoslovakia, dreamed that a Polish Dubček would appear to save Polish socialism. But such a scenario never unfolded, and Polish reality took the form of arrests, humiliation, and mounting anti-Jewish policies.

The last chapter examines the final stages of the "anti-Zionist" purge. The regime encouraged anyone implicated in the March events and Jews involved in Jewish organizations to leave Poland; between 13,500 and 15,000 Jews indeed immigrated and scattered around the world. In this chapter I clarify how and why the campaign died away, revealing the sudden fear that leading party members felt when Poles reacted in an unpredicted way to the anti-Zionist campaign. The hunt for Zionists transformed into a search for communists as hidden Jews, releasing the demons of *Żydokomuna*, the belief that the communist party was at its core a Jewish party. The regime could not allow such ideas to emerge, as they pulled the rug out from under the communist attempts to present themselves as the true Polish patriots. Already in late April 1968 Gomułka was expressing deep concerns about the direction of the anti-Zionist campaign, and by the summer he had ordered party members to stop seeking out "Zionists."

The anti-Zionist campaign achieved some of its goals. Citizens of Jewish descent left the ranks of the party and state mechanism, Polish Jewish institutions dwindled, and many Polish Jews emigrated from Poland. Student demonstrations stopped. The left-wing intelligentsia weakened, as some of its central figures left the country. Among the immigrants were Janina and Zygmunt Bauman with their three daughters, as well as the Sfards, David, Regina, and Leon. They had picked different paths to living in Poland, but all found themselves out of their homeland. The communist regime cast Jews in the role of security threat and drove them out of Poland. The vision of a homogeneous, exclusionary nation-state triumphed over socialist dreams and hopes of tolerance in a "republic of many nations." In 2018, on the fiftieth anniversary of the March events, Polin, the Jewish museum in Warsaw, staged an exhibit to commemorate the events. In the accompanying book, the two curators write, "Fear stemming from being stigmatized as 'a stranger at one's own home' was revived today, along with rhetoric familiar from March '68 and eagerly replayed in our day by the extreme right, the true heirs to the antisemitic faction of the United Polish Workers' Party. We have designed our exhibit . . . to include uncomfortable issues that are slowing being disappeared today, veiled by an increasingly popular narration about 'true Poles.'"[44] European nationalism has not disappeared; new (and old) "security threats" are still seen as threatening the body of the nation all around the continent. The year of 1968 has been considered a time of global rebellion, of generational struggle. But optimism about the achievements of this rebellion has waned, as the American Historical Review explained in a section dedicated to fifty years after 1968: "Finally, more than a few of these reflections [in the issue] have an elegiac quality, wistfully mourning the gradual dissolution of the utopian hopes that 1968 represented for both its participants and its inheritors—including this generation of historians. Here, perhaps, the 'legacy' of 1968 appears far more sobering."[45] In Poland, for one, despite decades-long efforts by intellectuals and politicians, the spirit of 1968 ethnonationalism is still alive in public life and in the highest echelons of the Polish State.

---

44. Justyna Koszarska-Szulc and Natalia Romik, "Estranged," in *Estranged: March '68 and Its Aftermath*, ed. Justyna Koszarska-Szulc and Natalia Romik (Warsaw: Polin and Onico, 2018), 27.
45. "AHR Reflection 1968 Introduction," in *American Historical Review* 123, no. 3 (2018): 709.

1

FROM INCLUSION TO EXCLUSION

Jews and Communism in Poland

THE HISTORY OF POLISH JEWS AND COMMUNISM IS contested, debated, and contentious. Volumes have been written on a variety of issues—from the question of overrepresentation of Polish Jews in the communist leadership and the security apparatus to the antisemitism of late communism and Soviet involvement in Polish-Jewish relations. In Poland, political divisions have colored the historiography on Jews and communism, with some portraying communism as a Jewish affair and others pointing to antisemitism in Polish society and to the regime's subsequent anti-Jewish policies. The question arises of how to write a history of the communist regime and its relationship with the Jews. Who are the Jews we are considering? Are they part of the "regime," or are they objects of communist repression? Or perhaps we should look at the particulars of Polish communism and its turbulent relationship with the categories of Jews and antisemitism. When we examine closely outbursts of anti-Jewish violence in the communist period, we see that they resulted from wider contexts of Polish history and communist policy. In 1956–57, as I argue in this chapter, Władysław Gomułka's return to the "Polish path to socialism" and to Polish "values" led to attacks on women, minorities, and Jews, which in turn led to a large-scale wave of migration. The secretary's program to homogenize communist Poland, or to rid it of its remaining minorities—a plan he had already begun to implement in the 1940s—brought about a surge in violence against Jews and the emigration of tens of thousands of Jews.

The multifaceted relationship between communism and Jews in Poland began in the interwar period, when the Communist Party of Poland (KPP) was a small and marginalized party that enjoyed little popular support. The higher echelons of the KPP included members of Jewish descent who dreamed of a large communist bloc from the Soviet Union to Germany where their Jewishness would become inconsequential and nationalism would not be the key to politics. For them, Marxist socialism offered a secular alternative to rising nationalism and political antisemitism. Only a tiny minority of Polish Jews joined the party, but they became visible symbols of the alleged "Jewishness" of communism. By the 1920s, the belief that communism was essentially Jewish took hold in Poland, as it had in many other European countries. Polish right-wing nationalists promoted the idea of Judeo-Bolshevism, particularly after the October Revolution, and during the Polish-Soviet War Jews suffered from pogroms and mass violence as suspected Bolsheviks. Anticommunist feelings in Poland also stemmed from fear of another Russian occupation as Soviet communism sought to expand the revolution westward.[1] In 1937, Stalin decided to liquidate the KPP, as part of the Great Purge of the late 1930s. He summoned the heads of the party to Moscow, where they were tried and executed. Possibly, Stalin saw the Polish party as "overrun" by Jews and wanted it to assume a more ethnically Polish character.[2] It was the first sign that some communists, particularly in Poland, would like to escape the association with Jews and Judaism. As communism moved away from universalism to nation building, this desire, for communism to be seen as part and parcel of the nation and not as an alien element, would become a guiding principle for Polish communism. In 1939, following the Molotov-Ribbentrop Pact and the division of Poland between the Third Reich and the Soviet Union, a Polish communist party had no raison d'être. Stalin wanted to erase Polish sovereignty, and the Soviet Union incorporated the eastern parts of Poland; Polish communists were expected to become part of the Soviet project.[3] Prominent Polish communists, some of Jewish descent, traveled to Moscow, where they spent the war years. As a result, a new Polish communist party emerged in two locations after the Germans started the war on the

---

1. Paul Hanebrink, *A Specter Haunting Europe: The Myth of Judeo-Bolshevism* (Cambridge, MA: Belknap, an imprint of Harvard University Press, 2018), chap. 1, Kindle. I am not addressing the statistical debate of how many Jews were in the party because I consider it problematic: How do we count how many Jews? By their birth mothers? Or by their own definitions? Many communists of Jewish origins did not see themselves as Jews. Communism was their break with Judaism.

2. Marci Shore, *Caviar and Ashes: A Warsaw Generation's Life and Death in Marxism, 1918–1968* (New Haven, CT: Yale University Press, 2006), 149. This was in contrast with the Great Purge of the Soviet party, which did not have anti-Jewish undertones.

3. Andrzej Paczkowski, *The Spring Will Be Ours: Poland and the Poles from Occupation to Freedom*, trans. Jane Cave (University Park: Pennsylvania State University Press, 2003), 48–49.

eastern front in 1941: occupied Poland and the Soviet Union. The Polish communist intellectuals in Moscow formed the latter group. The former, founded in 1942, was the Polish Workers' Party, which operated as a clandestine group with a small armed underground militia, the Armia Ludowa (AL); for most of the war, Władysław Gomułka headed it. The Moscow group, joining hands with the Armia Ludowa, swept back into the Polish homeland with the Soviet Army and, in July 1944, became a provisional self-appointed government.[4]

The advancing communist forces faced both the German Army and the Home Army, a large and staunchly anticommunist underground organization affiliated with the Polish government in exile. Famously, in August 1944, the Home Army staged an uprising against the German occupiers in Warsaw: the Germans crushed the revolt, killing thousands, deporting hundreds of thousands to concentration camps, and destroying Warsaw. The Soviet Army did not assist the rising Poles,[5] the Home Army never recovered, and the calamity further tarnished communism in the eyes of Poles. After the Nazi and Soviet occupations all but wiped out Polish military, religious, and intellectual elites, the failed uprising and subsequent destruction of the capital facilitated the communist takeover. When the war ended, Polish communists, leading the provisional government, faced less resistance from the decimated population. Besides large-scale political violence, to gain support, the Polish authorities used slogans of national unity and emphasized their success in expelling millions of Germans and Ukrainians from Poland, fulfilling the desire of many interwar nationalists to create a minority-free, homogenous Poland. The expulsion of Germans, sanctioned by Moscow and supported by the Allies, was designed to remove the population from the newly acquired territories and to prevent the creation of a large German-speaking minority in Poland.[6] On this project, very much in concert with nationalist aspirations, Gomułka and the Moscow group worked together, with Gomułka serving as minister of the Recovered Territories, coordinating the removal of Germans and the distribution of their property.[7]

---

4. Paczkowski, *Spring Will Be Ours*, 95–99, 106–20.

5. Paczkowski, *Spring Will Be Ours*, 121–29.

6. R. M. Douglas, *Orderly and Humane: The Expulsion of the Germans after the Second World War* (New Haven, CT: Yale University Press, 2013).

7. Norman M. Naimark, *Stalin and the Fate of Europe: Postwar Struggle for Sovereignty* (Cambridge, MA: Belknap, 2019), chap. 6, Kindle.

The communist takeover and expulsion of the Germans coincided with the return of Polish Jews to their homes at the end of the war. Survivors, mostly from the Soviet Union, made their way back to Poland to see what remained of their shtetl and the Polish-Jewish civilization. The Germans and their collaborators murdered more than three million Jews living in the prewar boundaries of independent Poland, more than 90 percent of Poland's Jewry.[8] Most of the Polish survivors had fled to the Soviet Union at the beginning of the war; only a small number of Jews survived in hiding on Polish soil or in German camps.[9] Many Poles met the Jewish survivors with indifference, anger, and violence. Jews were often assaulted, dragged off trains and beaten, and physically or verbally attacked when trying to return home. Poles who had taken over stolen Jewish property, had turned over Jews to the Germans, or had collaborated in other ways with the killing of the Jews were less then pleased to see returning Jews. They feared that Jews would demand compensation or expose their crimes. Others may have acted out of a desire to see a Poland free of Jews. It has been estimated that as many as 1,500 Jews were murdered in the years 1945–48.[10] This unwelcoming of Jews also fitted with the communist agenda. Certainly, the communists did not support the killing of Jews, and they did not encourage public disorder—the party condemned antisemitism and mob violence—but they did encourage Jewish emigration and did utilize the battle against antisemitism for their own goals. With the silent approval of the regime, Zionist groups operated at the time in Poland, aiding Jewish emigration and even opening a military training facility for future soldiers in the Israel Defense Forces.[11] Polish Jews also organized in self-help groups and attempted to rehabilitate their lives and their community. In 1944, Jewish leaders formed the Central Committee of Jews in Poland (Centralny Komitet Żydów w Polsce, or CKŻP), which welcomed communists,

---

8. Collaborators in the broad sense that includes several lingual-ethnic groups, among them Poles, Ukrainians, Latvians, Lithuanians, and others in the prewar borders of Poland (in no special order).

9. Camp survivors often did not go back to Poland but rather remained in displaced-persons camps in the Allied-controlled sections of Germany. Generally, the issue of how many Jews survived in Poland remains contested and is well beyond the scope of this study. On some of the current debates, see Jörg Hackmann, "Defending the 'Good Name' of the Polish Nation: Politics of History as a Battlefield in Poland, 2015–18," *Journal of Genocide Research* 20, no. 4 (2018): 587–606.

10. Gross, *Fear*, 31–80. Estimates vary, and this too is hotly debated in Poland. See Marcin Zaremba, *Wielka trwoga: Polska 1944–1947: ludowa reakcja na kryzys* (Warsaw: Znak, ISP PAN, 2012).

11. Bożena Szaynok, "Obóz ochotników do Hagany w Bolkowie (Polska, Dolny Śląsk)," in *Parlamentaryzm, konserwatyzm, nacjonalizm. Sefer Jowel. Studia ofiarowane profesorowi Szymonowi Rudnickiemu*, ed. Jolanty Żyndul (Warsaw: Wydawnictwo Sejmowe, 2010).

Bundists, and Zionists.[12] The Central Committee organized material help, orphanages, health care, and legal aid in the hope of reviving the social, cultural, and communal life of Polish Jews. One of the directors of the committee was Adolf Berman, brother of the prominent communist and Politburo member Jakub Berman, in charge of the newly established Security Services (Urząd Bezpieczeństwa). During the hectic years of the communist takeover of Poland, the CKŻP afforded Jews some relief and a measure of self-rule.[13] Yet most Jewish survivors indeed decided to emigrate: between 1945 and 1951, at least 150,000 Jews emigrated from Poland to Palestine/Israel.[14] Thus, in the postwar era, Poles forcibly expelled Germans and Ukrainians while pushing out the Jews, turning Poland into an ethnically homogeneous state, with few small minority populations. The new and uniform Poland was a project in which Gomułka played a central role and one that he would resume in the mid-1950s.

During the same period, the communists, with "Moscow communist" Bolesław Bierut serving as head of state and Gomułka as first secretary (in addition to his post as minister), quickly and forcefully eliminated rivaling left-wing parties, incorporating them in 1948 into the expanded Polish United Workers' Party (PUWP). In 1947, the communists falsified the election results in their favor, clearing the way for the establishment of a Stalinist-style state. By 1948, the communist regime was fully installed, and Bierut replaced Gomułka, becoming both head of state and first secretary of the PUWP. In 1949, a Soviet war hero of Polish descent became head of the Polish Army as Konstantin Rokossovsky was named minister of national defense and marshal of Poland, cementing Soviet presence in Poland. During 1949, the party also purged Gomułka for "nationalist deviation."[15] Gomułka, in a letter to Stalin shortly before his removal, complained that the members of Jewish origins lacked "attachment" to the Polish nation, thus doubting the loyalty to Poland of Beirut and his circle, who had spent the war years in the Soviet Union. Furthermore, he wrote that the number of Jews in the

---

12. The Zionists came from the socialist wing of the Jewish national movement, while the Bund was a prewar Jewish autonomous socialist party.

13. Anna Cichopek-Gajraj, *Beyond Violence: Jewish Survivors in Poland and Slovakia, 1944–48* (Cambridge, MA: Cambridge University Press, 2014).

14. Dariusz Stola, "Jewish Emigration from Communist Poland: The Decline of Polish Jewry in the Aftermath of the Holocaust," *East European Jewish Affairs* 47, no. 2–3 (2017): 169–88; Anna Cichopek-Gajraj, *Beyond Violence*, chap. 4.

15. A. Kemp-Welch, *Poland under Communism: A Cold War History* (Cambridge: Cambridge University Press, 2008), 17–35; Naimark, *Stalin and the Fate of Europe*, chap. 6.

party should be reduced. The warnings did not change Gomułka's situation; Stalin stood behind the current leadership of the party, and the Security Services arrested Gomułka in 1951. The former first secretary remained imprisoned until the end of 1954, but he did not stand trial.[16] For now, the Polish communist regime moved away from its previous minorities policies and began limiting emigration from Poland. About seventy thousand Jews remained in Poland in 1950, and for the next five years the regime prohibited them from leaving, along with other minorities.[17]

In 1948–56, Poland followed the model of the Soviet bloc: single-party rule, state terror against the "enemies of socialism," a cult of personality, and a centrally planned nationalized economy aiming for large-scale industrialization. The communist regime engaged in collectivization of farms and tried to transform and "modernize" Polish society.[18] It battled "revisionism," "national chauvinism," and "German militarism," suggesting to Poles that communism would guarantee peace and stability in the region that had been the battleground for two world wars.

As the communists took control of the Polish government, so the communists in the Jewish Central Committee pushed out the Zionists and Bundists. They railed against "national sectarianism" and opposed the existence of a unique Jewish section in the ruling party. After all, under communism, everyone was equal and there was no need for "special interest" groups within the party.[19] In October 1950, the Jewish Central Committee (founded in 1944) merged with the smaller Jewish Cultural Society (Żydowskie Towarzystwo Kultury w Polsce, or ŻTK) to create the Social Cultural Association of Jews in Poland (Towarzystwo Społeczno-Kulturalne Żydów w Polsce, or TSKŻ), an organization controlled solely by communists. Its charter was to "engage the Jewish people in the building of socialism in Poland and in the Polish national struggle for the peace and the erecting of socialism."[20] Until 1968, the TSKŻ dominated Jewish life in Poland, operating somewhat

---

16. For more on Gomułka and Jews in the party leadership, see Naimark, *Stalin and the Fate of Europe*, chap. 6; Audrey Kichelewski, "Imagining 'the Jews' in Stalinist Poland: Nationalists or Cosmopolites?," *European Review of History: Revue europeenne d'histoire* 17, no. 3 (2010): 505–22.

17. Marcos Silber, "Foreigners or Co-nationals? Israel, Poland, and Polish Jewry (1948–1967)," *Journal of Israeli History: Politics, Society, Culture* 29, no. 2 (2010): 213–32.

18. For more on this effort, see Malgroszata Fidelis, *Women, Communism and Industrialization in Postwar Poland* (New York, NY: Cambridge University Press, 2010).

19. Marci Shore, "Children of the Revolution: Communism, Zionism and the Berman Brothers," *Jewish Social Studies* 10, no. 3 (2004): 23–86.

20. Grzegorz Berendt, *Życie żydowskie w Polsce w latach 1950–1956* (Gdańsk: Wydawnictwo Uniwersytetu Gdańskego, 2006), 143.

independently; the regime considered its leadership loyal communists.[21] Many of the communist Jews at the helm of the TSKŻ had spent the war years in the Soviet Union, where they had witnessed the rise of the Jewish Antifascist Committee, a group of prominent intellectuals promoting Jewish culture in the Soviet Union.[22] For a short period in the 1940s, as part of the Soviet war propaganda effort, the regime allowed Jews to advance Yiddish culture within a broader Soviet context, "national in form and socialist in content." Turning away from the nationalities policies of the late 1930s, which strove for integration and the shutdown of ethnic institutions, the communists now encouraged certain Yiddish cultural production, believing it would help raise Jewish American money. The Anti-Fascist Committee went as far as to envision the creation of a Jewish Soviet Socialist Republic in the Crimea, which would provide safe haven for wartime refugees and give Jews a new beginning.[23] The plan never came to fruition; Stalin had the committee's heads murdered or executed in the postwar period. But the vision of an autonomous and flourishing communist-Jewish culture stuck: on returning to Poland, refugee Jews founded a Yiddish language newspaper, *Folks Sztyme*; a Yiddish theater; Yiddish-language Jewish schools; and a Yiddish publishing house. At the first meeting of the Jewish Cultural Society, one of its founders, David Sfard, spoke about the "new classics of the culture of the Jewish people," meaning secular Yiddish literature by the likes of Sholem Aleichem, Y. L. Peretz, and Mendele Mojcher Sforim. Until 1968, the TSKŻ worked to keep Yiddish culture alive in Poland.[24] On the tenth anniversary of the establishment of the publishing house, Sfard reported that so far it had published 165 titles in 817,500 copies.[25] Since the censors in charge of monitoring TSKŻ publications and activities were Yiddish speakers and belonged to the same social milieu, communist Jews enjoyed a degree of cultural autonomy in Stalinist Poland. This is not to say

---

21. Kichelewski, "Imagining 'the Jews.'"

22. Berendt, *Życie żydowskie*, 147–56.

23. Joshua Rubenstein and Vladimire P. Naumov, eds., *Stalin's Secret Pogrom: The Postwar Inquisition of the Jewish Anti-Fascist Committee*, trans. Laura Ester Wolfson (New Haven, CT: Yale University Press, 2001), 63, 84; Shimon Redlich, *War, Holocaust and Stalinism: A Documented History of the Jewish Anti-Fascist Committee in the USSR*, ed. K. M. Anderson et al., vol. 1 of *New History of Russia* (Luxembourg: Harwood Academic, 1995), 147. The history of Yiddish culture in the Soviet Union is of course complex and convoluted and beyond the scope of this book.

24. Berendt, *Życie żydowskie*, 50, 138.

25. Joanna Nalewajko-Kulikow, "The Last Yiddish Books Printed in Poland: Outline of the Activities of Yidish Bukh Publishing House," in *Under the Red Banner, Yiddish Culture in the Communist Countries in the Postwar Era*, ed. Elvira Grözinger and Magdalena Ruta (Wiesbaden: Harrassowitz, 2008), 117.

that they diverted from the party line; the Yiddish press rejected Zionism, defined as Jewish nationalism. Zionist organizations were shut down, and suspected Zionists came under attack. Yet the Polish communist government showed less interest in a purge of Jewish intelligentsia and party members of Jewish origins, in contrast to the rest of the Soviet bloc. Research has shown that in Poland the struggle against "cosmopolitanism" did not mean a battle against Jewish party members.[26]

Stalin's death in March 1953 was a turning point in the history of the Soviet bloc. A power struggle arose in the Soviet Communist Party, and the terror that had long been the rule in the Soviet Union and its satellites greatly lessened. Nine months after Stalin's funeral, long before Khrushchev's secret speech, a high-ranking Polish Security Services officer, Józef Swiatło, defected to the West. In 1954, speaking on Radio Free Europe, Swiatło, who was of Jewish descent, revealed the inner workings of the Ministry of Public Security and the extent of Stalinist terror, affirming to some Poles that Jews had been responsible for Stalinism.[27] To prove that times had changed, the Polish Central Committee launched an investigation into the practices of the Ministry of Public Security, which was in charge of the secret police and the harsh repression that typified the Stalinist era. The committee shut down the ministry, replacing it with the Committee for Public Security, a relatively spindly institution. The Central Committee also released several political prisoners, including many arrested by Swiatło himself. At the same time, in June 1954, Khrushchev and the Soviet new leadership recognized the legitimacy of different national paths to socialism. The declaration in effect exonerated Władysław Gomułka of charges of

---

26. Kichelewski, "Imagining 'the Jews'"; Naimark, *Stalin and the Fate of Europe*. The TSKŻ's activity contrasted with the situation at the time in the Soviet Union. Until Stalin's death in 1953, Soviet Jews found themselves under attack as prominent intellectuals and party members stood accused of either "cosmopolitanism" or "nationalism." In December 1952, Stalin accused a group of doctors, many of Jewish descent, of plotting to kill Andrei Zhdanov, a senior member of the Central Committee, who had died in 1948. Between 1951 and March 1953, the authorities arrested doctors and their wives in suspicion of involvement in the plot. The secret police interrogated them harshly, attempting to build the case for a widespread conspiracy directed by the United States. Stalin grew increasingly worried about the loyalty of Soviet Jews and their ties to America. In turn, Jews across the Soviet bloc feared that the communists planned a large-scale anti-Jewish purge. The doctors' plot and Jewish purge came to an end with Stalin's death in 1953. Jonathan Brent and V. P. Naumov, *Stalin's Last Crime: The Plot against the Jewish Doctors, 1948–1953* (New York: HarperCollins, 2003).

27. Zbigniew Błażyński, *Mówi Józef Światło: Za kulisami bezpieki i partii 1940–1955* (London: Polska Fundacja Kulturalna, 1985); Pawel Machcewicz, "Social Protest and Political Crisis in 1956," in *Stalinism in Poland, 1944–1956: Selected Papers from the Fifth World Congress of Central and East European Studies, 1995*, ed. A. Kemp-Welch (London: Macmillan, 1999), 99–118.

nationalist deviations, a crime for which he had been jailed since late July 1951; in December 1954, Gomułka was freed.[28]

In February 1956 in Moscow, during the shocking Twentieth Congress of the Soviet Communist Party, in which Khrushchev condemned Stalin's crimes, the first secretary of the PUWP, Bolesław Bierut, suddenly died. Khrushchev flew to Warsaw for Bierut's funeral and met with local party leaders to discuss the future of the regime. Instead of their choice for first secretary, Roman Zambrowski, a high-ranking member of Jewish origins, Khrushchev insisted on his own candidate, Edward Ochab, who was an ethnic Pole.[29] This appointment failed to bring stability to the party or the state. The PUWP secretariat circulated among its members Khrushchev's "secret speech" about Stalin's crimes, encouraging rank-and-file party members and leading intellectuals to criticize the party and the Soviet Union. Many spoke for greater openness and more public participation in the party's decisions.[30] Early in 1956, a rivalry emerged between two groups within the party's Central Committee. As Zbigniew Brzezinski, then a Harvard professor of political science, observed in 1957: "For the first time since the Bolshevik disputes of the early twenties . . . and more particularly in Poland, we find an active communist debate on the nature of communist ideology, a debate with all the earmarks of an honest search for answers within the somewhat loose framework of Marxist thought."[31] The Natolin group, named after a suburb of Warsaw where party officials vacationed, insisted that the state had to keep a firm grip on society. They blamed Jewish party members for the crimes of Stalinism and resisted talk of freedom of speech and internal democracy. They believed that if the party could only pry Jewish hands from the levers of power, its problems would be solved. One of the faction's supporters, Politburo member Aleksander Zawadzki, accused Jakub Berman, in charge of the security mechanism since the establishment of the regime, of overlooking senior Polish party members and handing the best jobs to unqualified Jews. Berman and his Jewish

28. Pawel Machcewicz, "Social Protest and Political Crisis in 1956." The reforms went only so far. For example, Cardinal Stefan Wyszyński, head of the Polish Catholic Church, remained in prison until 1956. Jerzy J. Wiatr, "Pokolenie '56," *Przegląd Humanistyczny* 5/6 (2006): 65–72.

29. Marcin Zaremba, *Komunizm, legitymizacja, nacjonalizm: nacjonalistyczna legitymizacja władzy komunistycznej w Polsce* (Warsaw: Wydawnictwo TRIO, 2001), 227–29.

30. Tony Kemp-Welch, "Khrushchev's 'Secret Speech' and Polish Politics: The Spring of 1956," *Europe-Asia Studies* 48, no. 2 (1996): 181–206.

31. Zbigniew Brzezinski, "Communist Ideology and Power: From Unity to Diversity," *Journal of Politics* 19, no. 4 (1957): 549–90.

comrades were blamed for the crimes and deviations of Stalinism and for the persecution of innocent Poles.[32] The members of the Puławian reformist faction, named after another vacation town, were former Stalinists and young socialists. The Puławians wanted reforms in keeping with their vision of Marxism-Leninism; as Khrushchev had indicated in his programmatic speech, a return to Lenin's ways would put socialism back on track. For the Puławians, this meant a return to internal democracy: real debates within the party, internal elections, and freer discussions. Many intellectuals boldly and publicly expressed their views in support of the faction and its goals of reforming communism.[33] During this factional struggle in the party, the "Jewish problem" came up repeatedly as hard-line Polish communists turned to anti-Jewish language and blamed Jews for Stalinism. Several anti-Jewish incidents occurred across Poland: Jews were accused of Stalinist crimes and attacked, verbally and physically.[34] At the same time, the party set out to homogenize the state apparatus by encouraging Jewish emigration, particularly of Jews connected to the Soviet Union and Stalinism. Convinced that communism had been tainted through its association with Jews, the leadership hoped "ethicizing" the party would shift popular perceptions.[35]

In late June 1956, workers in Poznań protested low wages and rising prices. In the dramatic days that followed, they besieged the town hall and the regional security building, grabbing weapons and attempting to hurt police officers. The workers chanted nationalist slogans, sang the national anthem, and called for an independent Poland. The rally turned into a massive anti-government riot. The authorities sent armored troops to disband the protests, and when the army opened fire, dozens of people were killed.[36] It became evident that First Secretary Ochab could not peacefully rein in discontented Poles. After the events in Poznań, Gomułka aligned with the Puławians,

---

32. Marcin Zaremba, *Komunizm, legitymizacja, nacjonalizm*, 229–31, 236–38.

33. Some of them were Central Committee members Jerzy Albrecht, Władysław Matwin, and Jerzy Morawski, as well as Roman Zambrowski. Paweł Machcewicz, "Social Protest and Political Crisis in 1956."

34. Bożena Szaynok, "The Role of Antisemitism in Postwar Polish-Jewish Relations," in *Antisemitism and Its Opponents in Modern Poland*, ed. Robert Blobaum (Ithaca, NY: Cornell University Press, 2005), 265–83.

35. Marcin Zaremba, *Komunizm, legitymizacja, nacjonalizm*, 223–63; Joanna B. Michlic, *Poland's Threatening Other: The Image of the Jew from 1880 to the Present* (Lincoln: University of Nebraska Press, 2006), 233–35.

36. Numbers are disputed; probably somewhere between 57 and 74 people were killed. Paweł Machcewicz, "Social Protest and Political Crisis in 1956."

making a bid to regain the position of first secretary. He positioned himself as a man of the people and a true Polish patriot. For many Poles, Gomułka's return would signal an opportunity for reform and for a more *Polish* form of socialism. After all, Gomułka, during his first tenure as secretary, had secured the new western territories and had cleansed them of Germans.[37] On October 19, 1956, during its eighth plenum, the party's Central Committee was to vote on Gomułka's appointment. On that very day, the chiefs of the Soviet Communist Party, including Khrushchev, landed in Warsaw as Soviet tanks stationed regularly in the Polish regions of Silesia and Pomerania converged on the capital. The message was clear: the soviet leadership wanted Ochab to remain in power. Still, the plenum convened as scheduled, and Ochab spoke, informing his colleagues of the aggressive Soviet moves and imploring them to reject Gomułka's bid. As a compromise, he asked the plenum to admit Gomułka and others to the Central Committee.[38]

After the four candidates had been approved, Gomułka, Ochab, Zambrowski, Józef Cyrankiewicz (the president), and Aleksander Zawadzki (chairman of the State Council) met with the Soviet delegation. Concurrently, party cells organized protests and marches demanding Gomułka's appointment; newspapers and radio chimed in. A settlement proved possible; after all, Gomułka was a loyal communist, a founding member of the party and one of its heads during the communist takeover. He assured the Soviets that Poland would remain in the Warsaw Pact and would follow Moscow's lead in matters of foreign policy. The Soviets agreed to return to Moscow most of the Soviet military advisers stationed in Poland and remove the Russian general who served as Poland's minister of defense, thus creating the semblance of greater freedom from Soviet influence. Apparently, Khrushchev had correctly determined that Gomułka would rein in the reformers, rendering Soviet military action unnecessary. On October 20, Gomułka was appointed first secretary.

Gomułka's ascent opened a new chapter of Jewish life in communist Poland as he transformed minority politics. The new post-Stalinist and reform-oriented government permitted and encouraged immigration to Israel: within two years, about fifty thousand Jews emigrated in what came to be known in Israel as the "Gomułka immigration" (*Aliyat Gomułka*). At the same time, the Soviet government allowed for Polish citizens still living

---

37. Pawel Machcewicz, *Władysław Gomułka* (Warsaw: Wydawnictwa Szkolne i Pedagogiczne, 1995), 35–48.

38. The others were Zenon Kliszko, Marian Spychalski, and Ignacy Loga-Sowiński.

in the Soviet Union to return to Poland, among them about thirty thousand Jews who mostly moved on to Israel. In October 1956, when describing the atmosphere surrounding the repatriation of Poles, the first secretary of the Israeli legation in Warsaw, Jacob Barmor, claimed that the slogan "Poland for Poles" was "tossed in the air"[39]—the very same words that interwar right-wing nationalists used, he further pointed out. Barmor, born and raised in interwar Warsaw, also maintained that Jews had served in the security apparatus during Stalinism and that they had become synonymous with the communist regime. "The regime wants to get rid of Jews to show that it is not under the control of Jews," he wrote. As mentioned, Gomułka saw Jews as responsible for the crimes of Stalinism and believed that Jews had too much influence. After 1956, as Barmor correctly described, Jews were being removed from the party. These changes in leadership and the internal struggle against party members of Jewish descent led to widespread outbursts of anti-Jewish violence, as anger toward the regime turned against Polish Jews.[40]

Lower Silesia witnessed a particularly harsh attack. Poland acquired the region after World War II and expelled the majority of its German inhabitants (with Gomułka as minister of Recovered Territories), making it a center of resettlement for Jews and Poles returning from the Soviet Union. The repatriates, Poles and Jews, moved into formerly German housing and took over German businesses. The Jewish communities in the towns and cities flourished and even enjoyed a certain level of autonomy in the immediate postwar period. These Jews, many of whom had survived the war in the Soviet Union and therefore were tarnished by communism, came to symbolize communist power in the region. Much of the violence in 1956 revolved around removing Jews from the workplace, where they were seen as foreign elements and promoters of Stalinism. Poles berated, verbally assaulted, and publicly humiliated Jews. Anti-Jewish violence spread from factories and government offices to schools, clubs, shops, and city streets.[41] In cities such as Wrocław, where antisemitic leaflets were circulated, Jews found on their doors signs calling for them to leave Poland.[42] In Wałbrzych,

---

39. Document 237, in *Documents on Israeli-Polish Relations 1945–1967*, ed. Marcos Silber and Szymon Rudniciki (Jerusalem: Israeli State Archives, Government Printer, 2009), 485.

40. Pawel Machcewicz, "Antisemitism in Poland in 1956," in *Jews, Poles, Socialists: The Failure of an Ideal*, ed. Antony Polonsky et al. (London: Littman Library of Jewish Civilization, 2008).

41. Document 237, in *Documents on Israeli-Polish Relations*.

42. Eva Węgrzyn, "Reasons for Emigration of Jews from Poland in 1956–1959," in *Postwar Jewish Displacement and Rebirth, 1945–1967*, ed. Françoise S. Ouzan and Manfred Gerstenfeld (Leiden: BRIL, 2014).

the police had to stop an anti-Jewish riot from turning into a pogrom in September 1956.[43] At the same time, it has been claimed that the ethnic violence in the region extended beyond the Jewish minority to other ethnic groups. As the historian Paweł Wieczorek puts it: "To the conciseness of the heads of the party and the city returned the memory of the presence in the city [Wałbrzych] of: Jews, Germans, Greeks, Roma and native population."[44] With the removal of the Stalinist leadership that publicly battled Polish nationalism and propagated national unity and the emergence of a much more national communism, the idea to make the "new territories" more "Polish" was taken up and Polish Jews were driven out of Lower Silesia. Not only Jews became eligible for immigration in 1956; the borders also reopened for the German minority, some of whom still lived in formerly German regions, and they too emigrated. Like Jews, until 1950–51, the regime allowed for ethnic Germans to leave under a reunification-of-families program. In 1955–56, the scheme was gradually revived and expanded to include most citizens of German origins who had relatives in Germany, East or West. As Dariusz Stola points out, by 1959 about 270,000 Germans immigrated to either of the Germanies; 95 percent of emigrants in this period belonged to ethnic minorities, while Catholic Poles could not easily emigrate. The government saw both Jews and Germans as holding allegiances to external homelands, and they had to give up their Polish citizenship upon emigrating.[45]

As would be the case in 1968, the communist regime was not one in its policies in 1956, and while many in the Ministry of Internal Affairs and in the army supported the nationalizing policies, there were other voices in the PUWP that called for an end to discrimination and action against "nationalist" party members.[46] In lengthy reports condemning fellow communists for "succumbing" to antisemitism, racism, and nationalism, these voices provide us with a glimpse into the extent of discrimination against minorities. Not

43. This was while Edward Ochab was still first secretary. Paweł Wieczorek, "Przed październikiem był wrzesień. Wystąpienia antyżydowskie w Wałbrzychu w 1956 roku," *Kwartalnik Historii Żydów* 4, no. 236 (2010): 449–61.

44. Paweł Wieczorek, *Żydzi w Wałbrzychu i powiecie wałbrzyskim 1945–1968* (Wrocław–Warsaw: IPN, 2017), 245.

45. Some German speakers were denied permission to leave, particularly those deemed necessary for certain industries, such as mining. Dariusz Stola, "Opening a Non-exit State: The Passport Policy of Communist Poland, 1949–1980," *East European Politics and Societies* 29, no. 1 (2015): 96–119.

46. Eugeniusz Mironowicz, *Mniejszości narodowe w Polsce. Państwo i społeczeństwo polskie a mniejszości narodowe w okresach przełomów politycznych, 1944–1989* (Bialystok: Wydawnictwo Bialoruskiego Towarzystwa, 2000), 145.

only Jews but also Germans, Ukrainians, Slovaks, Czechs, and other ethnic and linguistic groups all suffered from various forms of persecution. A 1957 internal party report claimed that chauvinism and nationalism ran rampant among certain party members and that minorities were discriminated against in several fields, including employment, education, and religion.[47] While preexisting antisemitic prejudices played a role in anti-Jewish violence, it exploded in 1956–57 as a result of both a deliberate attempt to blame the regime's crimes on Jews and a larger program of making Poland "for the Poles" and making Polish communism more ethnically homogeneous.

Similar trends appear in changes in gender politics during de-Stalinization. The communists engaged in returning women to their traditional roles, for they represented Polish national identities. Like Jews, women had become too visible and "taken jobs" from Polish men, and now they were asked to make room for new cadres and for Polish male supervisors. The entry of women into the workforce was perceived as an imposition from Moscow, as something alien to Polish values. Historian Malgorzata Fidelis writes, "In the popular mind, mass female employment and women in men's jobs were the most powerful symbols of a hated system."[48] The same words could have been used to describe the situation of Jews in 1955–56 Poland. As the communist state was moving away from Stalinist policies, it experienced a backlash of sorts: the party sought greater popular support and a more "Polish" way of practicing communism, which meant that women, Jews, and other social/ethnic groups had to return to their previous positions. The broader history of de-Stalinization and its impact on Polish society shows that the history of Jews in Poland has to be understood in the wider context of Polish history as well as minority and gender politics.

The violence against Jews, along with a desire to leave the communist state and a fear of retribution against party members, drove Jewish emigration from all over Poland. As mentioned, about fifty thousand Jews made their way out, among them university professors, prominent journalists, medical doctors, engineers, and other professionals, as well as party and state officials. Joining them were thousands of repatriates from the Soviet Union, who upon arriving in Poland "fell into a psychosis of immigration" and submitted requests to emigrate to Israel.[49] To facilitate this immigration and the Jewish repatriation from the Soviet Union, the Polish government

---

47. Mironowicz, *Mniejszości narodowe w Polsce*, 141.
48. Fidelis, *Women, Communism and Industrialization in Postwar Poland*, 216.
49. Document 243, in *Documents on Israeli-Polish Relations*.

accepted financial aid from the American Joint Distribution Committee (JDC).[50] To pave their way from Poland to Israel, the JDC provided material and bureaucratic aid to returning Polish Jews, who had come from the Soviet Union with very little. Poland wanted Jews to leave, and Israel demanded that Jews immigrate only to Israel. As the historian Marcos Silber pointedly writes, "These Jews were caught between two mutually exclusive nationalisms" and were forced to seek a new homeland in Israel.[51] To allow for the continued stream of immigration, Israeli officials made sure that news of the exodus from Poland emerged only after it ended. In September 1956, the Israeli Ministry of Foreign Affairs wrote to the Israeli delegate in Warsaw, Katriel Katz, that "there is irreversible damage to the *aliyah* [immigration] from Poland by the reckless publications in the Israeli press."[52] For, as would also be the case in 1967, Gomułka's emigration policies were not in concert with Soviet policies. The Soviet Union had put in place strict limits and objected to the emigration of specific ethnic groups (though the policy changed for certain groups at certain periods); it also sought an alliance with Israel's Arab neighbors, who objected to Jewish immigration to Israel.[53] In an attempt to slow down the emigration of repatriates, the Soviets demanded that Jewish returnees receive Polish citizenship before leaving.[54] Polish communists had different goals and pursued their own policies. This is not exceptional to Poland; other countries in the communist bloc, such as Romania and Hungary, had allowed or banned Jewish emigration in accordance to changing national and international circumstances. The post-Stalinist regime demanded that Soviet bloc countries uphold the party-state system and remain loyal to Moscow in international politics while retaining some independence in internal affairs.

Those charting the history of "Jews" in Poland in the decade of 1957–67, after the immigration subsided, face a few challenges. First, the question of identity must be raised: Who are Jews in this context; how are they defined

---

50. The JDC, an American-based Jewish relief organization, had operated in postwar Poland until 1949. Audrey Kichelewski, "A Community under Pressure: Jews in Poland, 1957–1967," *Polin: Studies in Polish Jewry* 21 (2008): 159–86.

51. Silber, "Foreigners or Co-nationals?," 213–32.

52. Document 235, *Documents on Israeli-Polish Relations*.

53. In all of 1957, the Soviets allowed one hundred Jews to immigrate to Israel (not as part of the Polish repatriation); see Boris Morzov, *Documents on Soviet Jewish Emigration*, Cummings Center Series (London: Rutledge, 1999).

54. Israeli diplomats claimed that the Egyptians pressured Khrushchev, who then pressured the Poles to end Jewish immigration. Document 249, *Documents on Israeli-Polish Relations*.

here? After the dust of political changes had settled, about thirty-five thousand self-identifying Jews (those who in official censuses defined themselves as such) remained in Poland. By 1967, their numbers had dwindled, as about ten thousand emigrated throughout the decade.[55] The actual number of Polish citizens of Jewish background or of "mixed" marriages remain unknown and is an object of debate in Poland. After the Holocaust, some Jews chose to remain with "Aryan" identities used during the war; others joined the communist party and moved away from their Jewish roots; and yet others feared that being Jewish would only turn them into victims again. They embraced Polish identities, often not revealing their Jewish past to their children. To label them as Jews would ignore their own identification. Jews who did define themselves as Jews also assumed various identities: Jews, Polish Jews, or Poles of Jewish descent/origins. Each category carried religious, cultural, and political meanings. Another challenge is the problem of Jews and communism: when writing about the regime and "the Jews," is it possible to separate "the Jews" from Jews serving in the regime or communist Jews? Post-Stalinist communism was not a monolithic system; the abolition of internal party terror meant that disagreement was possible, as long as arguments remained within the boundaries of Marxist-Leninist discourse. The archives show that communist Jews and Jews within the party promoted equality and demanded that the regime combat antisemitism and racism, and they held on to the idea that communism meant the eradication of nationalism and chauvinism. The TSKŻ remained antinationalist and opposed to both Polish and Jewish nationalism (i.e., Zionism). This was in stark contrast to voices rising within the party, particularly in the Ministry of Internal Affairs, that sought to "nationalize" communism and actively worked to cleanse party and state institutions of Jews. On the ground, discrimination and prejudice against Jews (and other minorities) persisted, and the regime ebbed and flowed in its responses.

The decade of 1957–67 saw some improvement for Jews living in Poland. Two organizations oversaw Jewish life in Poland, the TSKŻ and the ZRWM (Zwązek Religijny Wyznania Mojżeszowego, Religious Union of the Jewish Faith), which was responsible for the religious needs of the community, such as High Holiday services, Jewish burials, and kosher food. The TSKŻ had about seven thousand members and the ZRWM about five thousand (by 1966).[56] As mentioned, the regime allowed a Jewish charitable organization,

---

55. Kichelewski, "A Community under Pressure."
56. Audrey Kichelewski, "A Community under Pressure."

the JDC, back in the country. With it returned the World Jewish Congress and the Organization for Rehabilitation through Training (ORT), which operated professional schools in Poland. This foreign money funded the activities of the TSKŻ and ZRWM: millions of dollars funneled in 1956–67 kept Jewish institutions alive, providing material aid to an aging population and creating a cultural haven of sorts. At the same time, as historian Audrey Kichelewski has also suggested, the image of a "golden age" for Polish Jews has been exaggerated both by contemporaries and by scholars. Many literary and cultural figures emigrated in 1956–57, and the emigration continued throughout the decade as a third of the Jewish population, about ten thousand Jews, left. The younger generation of Polish Jews either assimilated into Polish society or departed the country, while older Jews often suffered from poverty and loneliness, factors that complicate the picture of a thriving community. Certainly, Jewish life persisted in Poland and Yiddish literature continued to be published, but it increasingly became clear that a revival of pre-Holocaust Jewish life would be impossible in a homogeneous Poland that was home to a tiny Jewish minority. Poland in the 1960s was not the multilingual, multinational country it had been in the 1920s, when Yiddish culture reached its height. In spite of the decline and marginalization of the Jewish community in Poland, in 1967–68, Gomułka and his close allies felt that Jews still had too much power and influence in communist Poland.

2

NOT TO BE TRUSTED

Polish Jews in the Aftermath of the June 1967 War

O N JUNE 6, 1967, THE DAY AFTER THE June 1967 War broke out in the
Middle East, the Polish government issued a statement expressing
"full support for the just struggle of the United Arab Republic and the Arab
states against [Israeli] aggression, in defense of their territory and their
sovereign rights."[1] The announcement reflected the official position of the
Soviet Union and its allies, yet its effects went beyond the sphere of the Cold
War. The June 1967 War changed the face of the Middle East and sent ripples
around the world. When the Polish press settled on a set of visual images
to represent the war, it depicted the Israelis as Nazis and the Arabs as Jews
being marched to camps. Articles, caricatures, and propaganda pamphlets
compared the rapid Israeli occupation of the West Bank to the Nazi blitz-
krieg and the sacking of Poland in 1939.[2] On June 19 the first secretary of the
Polish United Workers Party, Władysław Gomułka, rounded out the meta-
phor by referring to Polish Jews as a "fifth column" (Piąta kolumna), traitors
to the nation. At that moment, Poland's ruling party turned against the
country's tiny Jewish population. This chapter traces how the communist
government moved from a condemnation of Israel to an internal struggle
against "Zionist infiltrators and spies." In the culmination of a process that
began in the mid-1960s, in the eyes of the party Polish Jews, previously seen
as trustworthy, became Zionists and representatives of the State of Israel,
regardless of their political affiliation. My focus here is not on Polish-Israeli
relations but rather on the ways international affairs inform internal perceptions and measures.

---

1. *Żołnierz Wolności*, June 7, 1967, front page. All translations are mine, unless noted otherwise.

2. Agnieszka Skalska, *Obraz wroga w antysemickich rysunkach prasowych marca '68* (Warsaw: Narodowe Centrum Kultury, 2007).

Scholarship on trust often portrays communist regimes as based on mutual distrust between the government and the population, and it stresses the persistence of feelings of distrust and suspicion into the postcommunist period. Studies examining postcommunist societies tend to infer from the present to the past and to assume that during the communist era citizens distrusted state institutions and that, in turn, the state suspected the populace of disloyalty to the regime. Much of the literature on trust revolves around questions of trust placed in governments and institutions: how trust is constructed and how society operates through trust. Less room is given to the other side of the relationship—the trust governments and state authorities put in citizens and the groups considered trustworthy. And while political psychologists have examined trust between and within groups, historical and cultural perspectives have received limited attention.[3] This chapter shows how, even in a political system based initially on coercion and terror, state institutions expected loyalty, particularly on national grounds, and trusted certain groups more than others. Loyalty to the nation, which the communist regime wanted to equate with loyalty to communism, ensured the functioning of the state in the post-Stalinist world, where the Eastern-bloc states found their "national roads to socialism." In the 1960s, the regime's trust shifted to ethnic Poles, a fundamental change in the relationship between state and citizens. If at first the communist regime saw ethnic Poles as a suspect group and kept them under surveillance, during the 1960s Jews became so deeply distrusted that state authorities no longer considered them legitimate citizens of People's Poland. At the beginning of the decade, changes within the communist party brought into high-ranking circles ethnically Polish members who espoused a worldview that merged socialism and nationalism. By the end of the decade, most of Poland's Jews had been cast aside by the government and had left the country for other shores.[4]

---

3. See Piotr Sztompka, *Trust: A Sociological Theory* (Cambridge: Cambridge University Press, 2009); Besir Ceka, "The Perils of Political Competition: Explaining Participation and Trust in Political Parties in Eastern Europe," *Comparative Political Studies* 46, no. 12 (2013): 1610–35; William Mishler and Richard Rose, "Trust, Distrust and Skepticism: Popular Evaluations of Civil and Political Institutions in Post-Communist Societies," *Journal of Politics* 59, no. 2 (1997): 418–51; for a social psychology overview, see Katie N. Rotella, Jennifer A. Richeson, Joan Y. Chiao, and Meghan G. Bean, "Blinding Trust: The Effect of Perceived Group Victimhood on Intergroup Trust," *Personality and Social Psychology Bulletin* 39, no. 1 (2013): 115–27.

4. Of the 25,000 registered Jews, 13,500–15,000 emigrated. The numbers, as is usually the case for Polish Jews, are only an approximation, and the exact number of Jews living in Poland at the time, however defined, is unknown. Jerzy Eisler, *Polski Rok 1968* (Warsaw: IPN, 2006).

The driving force behind the shift in attitude toward the Jewish minority was the Ministry of Internal Affairs, especially in the wake of the June 1967 War. The minister of internal affairs, Mieczysław Moczar, and his appointees rejected the view of Jews as part of the Polish *socialist* nation, regarding them as a subversive minority to be distrusted and ejected from any position of influence. They grew convinced that Jews were undermining the socialist government and posing a threat to the future of communist Poland.[5] Gomułka's decision to launch a public campaign against Polish Jews stemmed from his belief that Jews threatened his authority and were no longer allies of the regime, a position he had held in the past. I here offer a new analysis of the anti-Zionist campaign in Poland that goes beyond the conventional discussion of factional struggles within the communist party and of contrived antisemitism, and it explains why the head of Poland's communist party decided to begin a public campaign against the country's Jews at a specific juncture, in 1967.[6]

Scholars have pointed to the admission into the communist party of former members of the Polish interwar right-wing movement, the *Endecja*, who brought with them antisemitic ideas, as a primary cause for the anti-Zionist campaign of 1967–68. Scholarship also suggests that intraparty struggles between new members and veteran ones (sometimes Jewish) drove Gomułka to side with the up-and-comers and purge the party of Jews.[7] Though the party's membership transformed in the late 1950s, these explanations overlook the worldview that became prevalent throughout the Eastern bloc, which merged ethnonationalism and communism, differentiating it from the political antisemitism of the 1930s. They also underestimate the

---

5. This work examines closely the language of the security apparatus and does not disregard it as a propaganda tool or a cover for the true intentions of the regime. Though scholars have analyzed the propaganda used in 1967–68, they have treated it as just that—propaganda, words and images manufactured to create a wedge between protesting students and the general public. Both the historian Dariusz Stola and writer Michał Głowiński have analyzed the language used by the regime assuming that the communists manipulated the language for certain political gains. Głowiński in particular wants to "expose" what is hidden behind the expressions used during the period. Dariusz Stola, "Anti-Zionism as a Multipurpose Policy Instrument: The Anti-Zionist Campaign in Poland, 1967–1968," *Journal of Israeli History* 25, no. 1 (2006): 175–201; Michał Głowiński, *Marcowe Gadanie, komentarze do słów, 1966–1971* (Warsaw: Pomost, 1991).

6. For studies on 1968 in Poland, see, for example, Dariusz Stola, *Kampania antysyjonistyczna w Polsce 1967–1968* (Warsaw: Instytut Studiów Politycznych Polskiej Akademii Nauk, 2000); Eisler, *Polski Rok 1968*; Piotr Osęka, *Marzec '68* (Warsaw: Znak, 2008).

7. For example, Joanna Beata Michlic, *Poland's Threatening Other: The Image of the Jew from 1880 to the Present* (Lincoln: University of Nebraska Press, 2006).

shift in attitude toward communist Jews within the regime.[8] Certain circles in the Polish communist regime at the time genuinely feared that Polish Jews compromised the regime and conspired with foreign Zionists. After the June 1967 War, Moczar and his followers gathered what they considered proof of Jewish disloyalty and succeeded in convincing the party's first secretary to launch an anti-Zionist campaign. Communist Jews went from being a generally trustworthy group in the 1950s to becoming the object of suspicion and fear. By the mid-1960s about twenty-five thousand Jews remained in Poland. In June 1967, these Jews, registered and self-identifying as Jews, came under attack as Gomułka launched the public campaign against them.

The secretary himself had been quietly pursuing the "Polonization" of the party since the early 1960s, reflecting anti-Jewish sentiments he had already expressed in the 1940s. This policy of replacing non-Catholic Poles with Catholic Poles had two aims. First, the crimes of Stalinism came to be associated with party leaders of Jewish descent, such as the man in charge of the secret police at the time, Jakub Berman; and Gomułka wanted to distance his regime from veteran Stalinists. He and his close advisers assumed that a more "Polish" party would render the regime more acceptable in the eyes of Poles. Second, Gomułka assumed ethnic Poles would be more loyal to him and to "national communism" and therefore chose them to form his cadre. He and his men believed that without Jews socialism would thrive in Poland. In this, Gomułka was following in the footsteps of the Soviet Communist Party, which had already undergone a process of Russification and suspicion toward comrades of Jewish descent. Similarly to the Polish case, Soviet high-ranking party officials saw "too many" Jews among the communist elites—Jews that they could not fully trust.[9] The Israeli state, which claimed all Jews as potential citizens and actively encouraged immigration to Israel, played a role in the shift of attitude toward Jews in Poland. As Marcos Silber explains, "Israel, itself a nationalizing state defined as a Jewish state. Its political elite asserted that Israel had the right, or even an obligation, to monitor the conditions, promote the welfare, support the activities

8. For works on nationalism and communism, see Katherine Verdery, *National Ideology under Socialism: Identity and Cultural Politics in Ceausescu's Romania* (Berkeley: University of California Press, 1995); Mikołaj Stanisław Kunicki, *Between the Brown and the Red Nationalism, Catholicism, and Communism in Twentieth-Century Poland: The Politics of Bolesław Piasecki* (Athens: University of Ohio Press, 2012).

9. Yuri Slezkine, *The Jewish Century* (Princeton, NJ: Princeton University Press, 2004), 297–98.

and institutions, and protect the interests of their ethnonational fellows: the Jews worldwide, including in Poland. However, in the case of Polish Jewry the ultimate task in this context was to promote their Aliyah [immigration] . . . the Jews in Poland, an ethnocultural minority defined as a national minority by the Polish state as well as by Israel. These Jews were caught between two mutually exclusive nationalisms."[10] The June 1967 War and reactions to it among Polish Jews became proof that Jews were untrustworthy and had no place in communist Poland, forcing them to emigrate. Like the Russians a decade before, now Gomułka was creating an ethnically Polish communism; unlike the Russians, he could do so in an ethnically homogenous country, since the few left of the German and the Jewish minority were emigrating.[11]

The June 1967 War

The June 1967 War began on June 5 with an Israeli air raid on Egyptian bases. When the conflict ended, on June 10, Israel had overpowered its opponents on all three fronts, capturing parts of Jordan, Egypt, and Syria.[12] Recent scholarship has debated whether and why the Soviet Union deliberately heightened tensions that led to the outbreak of war between Israel and Egypt. It is agreed that it had sought greater influence in the area since the late 1950s, provided the Egyptian and Syrian armies with weapons and military technology, and reported to Arab governments information that accelerated the crisis.[13] In any case, Arab countries' failures in the armed conflict with Israel revealed Soviet military weaknesses.[14] On June 10 the

10. Marcos Silber, "Foreigners or Co-nationals? Israel, Poland, and Polish Jewry (1948–1967)," *Journal of Israeli History: Politics, Society, Culture* 29, no. 2 (2010): 213–32, quote page 214.

11. The Germans were certainly a larger minority then Jews, but they were still small in relation to the size of the population. Marcos Silber, "Foreigners or Co-nationals? Israel, Poland, and Polish Jewry (1948–1967)," *Journal of Israeli History* 29, no. 2 (2010): 213–32.

12. Benny Morris, *Righteous Victims: A History of the Zionist-Arab Conflict, 1881–1999* (New York: Knopf, 1999), 327.

13. In early May 1967, when Anwar Sadat, president of the National Assembly of Egypt, visited Moscow, Soviet officials informed him that Israel was planning to attack Syria on May 17; the rumor later proved unfounded. Morris, *Righteous Victims*, 304–5. When Sadat passed along the Soviet intelligence, the Egyptian president, Gamal Abdel Nasser, asked United Nations peacekeeping troops to leave the Israeli-Egyptian border and ordered in naval vessels that blockaded the Gulf of Aqaba to ships under Israeli flags, which quickly led to the outbreak of war. The reasons for the Soviet misinformation remain disputed. Rami Ginat, "The Soviet Union: The Roots of the War and a Reassessment of Historiography," in *The 1967 Arab-Israeli War: Origins and Consequences*, ed. Wm. Roger Louis and Avi Shlaim, (New York: Cambridge University Press, 2012), 193–218.

14. For more about Soviet-Israeli relations and the Six-Day War, see Yosef Govrin, *Israeli-Soviet Relations, 1953–1967: From Confrontation to Disruption* (London: Frank Cass, 1998), 276–325.

Soviet Union—later followed by all the Warsaw Pact countries, with the exception of Romania—cut its diplomatic ties with Israel. The Soviets continued to provide aid to Egypt in exchange for the use of harbors and military bases. The Americans, for their part, supported Israel, turning the Middle East into a central theater of the Cold War.[15]

In the days before the June 1967 War, the Israeli public felt growing anxiety about the fate of the State of Israel, as the press reported on Arab preparations for war. Twenty-two years after the end of World War II, many feared a second Holocaust. The Israeli media compared Nasser to Hitler and Israel to Czechoslovakia, stirring anxiety.[16] As one Israeli kibbutz member explained, "it's true that people believed that we faced annihilation if we would lose the war."[17] Jewish communities around the world expressed similar fears, declaring, "We don't want another Auschwitz!"[18] Jews across the world raised money and recruited volunteers who came to Israel to work, replacing the men sent to the battlefield.[19]

Polish Jews were no different: they too wrote anxious letters to their relatives and friends in Israel, wondering when Jewish suffering would end and hoping that a second Holocaust would not occur. Israelis who had emigrated from Poland were in many cases either Holocaust survivors or the last remaining members of their families. The Israeli ambassador to Poland, Dov Satat, claimed that during the war the embassy received 3,200 letters of support for Israel, and not only from Jews.[20] Department W of Poland's secret police regularly inspected letters sent to and from the country: before and during the June 1967 War, its officers recorded and reported passages from letters Polish Jews sent to Israel. N. P. from Wrocław wrote to P. M. in Petach Tikva, "We have suffered enough." I. C. from Szczecin wished D.

---

15. Morris, *Righteous Victims*, 344.

16. Irit Keynan, "Milhemet sheshet ha-yamim ke-mara le-idan tikshurti she-halaf," in *Shishah yamim—sheloshim shanah: maba·t ·hadash 'al Mil·hemet sheshet ha-yamim*, ed. Asher Susser (Tel Aviv: Am-oved, 1999), 216.

17. Interview with Yariv from kibbutz Ein Ha'horesh, in *The Seventh Day: Soldiers' Talk about the Six-Day War*, ed. Avraham Shapira (London: Andre Deutsch, 1970), 164.

18. Mordechai Bar-On, *Gevulot ashenim: iyunim be-toldot Medinat Yi·sra'el 1948–1967* (Jerusalem: Yad Izhak Ben-Zvi Press, 2001), 372.

19. Jeremy Robson, ed., *Letters to Israel: Summer 1967* (London: Mitchell Valentine, 1968, published for the Volunteers' Union). For more about Jews' reactions to the war, see Eli Lederhendler, ed., *The Six-Day War and World Jewry* (Bethesda: University Press of Maryland, 2000).

20. "Poland: The Jewish Question," *Time*, August 18, 1967, http://content.time.com/time /subscriber/article/0,33009,840966,00.html. The Security Services monitored these letters. See Archiwum Instytut Pamięci Narodowej [AIPN; Archives of the Institute of National Remembrance] 01299/996, 69–73, 94–98.

A. in Tel Aviv "an end to Haman's contemporary," and H. S., a doctor from Wrocław, declared in a letter to M. S. in Haifa, "I am with you with all my heart; every day I think of my brothers fighting for their existence. . . . My whole heart is with you, brothers of my blood and my life saved from the crematoria."[21]

Setting the Stage for the Anti-Zionist Campaign

The Polish Ministry of Internal Affairs kept tabs on the Jewish community in the same manner that it monitored all other "national minorities." It reported that at the end of 1966 about twenty-five thousand Jews resided in Poland and claimed that 30 percent of the country's Jews were members of the TSKŻ.[22] The TSKŻ enjoyed the largest budget among the minority associations: in 1966, it stood at 8,943,100 zł (approximately $124,210), and that mostly came from the Joint.[23] Before the June 1967 War, the Ministry of Internal Affairs' Department I, in charge of domestic intelligence, already described "World Zionism" as hatching an anti-Polish plot. In March 1967, it warned that "the State of Israel is using its Polish embassy for ideological and political infiltration."[24] The minister of internal affairs, Mieczysław Moczar, led the nationalist faction; they hoped to make socialism more ethnically Polish—that is, less Jewish. This could be achieved through a strong Polish socialist state with a powerful police mechanism. Moczar and his men believed in a solid alliance with the Soviet Union and in "national communism," which stressed local elements of the system and its suitability to Poland as well as the similarity between rulers and citizens, all ethnic Poles. Nicknamed "partisans" for their professed role in fighting the German occupation during World War II, they had managed to achieve positions of power in the party and in government by the mid-1960s. They saw Jews as contaminating Poland with foreign ideas about both reform and

---

21. AIPN 01299/901, 247–48. Initials appear in the original documents.

22. AIPN BU MSW II 51, 1–15. The Joint Distribution Committee (the Joint) estimated that the number of Jews in Poland at the time was closer to twenty thousand, while the Israeli embassy put the figure at twenty-three thousand. The American and Israeli figures are also speculative, as no one knows how many ceased to identify themselves as Jews after World War II. For a discussion of the number of Jews in Poland, see Daniel Blatman, "Polish Jewry, the Six-Day War, and the Crisis of 1968," in *The Six-Day War and World Jewry*, ed. Eli Lederhendler (Bethesda: University Press of Maryland, 2000), 291–310.

23. AIPN BU MSW II 51, 1–15.

24. AIPN BU MSW II 51, 7. The text in Polish: "O penetracji ideologicznej i politycznej państwa Izrael poprzez jego ambasadę w PRL."

Stalinism and as threatening the future of communism. They blamed Jews for the ills of the Polish socialist state and thought they could trust only ethnic Poles in the governing of the state.[25]

From the standpoint of the Ministry of Internal Affairs, the Joint's American money that funded Jewish activities came with an anticommunist pro-Zionist agenda.[26] In 1949, the Soviet authorities claimed that the Jewish Antifascist Committee (JAC), formed in the Soviet Union to help propaganda efforts during World War II, was conspiring with the Joint to establish a Jewish republic in the Crimea that would become an American stronghold. From 1949 to 1952, Soviet Security Services arrested and secretly tried fifteen people connected with the JAC; fourteen of them were executed. The details of the trials, revealed decades later, give us some idea of how a communist regime perceived Jewish philanthropy.[27] According to the indictment, the JAC had encouraged a brand of Jewish nationalism with strong links to American imperialism. The NKVD (People's Commissariat of Internal Affairs) saw the Joint, a Western nonpartisan charity organization, as a cover for American espionage and sabotage, a "bourgeois Zionist organization."[28] Similarly, twenty years later, the officials of Department I in the Polish Ministry of Internal Affairs viewed the Joint as part of a wider Zionist conspiracy, as an organization closely linked to American interests that promoted Jewish nationalism, and they worried about its influence on Polish Jews. The World Zionist Organization (WZO) also aroused fear of Jewish American conspiracies. In a secret document from April 15, 1967, a key researcher at the Ministry of Internal Affairs described the tenets, structure, and activities of the WZO, presenting it as an antisocialist movement operating clandestinely in Eastern Europe. The movement's strong connections with West Germany (Federal Republic of Germany, FRG) explained why it planned to attack Poland first, according to this analysis. The author of the document was probably Tadeusz Walichnowski, a section

---

25. Protokół nr. 002/67 posiedzenia Kolegium do Spraw Operacyjnych MSW [Protocol of the meeting of the committee for Operational Affairs Ministry of Internal Affairs], in Dariusz Stola, *Kampania*, 292–313. Sławomir Cenckiewicz, *Oczami Bezpieki: Szkice i materiały z dziejów aparatu bezpieczeństwa PRL* (Kraków: Wydawnictwo ARCANA, 2004), 269–78.

26. AIPN BU MSW II 51, 8.

27. Joshua Rubenstein and V. P. Naumov, eds., *Stalin's Secret Pogrom: The Postwar Inquisition of the Jewish Anti-Fascist Committee*, trans. Laura Ester Wolfson (New Haven, CT: Yale University Press, 2001), 63, 84. See also Shimon Redlich, *War, Holocaust, and Stalinism: A Documented History of the Jewish Anti-Fascist Committee in the USSR* (Luxembourg: Harwood Academic, 1995), 147.

28. Rubenstein and Naumov, *Stalin's Secret Pogrom*, 84.

head at Department I who had written several publications about Zionism and Israel and a doctoral dissertation (Warsaw University, 1967) entitled *The Role of the State of Israel in Forming the German Federal Republic's Foreign Policy (1945–1966)*.[29] His April report reveals that before the June 1967 War the Ministry of Internal Affairs harbored growing anxieties about Zionism. Walichnowski claimed that Zionists, working with "West German revanchists" and "American imperialists," had a growing influence over Polish Jews, who in turn undermined the socialist government. The ideas of the hard-liner nationalist group in the party, articulated in Walichnowski's work, shaped the Polish regime's political-ideological discourse on Jews during the June 1967 War and the March 1968 events.

The extensive April 1967 report begins by narrating recent Jewish history and politics: Jews worked mostly as store owners, bankers, and academics, occupations long associated with capitalism and nationalism. Since capitalism and Jewish nationalism (Zionism) went together and most Jews lived in noncommunist countries, it followed that most Jews were Zionists. But not all Jews admitted it: Zionist organizations often relied on innocuous front identities that enabled them to operate freely.[30] Uniting the Zionist movement, according to this narrative, was the World Zionist Organization (WZO); American Jews formed the majority of its members, and it sought mass immigration to Israel and the security of the Jewish state. To those ends, Zionists maintained close ties with imperialist forces—that is, with the United States—and together with the Jewish Agency, the WZO spread pro-Israeli propaganda and subsidized Jewish immigration.[31] From a socialist point of view, the WZO functioned almost like the Soviet Communist Party: it embodied the ideological truth, directed allied groups around the world, and controlled the state. As the Ministry of Internal Affairs failed to grasp the existence of civil society, its officials also could not see a diaspora organization such as the WZO as a voluntary group with waning influence since Israeli independence; rather, they perceived it as a powerful institution dominating world Jewry. To the Polish Security Services, a call by the WZO president, Nahum Goldmann, for Zionists to penetrate and influence Jewish organizations in order to aid Israel thus sounded like a threat from a powerful international force. And for Walichnowski, the WZO represented

29. AIPN BU 0194/2617, 20. The dissertation's title in Polish: "Rola Państwa Izrael w Założeniach Polityki Zagranicznej Niemieckiej Republiki Federalnej (1945–1966)."

30. AIPN 01288/29, 2–3.

31. AIPN 01288/29, 3–5.

more than just Zionists; it stood for the Jewish people.[32] He asserted that the WZO was waging war on communism and quoted several Zionist leaders who presented socialist states as harmful to Jews and Judaism. Zionists used Israeli and American embassies in the European People's Republics to spread Zionist materials encouraging emigration. Finally, claimed Walichnowski, the WZO signed a secret agreement with the American government to use Jewish philanthropic groups to collect information on socialist countries and distribute pro-American propaganda.[33] Israel, continued the narrative, had created the idea of "dual loyalty": every Jew, the world over, owed loyalty both to his or her country of residence and to Israel. Should a conflict between the loyalties arise, Israel should always come first. The belief that Jews were not completely loyal to their homeland was not unique to Poland, and it was harmful to Jewish communities in many countries, particularly ones in conflict with Israel. The establishment of Israel served only to exasperate distrust of Jews, since now the Jewish state claimed them as citizens.

In socialist countries, continued the extensive report, the Zionists pursued a threefold policy toward Jews: persuading them to emigrate, establishing strong national and ideological ties with Israel, and using them "knowingly and unknowingly" to promote Israeli interests.[34] In a similar vein, Department I sent a report to the Polish Ministry of Foreign Affairs about the Israeli Foreign Ministry's stance toward Poland, warning of an "anti-Polish atmosphere" and of Israeli attempts to gain the support of Polish Jews.[35] Though he believed that Jews enjoyed unusually good treatment in his country, Walichnowski maintained that Zionists used Poland as fertile ground for their activity, which could easily spread to the rest of the communist bloc. They employed a range of tactics to sway Polish Jews: strengthening ties with Jewish communist organizations, providing Jews with moral and material support while encouraging them to pursue more influential jobs, and establishing contacts with Jewish academics. The

---

32. AIPN 01288/29, 5–8.

33. AIPN 01288/29, 13–16. It should be noted that Israel and its embassies worked for Jewish emigration, which they saw as part of the Zionist mission. However, this policy was known to the Polish government, and it was not part of a conspiracy to topple communism. See Silber, "Foreigners or Co-nationals?"

34. AIPN 01288/29, 17.

35. The report, also from April 1967, is quoted in Stankowski, "Zerwanie stosunków dyplomatycznych z Izraelem przez Polskę w czerwcu 1967 roku," in *Rozdział wspólnej historii Studia z dziejów Żydów w Polsce* (Warsaw: Cyklady, 2001), 360.

leaders of the WZO even visited Poland in 1964, taking the opportunity to meet with the heads of the TSKŻ. And the Israeli embassy kept in regular contact with a variety of Jewish entities, including the TSKŻ, the Religious Association, and the Jewish Historical Institute.[36] Perhaps the most serious accusation in the April 1967 report was that Zionist groups tried to destabilize socialism and strengthen West Germany by publishing books on World War II that defile Poland's good name internationally.[37] According to this theory, Zionist organizations and Israel stood behind several publications that presented Poles as antisemites and collaborators with Nazi Germany, among them works of fiction such as *Exodus* (1958) by Leon Uris and *The Painted Bird* (1965) by Jerzy Kosinski, as well as memoirs and history books.[38] The report explained that these historical distortions stemmed from the relationship between Zionism and West Germany. Many Polish officials viewed West Germany as the main threat to Poland, an ally of the imperialist United States and part of the Western bloc. Postwar Poland, in accordance with the Yalta Conference, had incorporated former German territories and had expelled millions of Germans. Relations between the countries had been difficult.[39] The "hostile intentions" of West Germany and the United States figured prominently in socialist propaganda; the Polish press devoted many pages to describing the rearmament of West Germany and its malevolent plans for Poland.[40]

The Ministry of Internal Affairs advanced the idea that Israel and West Germany had entered into a secret pact to slander the Polish people and their government: to improve Germany's good name, Poland and the Poles were blamed for the Holocaust.[41] The ministry claimed that as part of the reparation settlement, Israel agreed to work for the rehabilitation of West

---

36. AIPN 01288/29, 16–18.

37. AIPN 01288/29, 20–21.

38. Works cited in the report include Oscar Pinkus, *The House of Ashes* (1964), Alexander Donat, *The Holocaust Kingdom* (1965), Jean-François Steiner, *Treblinka* (1966), and Chaim Kaplan, *Scroll of Agony* (1965); as well as history books Harry M. Rabinowicz, *The Legacy of Polish Jewry: A History of Polish Jews in the Inter-war Years, 1919–1939* (1965), Max I. Dimont, *Jews, God, and History* (1962), and Milo Anstadt, *Polen: Land, Volk, Cultuur* (1965). AIPN 01288/29, 19.

39. West Germany refused to recognize Poland's postwar western borders at the time, and Poland saw West Germany as the enemy at the gate, the heir to Nazi Germany. For an overview of the subject, see Tomasz Kamusella, "The Twentieth Anniversary of the German-Polish Border Treaty of 1990: International Treaties and the Imagining of Poland's Post-1945 Western Border," *Journal of Borderlands Studies* 25 (2010): 120–43.

40. Archiwum Akt Nowych, archives of New Records (AAN) 237/VIII-870, 237/VIII-869.

41. AIPN 01288/29, 21–23.

Germany's international reputation.[42] Upon signing the reparations agreement, the Israeli prime minister, David Ben-Gurion, said that West Germany had nothing in common with Nazi Germany, and the president of the
WZO, Nahum Goldmann, described it as one of Israel's best friends.[43] These
statements constituted proof of a plot, in the eyes of ministry officials, for
how could Israel forgive the past so quickly? This conspiracy theory rings
familiar since it has reemerged lately in connection with Polish legislation
regulating the research and memory of World War II. Israeli and Jewish
protests against new laws in contemporary Poland have led some right-wing
activists in Poland to revive the allegation that an Israeli-German ploy stood
behind "anti-Polish" publications. Clearly, the discourse of the communist
Ministry of Internal Affairs on Jews and Israel still carries power in Poland.

As indicated in studies on trust, feelings of victimization decrease trust
in others while increasing trust in one's own group.[44] In this case, the Polish officials felt under attack by "Zionism." The ministry's reports created a
sense of threat to the group, now delineated by ethnic criteria and not loyalty
to ideology, intensifying distrust toward the group of "others," the Jews. The
ideas of Walichnowski and like-minded officers in the Ministry of Internal
Affairs received a far larger audience when the June 1967 War broke out and
the Soviets sided with the Arab states. For ministry officials, the behavior of
Polish Jews during the crisis served as further proof that the Israeli embassy
and the WZO had succeeded in enticing Jews to serve Zionist interests and
turn against the Polish communist regime. Jews could no longer be trusted
to hold any position of influence, and party bureaucrats feared that the Jews
would triumph in undermining Gomułka's government.

In the days following the outbreak of war between Israel and its neighbors, the Soviet press devoted many articles to factory meetings condemning Israel and reported that hundreds of letters had been received cheering
on the Arab troops.[45] There could be no doubt which way the wind was

42. For more on the reparations agreement, see Ronald W. Zweig, *German Reparations and the
Jewish World: A History of the Claims Conference* (London: Frank Cass, 2001). East Germany (the
German Democratic Republic) rejected the idea of reparations and refused to participate in the
agreement. In September 1952, West Germany had acknowledged Germany's responsibility for the
Holocaust and subsequently pledged to pay billions of dollars in compensation to its victims, mostly
to Jews in Israel.

43. AIPN 01288/29, 22.

44. Rotella et al., "Blinding Trust."

45. Zvi Gitleman, "The Psychological and Political Consequences of the Six-Day War in the
U.S.S.R.," in *The Six-Day War and World Jewry*, ed. Eli Lederhendler (Bethesda: University Press of
Maryland, 2000), 249–67.

blowing: Polish communists quickly blamed only Israel for the war,[46] and on June 6, 1967, the Polish government officially announced its support for the Arab states.[47] The Central Committee's organizational department informed the party leadership that Warsaw was abuzz with talk of the war.[48] At that point, the Security Services intensified its scrutiny of Jews, monitoring their activities and distinguishing them more rigorously from non-Jewish Poles. Reports were passed along to the minister of internal affairs, his departmental directors, and First Secretary Gomułka.[49] In its correspondences, the Ministry of Internal Affairs described Polish Jews as citizens "of Jewish decent" (osoby pochodzenia żydowskiego) or "of Jewish nationality" (osoby narodowości żydowskiej) while referring to other Poles simply as "Poles." These categories are not new. During the interwar period, as determined by the minority treaties of the early 1920s, Jews had been defined as a national minority, an entity that earned its rights collectively. Many Poles in the 1920s and 1930s did not view Jews as an integral part of the Polish nation, but rather as a hindrance to full independence. The majority of Polish Jews also kept to themselves, with only a minority perusing Polonization and integration into Polish society.[50] Noticeably, some in the party still refused, two decades later, to consider Jews as part of the Polish socialist nation, which in theory was to encompass all ethnic groups living in Poland.

The Ministry of Internal Affairs' reporting focused on the five thousand members of the TSKŻ, a tiny group that identified as communists and as Jews. Since they were professed communist believers, they could potentially constitute an opposition group—that is, a particularly dangerous

46. AIPN BU MSW II 7275, 440–41

47. "Oświadczenie Rządu Polskiej Rzeczypospolitej Ludowej," *Żołnierz Wolności*, June 7, 1967.

48. KC PZPR Wydział Organizacyjny Informacja [Central Committee Polish United Workers Party Organizational Department] nr. 19/A/4317, 6 czerwca 1967, in *Marzec '68: Między tragedią a podłością*, ed. Grzegorz Sołtysiak and Józef Stępień (Warsaw: Profi, 1998), 9–10.

49. Protokół nr. 002/67 posiedzenia Kolegium do Spraw Operacyjnych MSW, in Stola, *Kampania*, 292–313.

50. Joanna Beata Michlic, *Poland's Threatening Other: The Image of the Jew from 1880 to the Present* (Lincoln: University of Nebraska Press, 2006); Alina Cała, "Mniejszość żydowska," in *Mniejszości narodowe w Polsce: państwo i społeczeństwo polskie a mniejszości narodowe w okresach przełomów politycznych (1944–1989)*, ed. Piotr Madajczyk (Warsaw: Instytut Studiów Politycznych Polskiej Akademii Nauk, 1998), 245–89; Yfaat Weiss, *Etniyut ·ve-ezra·hut* (Jerusalem: Hotsa'at sefarim 'a. sh. Y. L. Magnes, ha-Universi·tah ha-'Ivrit: Mekhon Leo Be·k, 761, 2000); Carole Fink, *Defending the Rights of Others: The Great Powers, the Jews, and International Minority Protection, 1878–1938* (New York: Cambridge University Press, 2006); Jerzy Ogonowski, *Sytuacja prawna Żydów w Rzeczypospolitej Polskiej 1918–1939* (Warsaw: Żydowski Instytut Historyczny, 2012).

enemy seeking to destroy the party from within.[51] Whether or not they had celebrated Israel's victory over the Arab countries became unimportant: regardless of their stated purpose, all the activities of these Jews—and very quickly this would apply to *all* Jews—became fraught with conspiratorial meanings. Historian Igal Halfin has shown that when communists discuss criminal guilt, intent far outweighs action.[52] And in this case the officials saw almost every Polish Jew as a Zionist, and every Zionist, by definition, cheered Israel. Reports sent from the Ministry of Internal Affairs to Gomułka and the heads of the communist party stressed the number of Jews who strayed rather than those who accepted the official stance of the Polish government. At the same time, they downplayed expressions of support for Israel in non-Jewish circles.

From the outbreak of the June 1967 War, the ministry issued reports on popular sentiments every twelve hours. The heads of the ministry learned from the first report (June 7) that professors and students from Warsaw University's Philosophy Department had expressed support for Israel.[53] The second bulletin that day mentioned that young Jews wanted to volunteer to serve in the Israeli Army: those with families in Israel saw the war as an attack on "their homeland" (na własną ojczyznę). And workers at the state publishing house defended Israel's actions, saying that the Jewish state had to take up arms in self-defense. The central event in the reports of June 7 was a "nationalistic" (or Zionist) discussion in Club Babel, the TSKŻ-run youth club. Named after the Soviet Jewish writer Isaac Babel, the club hosted political speakers as well as musical performances and amateur theater shows. It was where young Polish Jews shared ideas and discussed current issues openly. According to a report on the meeting, the club invited the editor of the weekly *Polityka*, Mieczysław Rakowski, to speak about "international problems of the communist movement" to a crowd of about a hundred people. According to the ministry's informant, the students were more interested in discussing the recent war in the Middle East than the history of the workers' movement. The students, who "clapped and laughed" when they heard of Israel's recent military actions, asked Rakowski why the Soviet Union had ventured into the Middle East. They also asked why

51. Igal Halfin, *Intimate Enemies: Demonizing the Bolshevik Opposition* (Pittsburgh, PA: Pittsburgh University Press, 2007), 18–32.
52. Igal Halfin, *Terror in My Soul: Communist Autobiographies on Trial* (Cambridge, MA: Harvard University Press, 2003), 10.
53. AIPN 01299–853, 18–21.

the Polish press was reviving "bad feelings" and "antisemitism." They commented, "The situation of the Palestinian Arabs can be compared to that of the Germans expelled from Poland: it is senseless to demand that they return to Israeli territory."[54] Natan Tenenbaum, an editor for the Polish-language TSKŻ magazine *Nasz Głos*, likened the coverage of the conflict in the daily Warsaw newspaper *Życie Warszawy* to the editorial stance of the Nazi *Völkischer Beobachter*. And others criticized the Soviet Union's position with regard to Israel.[55] This Club Babel meeting appears in several later reports as an example of the nationalism of young Jews, especially after the student protests in March 1968.

The report of June 8 described an anti-Israel rally by Arab students and an announcement of solidarity with Israel by a group of writers. It also stated that the heads of the Jewish community perceived the Polish condemnation of Israel as "unfair." In the Yiddish-language newspaper *Folks Sztyme*, workers claimed that the Polish press exhibited a "one-sided" approach, and some journalists wondered who had organized the Arab students' demonstration in Warsaw. In addition, the Israeli embassy had received telephone calls from Polish citizens offering their support, including two students who had volunteered to quit their studies and join the Israeli Army.[56] On the next day, June 9, the Security Service's Warsaw bureau informed the head of the ministry's Department II of Jewish lawyers who sided with Israel: they believed that Israel had been obliged to attack first to avoid destruction.[57] Jewish journalists working for the Polish News Agency and the daily *Kurier Polski* also showed concern for their relatives and friends in Israel. The journalists blamed the Arabs for the war, and one suggested changing a headline from "Israeli Aggression in the Middle East" to "Conflict in the Middle East." Finally, Jewish students in Warsaw distributed a map showing Israel's progress in the war.[58]

The extent to which these accounts reflected reality remains irrelevant: the point here is that officers of the Polish secret police accused Jews of "dual loyalty," and they reported this to their superiors. They did not report

54. "Sytuację arabów palestyńskich można porówać do sytuacji Niemców wysiedlonych z Polski i dlatego nie ma żadnego sensu występowanie o ich powrót na teren Izraela." AIPN 01299/996, 26.
55. Notatka Ministerstwa Spraw Wewnętrznych 8 czerwca 1967, in *Marzec '68: Między tragedią a podłością*, ed. Grzegorz Sołtysiak and Józef Stępień (Warsaw: Profi, 1998), 10–12.
56. AIPN 01299/996, 33–34.
57. AIPN 01299/996, 37.
58. AIPN 01299/996, 35–39.

on Jews condemning Israel, and the evidence against Polish Jews mounted. On June 9, the Ministry of Internal Affairs summoned the TSKŻ leadership to a meeting. In attendance were David Sfard, the TSKŻ vice president, and Leopold Domb, the association's president, among others.[59] In his memoir, Sfard claimed that Gomułka had been furious at the TSKŻ and that the Ministry had therefore asked them to come in: "'What sort of association is this?' Gomułka shouted, 'It has to decide whether it is with us or against us.'"[60] The secretary's anger testified to his disappointment in the previously loyal association and to his fading trust in it. The meeting in the ministry quickly turned into an interrogation, but the undersecretary of state, Zygfryd Sznek, still asked the TSKŻ delegation to condemn Israel's "imperialist politics" and to try to convince Jewish circles to adhere to the official Polish policy.[61] Domb replied passionately that Nasser planned to "liquidate the State of Israel and the Israeli people." Jews were unhappy about the government's stance, and some took to calling the TSKŻ "Judenräte," a reference to the Jewish councils that the German occupiers had created to administer the ghettos. Sfard excoriated the Polish press, arguing that it left Jews no choice but to get their information from Western sources: "We refuse to adopt many of the phrases in the Polish press." Yet, Sfard denied accusations that Jews were disloyal to the regime: "Many of our young people are patriots, and some of them cried because of what happened during the meeting in Club Babel." Sfard warned the ministry officials that the government triggered a rise in antisemitism when it announced that Israel had been the aggressor.[62]

The invitation to the Ministry of Internal Affairs did not alarm Domb or Sfard. The Security Services could not easily rattle the sense of belonging that veteran communists who had survived World War II and Stalinism

---

59. AIPN BU MSW II 7282, unnumbered document, June 1967, 1. During World War II, Leopold Domb (under the name Leopold Trepper) had been the head of the "Red Orchestra," an underground organization that operated in Germany and France, sending information to the Soviet Union. Domb returned to Moscow after the war, only to be arrested and imprisoned until 1954. He returned to Poland in 1957. See V. E. Tarrant, *The Red Orchestra: The Soviet Spy Network inside Nazi Europe* (New York: John Wiley & Sons, 1996).

60. David Sfard, *Mi·t zikh un mi·t andere: oy·tobiografye un li·terarishe eseyen* (Jerusalem: Farlag Yerusholaimer almanakh, 1984), 286.

61. AIPN BU MSW II 7282, unnumbered document, June 1967, 1. The ministry's demand is also mentioned in Sfard's memoir: Sfard, *Mi·t zikh un mi·t andere*, 287. On Sznek, see Mirosław Piotrowski, *Ludzie Bezpieki w walce z narodem i Kościołem* (Lublin: Klub Inteligencji Katolickiej, 1999), 328.

62. AIPN BU MSW II 7282, unnumbered document, June 1967, 3.

felt toward the communist establishment in Poland. The TSKŻ chiefs interpreted the situation as a disagreement over foreign policy, not an internal Polish matter, and they expressed their dissatisfaction with the regime's stance on the Middle East. The ministry officials who attended the meeting understood it in a completely different way. They accused the TSKŻ presidium of collaborating with Zionist organizations in launching an anti-Polish campaign on the pages of its official publication, *Folks Sztyme*, and in the Western Zionist press.[63] Such accusations effectively transformed the Jewish leaders from allies to wreckers.

The Ministry of Internal Affairs did not seek out Jewish confessions as was the practice during Stalinism. Times had changed, and the officials had no interest in the souls of Jewish members. Anyway, the guilt of Polish Jews had been established a priori and collectively. Those who met with Sfard and Domb cared little whether or not they would admit that they had planned an anti-Polish campaign; they simply informed them of their transgressions. Guilt had ceased to operate at the individual level; it now belonged to the entirety of Polish Jews. Those who had registered as Jews and identified with other Jews belonged to a different nation, which rendered their loyalty to Poland questionable. Their conduct during the June 1967 War confirmed the ministry's ideas. While Moscow halted all emigration to Israel in June 1967, Warsaw was eager to get rid of "their Jews," who would always remain a band of outsiders and never a part of the Polish socialist nation.[64]

On June 10, the Warsaw Pact countries declared that they were severing relations with Israel, and on that same day, the June 1967 War ended with an Israeli victory and a cease-fire. The Ministry of Internal Affairs reported that many citizens commented on the weakness of the Arab armies and the vigor of Israeli forces. At the time, many Poles listened to Radio Free Europe, and they had come to believe that the Arab defeat compromised the Soviet Union's reputation.[65] Outside of Poland's Jewish communities, claimed government reports, responses varied: most workers supported the socialist government's line, while the intelligentsia tended to side with Israel.[66]

---

63. AIPN BU MSW II 7282, unnumbered document, June 1967, 4.

64. Memorandum of I. Andropov and A. Gromyko to the CPSU Central Committee, June 10, 1968, in *Documents on Soviet Jewish Emigration*, ed. Boris Morozov (Portland, OR: Frank Cass, 1999), 65. The memorandum discusses the yearlong ban and its effects.

65. AIPN 01299/ 996, 41, 67–68. To the displeasure of the censors and some party members, Poles, particularly in Warsaw, had access to foreign newspapers and magazines and could listen to Radio Free Europe. AAN, KC PZPR 237/V/671, 36; AAN, GUKPPiW 948, 3.

66. AIPN 01299/853, 69–70; AIPN 01299-853, 80.

The Catholic authorities in Poland supported Israel out of concern for the holy places in the war zone, doing much to sway popular sentiment in favor of the Jewish state.[67] On June 6, the head of the Polish Church, Cardinal Wyszyński, had led a prayer for peace in the Holy Land.[68] Sfard wondered: "As communists, how should we understand it when Cardinal Wyszyński prays for the safety of the holy places and peace for Israel, while the Soviet Union supports Nasser?"[69] The Warsaw police informed Department II that in the Jewish Religious Union and in the TSKŻ, "people of Jewish descent" celebrated Israel's success. Stefan Staszewski, one of the most important Stalinists in the party, said that Israel's victory showed the Jews' superiority over the Arabs. In Warsaw's main synagogue, moreover, a communal prayer of thanks was offered for Israel's survival.[70] When the Soviet decision to break relations with Israel was announced, Jews reportedly felt "nervous" and angry. Some, like David Sfard and Hirsch Smolar, *Folks Sztyme*'s editor, dismissed the announcement and recent overtures to Arab states as insincere actions masking geopolitical maneuvering. Others argued that Poland had no right to issue such a statement in the name of the entire nation or to compare the Israeli defense minister, Moshe Dayan, to Hitler. One Polish Jew was quoted as saying that if Poland expected Israel to withdraw from the occupied territories, then Poland should return its western parts to Germany.[71] In Tel Aviv, meanwhile, the manager of the Polish bank Polska Kasa Opieki (PeKaO) permitted an Israeli flag to be hoisted on the building.[72] A special report on reactions to the situation in the Middle East concluded that Polish Jews had a single view of recent events: they all criticized the decision to break off diplomatic relations with Israel. The Ministry of Internal Affairs labeled these words and actions as anti-Polish as well as anti-Soviet, proof of collective Jewish disloyalty to the regime.[73]

Warsaw's police chief wrote a report complaining that the Israeli embassy was trying to convince Polish Jews to declare their support for Israel and to emigrate.[74] On June 11, the police questioned fifteen people as they left the embassy. The Ministry of Internal Affairs' report mentioned

---

67. AIPN 01299/853, 53; AIPN 01299/ 996, 40.
68. Eisler, *Polski Rok 1968*, 638.
69. AIPN 01299/853, 53.
70. AIPN 01299/ 996, 67; AIPN 01299/853, 70.
71. AIPN 01299/853, 80–82.
72. AIPN 01299/853, 76–79.
73. AIPN 01299/996, 48.
74. AIPN 01299/996, 66.

doctors, students, writers, and intellectuals, including the sociologist (and future in-law of David Sfard) Zygmunt Bauman and his wife, Janina. Another was the sixty-year-old author Salomon Łastik, who told the officer who stopped him that the police should put up a sign forbidding entry to the Israeli embassy rather than ask upstanding citizens for their papers. Łastik's wife, who did not have her identification with her, was taken to the local police station. A young man from Wrocław complained that he had to show his papers only because he was a Jew, while an older Wrocławian protested that the officers behaved "like bandits."[75] In her memoir, Janina Bauman describes their encounter with the police that day: "When we finished our cakes and coffee and were returning to the car, we were suddenly stopped by two strangers. They said they were police officers and asked to see our identification cards. Outraged, we asked to see their documents first and demanded to know why we were being stopped. They willingly showed us their licenses but refused to explain what was wrong. They looked at Mother's Israeli passport for a while, wrote down all of her details and ours, then politely said goodbye and let us go."[76] The next day, the Israeli ambassador to Poland, Dov Satat, was asked to leave the country.[77]

On June 12, Gomułka met with the secretaries of the regional party committees to explain Poland's position (which he repeated in a public speech the following week).[78] He began his comments to local leaders by describing relations between Arab nations and Western powers, arguing that new "pan-Arab, anti-imperialist" governments threatened Western oil interests in the Middle East. Western states relied on Israel's "aggression" and "expansionism" to suppress Arab liberation movements and rewarded Israel with financial and military aid. Uninterested in pursuing peace with its neighbors, the Israeli government had started the June 1967 War to stop Syria's socialist Ba'ath Party from revising its oil policy. In this part of the speech, Gomułka mostly reiterated the Soviet party line. The first secretary also made some comparisons between Israel and Nazi Germany. Specifically, Israel's assault that began the war brought to mind the German invasion of Poland in 1939, and Israeli soldiers therefore behaved like Nazis. Gomułka only briefly dwelt on the comparison, but it was fundamental—equating

75. AIPN BU MSW II 5000, 77–81.

76. Janina Bauman, *A Dream of Belonging: My Years in Postwar Poland* (London: Virgo, 1988), 169.

77. Mordecai Palzor, "Polin hidosh ha-yahasim," in *Misrad ha-ḥutz: 50 ha-shanim ha-rishonot,* ed. Mosheh Yegar, Yosef Govrin, Ayreh 'Oded (Jerusalem: Keter, 2002), 56.

78. AAN 237/V/899, 33–56.

Israel to Nazi Germany would become a propaganda staple in the Polish press for a year.[79] Finally, Gomułka cautioned party leaders about hesitating in the fight against capitalist imperialism, which was intensifying its attack on socialism: "In many of *our rings* there are dangerous symptoms of liberalization, a lack of responsibility for the situation in which we find ourselves. This was visible in some Warsaw circles . . . at the time of the events in the Middle East. [We] cannot ignore the celebratory banquets certain institutions have organized to honor Israel's victory, nor can we ignore comments like the one made by the writer who said he had *two homelands*: Israel and Poland. These are not compatible with our state's policies on class and our anti-imperialist politics."[80] Gomułka here sent a clear message to the rank and file: toe the line or there will be consequences. His mention of "liberal rings" is telling: he did not mention Jews directly, preferring instead to talk about rings and "Warsaw circles," euphemisms generally understood in Poland to mean Jewish intellectuals. The idea of two homelands (*ojczyzny*), suggesting the dual loyalty of Jews, made its first public appearance in this speech. Rather than describe Poland as a nation (*naród*), Gomułka chose to refer to it as a state (*państwo*). Those who refused to subscribe to the state's stance had better change their views or they would cease to belong to the state. Jews, in this formulation, could not belong to the Polish nation, but they could still be citizens under certain conditions. Gomułka did not call the Jews traitors or ask them to leave, but he made it clear to the party that a significant change had occurred and that he placed Polish Jews under special scrutiny since his trust in them had been damaged.[81] Two days later, the Warsaw party committee's first secretary spoke to party activists and repeated Gomułka's message. He called the behavior of certain "Polish citizens of Jewish descent" unacceptable and reminded Warsaw's Jews of the paramount importance of loyalty to the party.[82]

However, information about Jewish defiance continued to pile up on Gomułka's desk. These reports increasingly juxtaposed the Poles' embrace of the government's stance with the Jews' rejection of official policy, providing yet more proof of Jewish untrustworthiness in comparison to ethnic

79. AAN 237/V/899, 33–56.

80. AAN 237/V/899, 54.

81. Gomułka's secretary later confirmed that Gomułka had been visibly upset by the reports of Polish Jews supporting Israel. See Stola, "Anti-Zionism as a Multipurpose Policy Instrument," 175–201.

82. AKW PZPR 404, 39–81.

Poles. Accounts emphasized workers' meetings with a pro-Arab consensus, while "workers of Jewish descent" still expressed pro-Israeli views. In Warsaw, intelligence bulletins noted that discussions about the Middle East became much less frequent, with the exception of "people of Jewish nationality," who continued to speculate about the situation.[83] The TSKŻ club in Kraków worked to give Israel "moral and financial" support, alleged the reports. A father and son at the Śląsk TSKŻ branch collected money for Israel, and in Legnica Jews who condemned Israel were verbally attacked (by other Jews).[84] Jews who appeared to accept the party line were described as hiding their real views; in Wrocław, as one account indicated, the TSKŻ leadership told students "not to reveal their views to Polish students."[85]

The names of more and more Jews holding midlevel positions in the party or in the state apparatus appeared in the reports of the Ministry of Internal Affairs. Antoni Zambrowski, son of the well-known Stalinist Party leader Roman Zambrowski, supposedly affirmed Israel's right to hold on to the newly occupied territories. At the *Czytelnik* publishing house, Jewish employees criticized Poland's decision to break off relations with Israel, complaining that "now Poland will have to send aid to Arab countries," and a factory manager referred to the diplomatic crisis as "scandalous and ill-conceived." A director at the Ministry of Health and two Ministry of Foreign Affairs officials objected to donating blood to Arab states and not to Israel. And at the *Książki i Wiedza* publishing house, Jews disapproved of the Soviet Union's position, as did Jews at the Documentary Film Studio, Jagiellonian University, Kraków's Academy of Fine Arts, and the Writers Union, as well as Jewish journalists, lawyers, librarians, writers, intellectuals, and many others.[86] Such lists confirmed the Jews' incorrigibility and their infiltration into every institute in the state, augmenting feelings of fear and the sense that a conspiracy was at work. Jews thus turned into a ubiquitous threat to the stability of the regime in the eye of its Polish heads.

On June 14, the Ministry of Internal Affairs and the party's organizational department issued a report summarizing the reaction of the TSKŻ and "Jewish circles" to the June 1967 War. In the first few days of the conflict, *Folks Sztyme* relied on Western press agencies rather than on the Polish News Agency (PAP) or TASS (Telegraph Agency of the Soviet Union,

---

83. AIPN 01299/996, 91.
84. AIPN 01299/854, 4–7, 15.
85. AIPN 01299/854, 1–3.
86. AIPN 01299/996, 91–93, 103–6; AIPN 01299/854, 7, 14–15, 22–27.

the Soviet news agency) and reported on Israel's decisive victory and its commendation by world Jewry. Meetings between Israeli officials, foreign guests, and the Polish Jewish leadership before the war, stated the report, laid the ground for the presidium's decision to support Israel.

Summing up, the report criticized the TSKŻ heads for their refusal to follow the party line: "Based on a general assessment of the situation in Jewish circles and the attitudes of TSKŻ activists, we note the persistence and strength of pro-Israeli and Zionist feelings in these circles. Many TSKŻ activists, members of the party, have shifted their political position or failed to struggle against pro-Israeli sentiments. Some engaged actively in irresponsible acts against the politics of the People's Republic of Poland and other socialist countries, while others simply acquiesced in these acts. We learned that the heads of the TSKŻ conducted large-scale work among Jewish youths without trying anything to correct their political orientation."[87]

The TSKŻ failed in its mission and deviated from the party line, and it made no attempt to correct the behavior of others or convince Jews to follow official policy, claimed the ministry's officials. Many had turned into Zionists, acting against the best interests of Poland. Jews, explicated the report, could not control their feelings toward Israel, their ethnonational state. Besides, the organization had established strong links with international Zionist organizations and received funds from an American group (the Joint). Something had to be done. To bring the TSKŻ leadership back in line, the report of June 14 proposed that the party call on the TSKŻ to criticize "officially and publicly . . . chauvinistic sentiments" among its members; *Folks Sztyme* would have to publish a denunciation of Israel's actions. TSKŻ leaders needed to get the rank and file of their organization behind the government: the defiance of young people, in particular, would have to be quelled. The association would have to prove it could be trusted. Finally, the report advised the government to halt the flow of money from the Joint, as well as the flow of foreign activists into Poland.[88]

Gomułka Launches the Campaign

The Ministry of Internal Affairs had sent Gomułka dozens of reports on Jews celebrating Israel's victory despite his warnings and following the TSKŻ leaders' professed disinclination to act on the party's criticism. Gomułka

---

87. AIPN 01288/29, 159.
88. AIPN 01288/29, 155–61, quote on page 160.

responded by taking the anti-Israeli campaign a step further. The Ministry had succeeded in spreading fear of a Jewish menace within the party and in raising Gomułka's guards. An opportunity presented itself on June 19. Until then, most party-organized rallies and newspaper articles had denounced Israel and its "imperialistic tendencies" without associating them with Polish Jews. It was during the first secretary's address at the Trade Union Congress that he infamously referred to Polish Jews as a fifth column, enemies within. After a long discussion of Middle Eastern history, Gomułka explained that Poland's stance toward Israel had been influenced by World War II. He went on to say: "We also wonder how the Israeli aggressors have forgotten that the very thing they glorify—the Luftwaffe's domination of the skies over Poland—also brought with it the virtual extermination of the Jews—Polish citizens. The only ones saved were those [Jews] whom the Poles concealed, at the risk of their own lives."[89]

Gomułka invoked the Holocaust, speaking explicitly about the genocide of Europe's Jews, to suggest that Polish Jews owed a debt to their fellow compatriots. He presented the Poles as the true heroes of the war: they gave their own lives to rescue Jews. In contrast, Israeli Jews followed in the footsteps of Germans. He then spoke of Polish Jews' recent behavior:

> In connection with the applause Israel's aggression has elicited in the Zionist milieu of Jewish citizens of Poland, I wish to declare the following: we never made it difficult for Polish citizens of Jewish nationality to move to Israel, whenever they wanted. But we maintain that all Polish citizens should have only one homeland—People's Poland. The government treats every citizen of People's Poland equally, regardless of their nationality. Every citizen of our country who takes advantage of equal rights bears similar responsibilities toward People's Poland. *We do not want a fifth column in our country.* So long as there is a threat to world peace and therefore to the security of our country and the peaceful work of all Polish citizens, it will be impossible for us to remain indifferent to those who support the aggressor, the destroyer of peace. Let those who feel that these words are directed at them draw the appropriate conclusions.[90]

In contrast to Soviet policy, Gomułka was telling Polish Jews to leave: he had lost trust in them; they were "fifth column" agents serving an enemy. In the face of mounting evidence against Polish Jews in the many reports of their disobedience, the secretary could not accept dual loyalty or sympathy for a

---

89. AAN 237/V/899, 85.

90. AAN 237/V/899, 85; Stola, *Kampania*, 41. Italics added by author; this part of the speech did not appear in official party publications.

state squarely entrenched in the Western imperialist camp. Even the Jews who had chosen to continue living in Poland, who had largely accepted the communist regime and had previously been considered loyal, were no longer welcome. Even these Jews could no longer subdue their feelings toward Israel, many in the higher echelons of the party believed. The first secretary turned a dispute over Polish foreign relations into a struggle against traitors; Jews who sided against Poland's allies damaged the country's stability, hardly a suitable response to the nation that had saved their lives and given them equal rights.

Gomułka chose the expression "Polish citizens of Jewish nationality" rather than "Jewish descent," indicating strongly that they were not part of the Polish *naród* or nation and demarcating the line between those "under threat," the non-Jewish citizens of People's Poland, and those "who threaten," the Jewish citizens.[91] At the same time, Gomułka—whose wife was of Jewish descent—made sure not to accuse *all* Jews of betrayal: the term Zionist (applied to anyone who had expressed pro-Israeli or antigovernment views) would henceforth refer to that section of Poland's Jewish population deemed unreliable and untrustworthy. Though the first secretary differentiated between the "Zionist milieu" and the rest of Poland's Jews, the Ministry of Internal Affairs blurred the distinction: any Jew could be a Zionist, a term that denoted an enemy in the Stalinist era.[92]

Interestingly, the version of Gomułka's speech that subsequently appeared in print lacked the paragraph that mentioned Jews as a fifth column, though the entire address was broadcast on the radio.[93] Apparently Gomułka felt unready to circulate his accusations and intimidations outside of Poland. Perhaps he realized that in the face of the Soviet refusal to let Jews leave, his words encouraging them to emigrate from Poland would seem out of place. Since his return to power in 1956, and as part of a larger policy against minorities, Gomułka had promoted Jewish emigration, in contrast to Soviet policies, which permitted only a small number of Jews to leave.

91. Ahmed, *Cultural Politics*, 72. *Naród* holds a different meaning than *nation* in the American or British sense. As in other eastern European languages, *naród* refers to *nation* in the ethnic sense, not as a civic group. Geneviève Zubrzycki, *The Crosses of Auschwitz: Nationalism and Religion in Post-Communist Poland* (Chicago: Chicago University Press, 2006).

92. Zionism constituted one of the main accusations in the Slanski trials in Czechoslovakia in the 1950s, for an important case. Alena Heitlinger, *In the Shadows of the Holocaust and Communism: Czech and Slovak Jews since 1945* (New Brunswick, NJ: Transaction, 2006).

93. The Western press reported this omission. See, for example, Henry Kamm, "Gomułka Warns Pro-Israel Poles," *New York Times*, June 20, 1967.

True to communist practices, the party apparatus organized state-wide meetings to commend Gomułka's speech. Local party organizations passed resolutions backing the government and sent enthusiastic letters to the first secretary. The heads of the Ministry of Internal Affairs, pleased that Gomułka had heeded their warnings of the Jewish threat, outlined ways to deal with the TSKŻ and submitted lists of people holding "Zionist and pro-Israeli" views. Moczar wanted to shut down the TSKŻ, close its schools and newspaper, and stop the flow of money from the United States.[94] On June 21, the director of Department III of the ministry, Henryk Piętek, declared Gomułka's speech a great success among Poland's workers, one of whom was quoted as saying, "The Polish people now love Gomułka more than ever."[95] As the memory of World War II occupied Poles' minds and hearts more than debates on the Middle East, Department I added that many were particularly pleased by the first secretary's retort to "the accusations made by Zionist elements that Poles were complicit in the murder of Jews during the [Nazi] occupation." But the speech had not changed the minds of Jews, they claimed, as officials continued to cite instances of Jewish defiance.[96]

On June 21, the TSKŻ presidium met once more with directors at the Ministry of Internal Affairs and the party. Domb, the head of the Jewish organization, was away on vacation. The government officials repeated to the TSKŻ leadership some of the demands enumerated earlier. These included publicly condemning the behavior of TSKŻ activists and youths; publishing a notice in *Folks Sztyme* critical of Israel's aggression, as well as articles and commentaries supporting the regime's position; and discussing the general attitude among Polish Jews during the next TSKŻ plenary session. At first, Vice President Sfard opined that there was "no difference" between what the government demanded and what the organization had already done. But when the officials asked to know when the TSKŻ would publish a condemnation, Sfard and the others replied that they disagreed with some of "Comrade Gomułka's statements" and would have to meet with the rest of the presidium before making any announcements. Sfard added that the presidium had "many chores" to attend to before it could

---

94. AIPN BU MSW II 52, 234–62; AIPN BU MSW II 7282, 386–400; AAN KC PZPR XIA/301, 82–88.

95. AIPN 01288/29, 71–72.

96. AIPN 01299/854, 36–40.

issue any statement. Exasperated, the government officials warned the presidium to comply promptly.[97]

When Sfard communicated the gist of the meeting to the TSKŻ presidium, the group stoutly refused to denounce either Polish Jews or Israel.[98] The presidium's members worried that if they condemned Israel in the name of Polish Jews, they would distance themselves from Jews around the world and much-needed foreign aid would cease; the elderly in the community heavily relied on it. TSKŻ officials were also concerned that Gomułka's speech would encourage antisemitism.[99] The public statement that the TSKŻ finally drafted was rejected by the Ministry of Internal Affairs and the party leaders, who accused the association of doing its best to look like a "branch of the Israeli Communist Party."[100] On June 26, during yet another meeting with officials from the Ministry of Internal Affairs, Sfard stressed that he saw no reason to fault Israel's recent actions; reports of brutality had yet to convince him. The more important issue, he said, concerned Gomułka's words that had hurt "many good communists—Jews, not only Jewish communists in Poland but also Jewish communists throughout the world." Sfard added that the announcement the government requested would damage the TSKŻ's reputation and drive many members to resign. Once more, it became clear to government officials that Sfard and his associates would not easily embrace the regime's position and could not be trusted to rectify the situation.

Yet the TSKŻ eventually capitulated, most probably hoping to put this chapter behind it. It condemned "the aggressive [i.e., Israeli] act, inspired and supported by Anglo-American imperialism" and "the deplorable expulsion of Arabs from the areas occupied by the Israeli army." The announcement called for an Israeli withdrawal from territories formerly held by Arabs and warned the Israeli government against the consequences of its "false politics" and aggressive behavior. Parts of Gomułka's speech, in which he spoke for Israel's independence and cooperation with the Arab states, were

---

97. AIPN BU MSW II 7282, unnumbered document, June 1967, 7–8. Sfard offered a similar description of the meeting in his memoir. Sfard, *Mi·t zikh un mi·t andere*, 286. For the situation in the TSKŻ, I relied mostly on Ministry of Interior reports, since they present the regime's point of view on the Jewish organization. Sfard's memoirs confirm events described in reports (which he obviously had not read).

98. Sfard, *Mi·t zikh un mi·t andere*, 287.

99. AIPN 01299/854, 48–52.

100. AIPN BU MSW II 7282, unnumbered document, June 1967, 8.

quoted. The statement, however, failed to restore trust, and party officials continued to view the Jewish organization with suspicion.[101]

On June 26, a week after the fifth-column speech, Department III circulated a secret list of the number of Jews in key political, cultural, and economic institutions. For instance, the Ministry for Chemical Industry employed one Jew as vice minister, two as advisers, three as deputy directors, and sixteen in other positions. At the Ministry of Arts and Culture, twenty "persons of Jewish nationality" worked as directors and fifty-eight held other posts.[102] This cataloguing of Jews testified once more to the ethnic nature of the anti-Zionist campaign, at least for those in the Ministry of Internal Affairs who sought a more Polish communist regime and distrusted the Jewish minority. They feared hidden Jews, Jews who had too much influence in state institutions and who imposed their "Zionist" agenda on the Polish people.

The "ethnic turn" could also be read in a document produced at the Ministry of Internal Affairs that summarized the national mood during the period from June 5 to July 12. Kazimierz Świtała, the report's author, had been appointed in June as undersecretary of state in the ministry (equivalent to vice minister). This review, in which Poles were contrasted with Jews again and again, clarified why those of Jewish descent could not be trusted and prepared the ground for a purge. Ethnic Poles who showed sympathy for Israel were referred to as "Catholics of Jewish descent," and news that Poles cheered Israel's victory always came from Israeli diplomats or Western journalists—so naturally it was untrue. Ongoing contacts between Jews in Poland and those in Israel strengthened the grip of Israeli diplomats over Jewish Poles. It was little wonder, then, that so many Jews sent letters to the Israeli embassy and to friends and family in Israel offering help and congratulations on the victory.[103] Świtała accused Jews in "prominent social positions, formerly in [state] service," of failing to condemn Israel and its imperialist politics.[104] The vice minister insisted that even after Gomułka's speech Poland's Jews had not balked; instead of recanting, they attacked the first secretary in a "hateful, aggressive, and offensive fashion."[105] He maintained that the party would simply be acting in self-defense if it were to

---

101. AAN 237/VIII–918, 440–41.

102. AIPN 01288/29, Zestawienie cyfrowe osób narodowości żydowskiej, June 26, 1967.

103. AIPN 1288/29, Informacja za okres od 5 czerwca do 12 lipca 1967r., 1–4.

104. AIPN 1288/29, Informacja za okres od 5 czerwca do 12 lipca 1967r., 6–8.

105. AIPN 1288/29, Informacja za okres od 5 czerwca do 12 lipca 1967r., 9. "nienawistny, napastliwy i obraźliwy sposób."

purge citizens of Jewish descent.[106] Members of the TSKŻ and the ZRWM, the Jewish religious association, proved the most defiant. Funded by the Joint and fed information by foreign contacts, these groups revealed their true colors on the pages of *Folks Sztyme* and in their meetings with the heads of the Ministry of Internal Affairs.[107] At the end of his report, Świtała stressed the loyalty of Poles and the treason of the Jews, conditioned by years of Zionist work in Poland.[108] For him, in the same manner that Poland aimed to be inhabited and governed by Poles, so Israel strove to bring together all Jews (which was indeed Israeli policy).[109] Thus, in the face of evidence of Jewish sentiments toward Israel, Świtała and other high-ranking officials rejected the idea of a Jewish identity disconnected from Zionism and ethnonationalism. He concluded with reassuring words: "At this time . . . [we] would like to inform the heads of the party that the Ministry of Internal Affairs stands ready to take the necessary steps to counter any irresponsible and provocative disturbances."[110]

At the end of July, Department III calculated that from June 5 to July 28, 1,232 people had revealed negative attitudes toward the government's position on the Middle East. The report detailed their professions and divided them by nationality: 994 Jews and 238 Poles. The majority in both groups, Poles and Jews, were either "intelligentsia" working as state bureaucrats or managers in the administration and economy.[111] By August the numbers had increased to 1,286 Jews and 267 Poles.[112] Although the ministry was preparing for a purge, the figures actually indicated that the number of citizens speaking out against the government remained tiny, about 1,500 out of 35 million Poles. This minuscule and imagined threat illuminates most strikingly the political discourse of security that marks the rise of the nation-state and still affects daily life in the early twenty-first century.[113]

---

106. AIPN 1288/29, Informacja za okres od 5 czerwca do 12 lipca 1967r., 9–10.

107. AIPN 1288/29, Informacja za okres od 5 czerwca do 12 lipca 1967r., 10–11.

108. AIPN 1288/29, Informacja za okres od 5 czerwca do 12 lipca 1967r., 16–17. He cites as examples the head of cadres and professional schools in the Central Geology Bureau, Bolesław Bursztyn, whose daughter had moved to Israel, and the head of a censorship department at the Central Committee, Wilhelm Strasser, whose brother served in the Israeli Army.

109. Silber, "Foreigners or Co-nationals?"

110. Silber, "Foreigners or Co-nationals?," 17.

111. AIPN 1288/29, Notatka danych liczbowych osób, które w okresie konfliktu na Bliskim Wschodzie zajęły postawę proizraelską, July 30, 1967.

112. AIPN 1288/29, Notatka, August 31, 1967.

113. For analysis of contemporary security discourse, see Lene Hansen, *Security as Practice: Discourse Analysis and the Bosnian War* (New York: Routledge, 2013); Jef Huysmans, "What's in an Act? On Security Speech Acts and Little Security Nothings," *Security Dialogue* 42 (2011): 371–83.

Beyond the specifics of the communist regime in Poland, we see here a case of how an "enemy" is constructed by surveillance and security authority figures who often believe they are working to protect society. Rather than simply an image meant to manipulate the masses, the enemy group also stems from ideas about nation and state—about who *in principle* can and cannot be trusted. The drive to consolidate the Polish communist state had led to the violent deportations of Germans after World War II, the expulsions and forced relocations of Ukrainians and Lemkos, and the thorough effort to "Polonize" the new territories gained from Germany.[114] The regime now turned to remove remaining Jews and complete the transformation of Poland into an ethnically homogenous state.

This chapter traced how official condemnation of Israel in Poland after the Six-Day War turned into denunciation of Polish Jews and how, in the process, the regime completed the transformation of Jews from trusted citizens of socialist Poland into a disloyal and subversive minority. This shift revealed the worldview of the heads of the Ministry of Internal Affairs, a blend of nationalist and communist ideas that portrayed Polish Jews as undermining the socialist project. The Ministry of Internal Affairs viewed Polish Jews with suspicion and searched for Zionist "enemies" before the student protests of March 1968.

---

114. Hugo Service, "Reinterpreting the Expulsion of Germans from Poland, 1945–9," *Journal of Contemporary History* 47 (2012): 528–50.

3

THE ENCYCLOPEDIA AND
"THE FALSIFICATION OF HISTORY"

IN THE SUMMER OF 1967, ON THE HEELS of Gomułka's dramatic June speech, a powerful dispute centering on the communist *Wielka Encyklopedia Powszechna's* (The great general encyclopedia) entries on World War II erupted in the Polish United Workers' Party (PUWP). In the entry on concentration camps, Janusz Gumkowski, the former director of the Central Commission for the Investigation of Hitlerite Crimes in Poland, described two types of camps: death camps and concentration camps:

> On what is today Polish soil, there were four main camps: Gross Rosen near Świdnica . . . Stutthof near Gdańsk . . . Oświęcim-Brzezinka (Auschwitz-Birkenau), and Majdanek. The last two were also sites of mass extermination. Called by the Nazis Sonderlager, meaning "special camps," and, unofficially, Vernichtungslager, meaning "death camps," they did not have the characteristics of [other concentration] camps and were a separate link in the chain of the Hitlerite policy of extermination. The only function of death camps was the mass killing of people—they were set up only on Polish soil for the mass extermination of Jews from the whole of Europe, as part of the realization of the "final solution of the Jewish question" (Endlosung der Judenfrage).[1]

The paragraph above easily could have appeared at the time in a Western European encyclopedia: in essence, the Nazi leadership planned the annihilation of Europe's Jews and murdered them in death camps set up during Operation Reinhard.[2] Twenty years of Polish historical research led to Gumkowski's words. They differed little from the Polish official memory of

---

1. *Wielka Encyklopedia Powszechna* (Warsaw: Panstwowe Wydawnictwo Naukowe, 1966), 8:87–89.

2. Saul Friedländer, *The Years of Extermination: Nazi Germany and the Jews, 1939–1945* (New York: HarperCollins, 2007), 346, 356–57, 431–32, 480. Operation Reinhard, or *Aktion Reinhard*, was the code name for the Nazi deportation of Jews to death camps in 1942–43 as part of the implementation of the "final solution." The Germans set up the camps for the sole purpose of killing Jews.

the Holocaust. By the 1960s, schoolchildren were learning a version of history that included the *final solution* and the death camps. But at a certain moment in the summer of 1967, the PUWP declared it would no longer tolerate such accounts: leading members expressed outrage and surprise that censors had overlooked Gumkowski's article and allowed its publication. They circulated a series of internal reports claiming that, in fact, there were no special death camps for Jews, that all camps functioned as death camps, and that Jews and Poles had shared the same fate during World War II. This marked the beginning of a campaign against the "falsification of history by world Zionism," with the encyclopedia and its Jewish editors singled out over the course of the next year for shrill criticism. In concert with the Ministry of the Interior, party members accused Jews of shifting the blame for the Holocaust from Germany to Poland and of trying to poison world public opinion against their own country. In addition to hounding and purging those involved in preparing and publishing *Wielka Encyklopedia Powszechna*, the party also scrutinized many recent publications that dealt with Polish Jews and World War II.

This chapter looks first at the ways in which World War II and the Holocaust were remembered in Poland before 1967, pointing to the emergence in the late 1950s of a narrative that focused on Polish heroism in the rescue of Jews during the war.[3] It then shows that the memory of World War II became central to the worldview of the politicians and writers behind the anti-Zionist campaign. For the minister of the interior and his supporters, World War II represented a moment of suffering for the cause of Polish freedom and of valor in the face of fascism. This image is a secularized reincarnation of the idea of Poland as "Christ among the nations," the long-held Polish myth of national sacrifice and victimhood. According to sociologist Geneviève Zubrzycki's analysis of the myth, "Poland is

---

3. A growing body of work now exists on Polish-Jewish relations during the war, which lies beyond the scope of this book. See, for example, Barbara Engelking, *Jest taki piękny słoneczny dzień: losy Żydów szukających ratunku na wsi polskiej 1942–1945* (Warsaw: Centrum Badań nad Zagładą Żydów IFiS PAN, 2011); Jan Grabowski, *Judenjagd: polowanie na Żydów, 1942–1945* (Warsaw: Centrum Badań nad Zagładą Żydów IFiS PAN, 2011); Jan T. Gross, *Neighbors* (Princeton, NJ: Princeton University Press, 2001); Gunnar S. Paulsson, *Secret City: The Hidden Jews of Warsaw, 1940–1945* (New Haven, CT: Yale University Press, 2002); Joshua D. Zimmerman, ed., *Contested Memories: Poles and Jews during the Holocaust and Its Aftermath* (New Brunswick, NJ: Rutgers University Press, 2003); Joshua D Zimmerman, *The Polish Underground and the Jews, 1939–1945* (Cambridge, UK: Cambridge University Press, 2017); Tomasz Frydel, "The Devil in Microhistory: The 'Hunt for Jews' as a Social Process, 1942–1945," in *Microhistories of the Holocaust*, ed. Claire Zalc and Tal Bruttmann (New York: Berghahn Books, 2016).

the bulwark of Christendom defending Europe against the infidel (however defined). A nation assailed by dangerous neighbors, its identity is conserved and guarded by its defender, the Roman Catholic Church. . . . Christ among nations, it was martyred for the sins of the world and resurrected for the world's salvation."[4] As Alon Confino has pointed out, memory not only shapes but also reflects national culture and should be understood within the "symbolic universe available to the society."[5] The idea of "Christ among the nations," sacrifice for the sake of others, corresponds with the perception of Poles as saviors of Jews and heroes of wartime Europe, which, as the chapter demonstrates, arose in the 1960s and gained dominance in the commemoration and study of World War II after the events of 1967–68. The party members behind the attack on the encyclopedia saw local Polish Jews as part of a Zionist conspiracy to utilize the memory of the Holocaust for the benefit of the Jewish state and its imperialist allies. They feared that "international Jewry" would obliterate the memory of Polish bravery and replace it with Jewish suffering and Polish collaboration as the Holocaust came to the fore of World War II remembrance in a globalizing world.

Historical Research and Commemoration of the Holocaust in Poland, 1945–67

In the years immediately after World War II, Jews who had remained in Poland commemorated and studied the Holocaust. Jewish organizations operated without much government supervision, assisting those who had survived the war and organizing memorial events.[6] On April 19, 1945, the second anniversary of the Warsaw Ghetto Uprising, the war was not over yet when activists held a ceremony on the ruins of the bunker occupied by the commander, Mordechai Anielewicz, at 18 Mila Street. A year later, survivors, government officials, and youth groups participated in another service and unveiled a small memorial. On it were engraved, in Hebrew, Yiddish, and Polish, these words: "For the heroes who gave their lives in the

---

4. Geneviève Zubrzycki, "History and the National Sensorium: Making Sense of Polish Mythology," *Qualitative Sociology* 34 (2011): 21–57.

5. Alon Confino, *Germany as a Culture of Remembrance: Promises and Limits of Writing History* (Chapel Hill: University of North Carolina Press, 2006), 174.

6. Grzegorz Berendt, "A New Life: Jewish Institutions and Organizations in Poland from 1944 to 1950," in *Jewish Presence in Absence: Aftermath of the Holocaust in Poland, 1944–2000*, ed. Feliks Tych and Monika Adamczyk-Garbowska (Jerusalem: Yad Vashem, 2014).

war for the honor and freedom of the Jewish people, for the liberation of Poland, and for man's salvation. The remnants of Poland's Jewry."[7]

The architect L. M. Suzin, who designed the small ghetto memorial, also created a plaque installed at the site of Warsaw's Umschlagplatz, the place where Jews were gathered before being sent to Treblinka. The inscription, also in Hebrew, Yiddish, and Polish, read: "From this place, the Hitlerite murderers led hundreds of thousands of Jews to martyrs' deaths in extermination camps between 1942 and 1943."[8] At Birkenau (Brzezinka), Jews placed a commemorative tablet near one of the crematoria: "To the memory of the millions of Jewish martyrs and fighters exterminated in Oświęcim and Brzezinka by the genocidal Hitlerites, 1940–1945."[9] Jewish art associations staged exhibitions presenting survivors' work on the Holocaust or the art of those who died during the war. The Jewish Society for the Encouragement of Fine Arts presented the exhibition *Rescued Works of Art of Jewish Artists*, which featured pieces the society had purchased from private owners; it toured throughout Poland, attracting more than ten thousand visitors.[10]

As these various acts of memory took place, Poland was in the midst of becoming the Polish People's Republic, a Soviet-style Stalinist state. During the Stalinist period, Jews just about vanished from public discourse. Following the example of the Soviet Union, official Poland mostly, though not entirely, ignored the Holocaust. When they did mention it, official narratives presented the murder of Jews as the result of capitalist interests and not as a racial crime.[11] At the same time, the regime turned the anniversary of the Warsaw Ghetto Uprising into a centerpiece in World War II commemoration. The yearly ceremony became the venue for honoring Polish

---

7. Yitzhak Zuckerman, *Sheva' ha-shanim ha-hen, 1939–1946* (Tel Aviv: ha-·Kibuts ha-me'u·had, 1990), 565–66.

8. See a picture of the plaque in Konstanty Gebert, "The Dialectics of Memory in Poland: Holocaust Memorials in Warsaw," in *The Art of Memory: Holocaust Memorials in History*, ed. James E. Young (New York: Prestel, 1994), 121–29.

9. Not much is known about the first memorial in Birkenau. See Marek Kucia, *Auschwitz jako fakt społeczny: historia, wspołczesność i swiadomość społeczna KL Auschwitz w Polsce* (Krakow: Universitas, 2005), 29. A photograph of the memorial is on an unnumbered page at the end of the book. In Polish the Germans are called "genocidal Hitlerites" ("hitlerowskich ludobójców") and in Yiddish and Hebrew "Hitlerite murderers."

10. Renata Piątkowska, "Jewish Artists in Poland after the Holocaust," in *Jewish Presence in Absence: Aftermath of the Holocaust in Poland, 1944–2000*, ed. Feliks Tych and Monika Adamczyk-Garbowska (Jerusalem: Yad Vashem, 2014).

11. Jonathan Huener, *Auschwitz, Poland and the Politics of Commemoration, 1945–1979* (Athens: Ohio University Press, 2003), 79–108.

antifascist armed struggle.[12] The leaders of the uprising, who belonged to left-wing youth movements, fitted the image of the underground fighter that the regime sought to foster: young, socialist, and heroic. More significantly, the uprising's heads did not belong to the Polish national underground and did not act in concert with the Polish exiled government in London, both of which were ostracized during the Stalinist period.[13]

In 1956, three years after Stalin's death, Nikita Khrushchev gave his famous "secret speech" at the twentieth Communist Party Congress; this opened the door to rethinking memories of World War II. Khrushchev allowed Soviet citizens to speak about wartime suffering and sacrifices.[14] The Polish first secretary, Bolesław Bierut, died in Moscow while attending the congress, facilitating the return of Władysław Gomułka to the post in late 1956. For Poles, Gomułka represented the "national road to socialism," and they hoped for greater independence from Moscow.[15] After 1956, with the de-Stalinization of Poland, the ways in which the events of the war were studied changed substantially. With the rise of a new kind of communist ideology that stressed Polish identity and unity came a new understanding of the war. At the helm of the regime now stood men who saw themselves as Polish patriots and socialism as the cure to Poland's past maladies and its current geopolitical problems. World War II for them represented a moment of sacrifice for the salvation of Poland and of heroism in fighting the German occupiers. De-Stalinization thus brought a revival of commemoration of World War II and a rehabilitation of the previously denounced national underground. The bravery of the fighting men and women of clandestine organizations, the national Armia Krajowa (AK, or Home Army) and the communist underground Armia Ludowa, became a dominant theme in public discourse. In 1956 and 1957 the government released former AK fighters from communist prisons and rehabilitated many others.[16] Several publications about the clandestine organization appeared, as did films, memoirs,

12. Renata Kobylarz, *Walka o Pamięć: Polityczne aspekty obchodów rocznicy powstania w getcie warszawskim, 1944–1989* (Warsaw: Instytut Pamięci Narodowej, 2009), 69–83.

13. Anat Plocker, "Atar Ha'zikaron be'Auschwitz Birkenau, 1947–1955" (master's thesis, Tel Aviv University, 2003).

14. William Taubman, *Khrushchev: The Man and His Era* (New York: Norton, 2003), 270–83.

15. Anthony Kemp-Wlech, *Poland under Communism: A Cold War History* (Cambridge: Cambridge University Press, 2008), 96–123.

16. Andrzej Friszke, "Przystosowanie i Opór: Rozważania nad postawami społecznymi, 1956–1970," in *Komunizm: Ideologia, System, Ludzie*, ed. Tomasz Szarota (Warsaw: Neriton, 2001), 139–55.

and journals.[17] The fighters of the AK came to be seen as courageous men and women misled by the political leadership and the Polish government in exile.[18] Popular culture portrayed ordinary Poles as battling against all odds for victory against a powerful Nazi enemy.

The new openness allowed for the publication in Polish of memoirs and diaries of Jewish Holocaust survivors throughout the 1960s. In 1960, for instance, two journals kept by residents of the Łódź ghetto appeared: that of sixteen-year-old Dawid Sierakowiak, who died in the ghetto, and of Jakub Poznański, who survived the war.[19] In 1962 the writer Adam Ostoja published a memoir by Abram Kajzer, a camp survivor.[20] Another Auschwitz survivor, Sara Nomberg-Przytyk, published her recollections of the Białystok ghetto, *Kolumny Samsona* (Samson's Columns), in 1966.[21] A year later, Halina Birenbaum, a Holocaust survivor who had immigrated to Israel, published her memoir, first in Polish and later in Hebrew and English.[22] The Holocaust also featured in several new works in Yiddish, both fictional and nonfictional, during this period, and it became the dominant topic in Yiddish literature.[23]

The official policy of commemorating the Nazi occupation changed as well: the Commission for the Protection of Sites of Suffering and Martyrdom (CPSSM) commissioned monuments at the sites of death camps, where often there was either no memorial or only a plaque or small tombstone.

---

17. Joanna Wawrzyniak, *ZBoWiD i Pamięć Drugiej Wojny Światowej 1949–1969* (Warsaw: TRIO, 2009), 263–64.

18. Marcin Zaremba, *Komunizm, legitymizacja, nacjonalizm: nacjonalistyczna legitymizacja władzy komunistycznej w Polsce* (Warsaw: TRIO, 2001), 289–90.

19. Dawid Sierakowiak, *Dziennik* (Warsaw: Iskry, 1960); Jakub Poznański, *Pamiętnik z Getta Łódzkiego* (Łódź: Wydawnictwo Łódzkie, 1960).

20. Abram Kajzer, *Za drutami śmierci* (Łódź: Wydawnictwo Łódzkie, 1962).

21. Sara Nomberg-Przytyk, *Kolumny Samsona* (Lublin: Wydawnictwo Lubelskie, 1966). Nomberg-Przytyk worked as a slave laborer in Auschwitz in Josef Mengele's hospital; her memoir of that period was published as *Auschwitz: True Tales from a Grotesque Land*, trans. Roslyn Hirsch, ed. Eli Pfefferkorn and David H. Hirsch (Chapel Hill: University of Northern Carolina Press, 1986). After the 1968 purges, she immigrated to Canada.

22. Halina Birenbaum, *Nadzieja umiera ostatnia* (Warsaw: Cytelnik, 1967) was published in English under the title *Hope Is the Last to Die: A Personal Documentation of Nazi Terror*, trans. David Welsh (New York: Twayne, 1971) and in Hebrew as *Ha'Haim Ke'Tikva*, translated by the author (Kibutz Lohamei Ha'Getaot: Ha'Kibutz Ha'Meohad, 1983). The story of the Birenbaum family is also recounted in the Israeli documentary film *Bigelal ha'milhamah ha'hi* [Because of that war], directed by Orna Ben-Dor (1989).

23. Monika Adamczyk-Garbowska and Magdalena Ruta, "Responses to the Holocaust in Polish and Yiddish Literature," in *Jewish Presence in Absence: Aftermath of the Holocaust in Poland, 1944–2000*, ed. Feliks Tych and Monika Adamczyk-Garbowska (Jerusalem: Yad Vashem, 2014).

The memorials gave Poles a place to mourn and commemorate the war without controversy, as they did not mention the Armia Krajowa or the Warsaw uprising. The construction of the memorials reflected both a public need to remember the war—hundreds of thousands attended the dedication ceremonies—and growing governmental control over acts of commemoration.[24] On the twentieth anniversary of the liquidation of the Lublin ghetto, in 1962, the city built a monument to the Jews murdered in extermination camps in the area. Inscribed on the monument were the words of the Jewish poet Yitzhak Katzenelson, who was killed in Auschwitz: "Where are my dear ones? I seek them in every heap of ashes."[25] Unlike in the previous and following periods, the Lublin monument explicitly commemorated the Jews who perished at Majdanek and Belzec.

At Treblinka, the sculptor Franciszek Duszeńko and the architect Adam Haupt created a memorial for those murdered in the camp.[26] Dedicated in 1964 and partly subsidized by the World Zionist Congress, the memorial included seventeen thousand stones reminiscent of gravestones; some were inscribed with the names of countries, while others bore the names of villages and towns from which Jews had been deported. One is reminded of old Jewish cemeteries.[27] As part of the commemoration, Gumkowski, the author of the *Wielka Encyklopedia Powszechna* entry on concentration camps, collaborated with historian Adam Rutkowski on a booklet about Treblinka. The authors stated that eight hundred thousand Jews from all over Europe died there as part of the Nazi "final solution." Gumkowski and Rutkowski gave a detailed account of the camp and its operation, down to the size of the gas chambers.[28]

24. For instance, the dedication of the monument in Treblinka: AAN 237/VIII–882, 27–30.

25. Robert Kuwalek, *Heritage Trail of the Lublin Jews*, trans. Adm Janiszewski, ed. Stanislaw Turski (Lublin: Lubelski Osrodek Informacji Turystycznej, 2002). The poem was written and later published in Yiddish; see Yitzhak Katzenelson, *The Song of the Murdered Jewish People*, trans. and ed. Noah H. Rosenbloom (Kibbutz Lohamei Haghetaot: Hakibbutz Hameuchad, 1980). It was published in Poland in the 1980s; see Icchak Kacenelson, *Pieśń o zamordowanym żydowskim narodzie*, trans. Jerzy Ficowski (Warsaw: Czytelnik, 1982).

26. James E. Young, *The Texture of Memory: Holocaust Memorials and Meaning* (New Haven, CT: Yale University Press, 1993), 186–87.

27. AAN 237/VIII–882, 27–30.

28. J. Gumkowski and A. Rutkowski, *Treblinka* (Warsaw: Rat f. Schutz d. Denkmäler d. Kampfes u. d. Heldentums, 1963). The number is estimated to be larger, but the difference is the result of decades-long research. The Germans destroyed the camp, and there were almost no survivors.

In the early 1960s, academic works about the extermination of the Jews also began to appear in Polish.[29] The head of the Jewish Historical Institute, Bernard Mark, took the lead in producing several books dealing with the Nazi treatment of the Jews.[30] The distinction between death camps and concentration camps emerged in several of these publications. The thirteenth volume of the *Biuletyn Głównej Komisji Badania Zbrodni Hitlerowskich w Polsce* (Bulletin of the Central Commission for the Investigation of Hitlerite Crimes in Poland), published in 1960, included an article entitled "The Extermination of the Jewish Population in Camps on Polish Soil" and forty-five translated Nazi documents.[31] The article described how the Nazi regime moved from forced resettlement to annihilation of the Jews. In the last paragraph, the editors made the claim that the documents stood as "indisputable proof of the genocidal crime perpetrated against the Jewish people."[32] The language is striking: the Central Commission for the Investigation of Hitlerite Crimes in Poland, the highest official authority dealing with World War II, called the murder of Jews *genocide* (*ludobójstwo*).[33] Nothing stopped Janusz Gumkowski and his fellow volume editors from noting in 1960 that the Nazis planned and executed a mass murder based on racial ideology. They did this without more general references to Polish suffering; the contemporary atmosphere allowed for a straightforward discussion of the "final solution."[34] Further research throughout the 1960s examined the road to Auschwitz and continued to comment on the differences between various camps in the Nazi system.[35]

---

29. See, for example, Tadeusz Berenstein, "Eksterminacja ludności Żydowskiej w dystrykcie Galicja," *Biuletyn Żydowskiego instytutu historycznego w Polsce* 61 (1967): 3–58; Szymon Datner, "Eksterminacja ludności Żydowskiej w okręgu białostockim," *Biuletyn Żydowskiego instytutu historycznego w Polsce* 60 (1966): 3–50; W. Orbach, "Sytuacja zdrowotna mieszkańców getta Łudzkiego," *Biuletyn Żydowskiego instytutu historycznego w Polsce* 65/66 (1968): 141–71.

30. Among them were *Struggle and Death in the Warsaw Ghetto* (1959); *Martyrdom, Struggle, and the Extermination of Jews in Poland, 1939–1945* (1960); *Life and Struggle among Youths in the Warsaw Ghetto during the Hitlerite Occupation, 1939–1944* (1961).

31. Szymon Datner, Janusz Gumkowski, and Kazimierz Leszczynski, eds., *Biuletyn Głównej Komisji Badania Zbrodni Hitlerowskich w Polsce*, vol. 13 (Krakow: Wydawnictwo Ministerstwa Sprawiedliwosci, 1960).

32. Datner, Gumkowski, and Leszczynski, *Biuletyn Głównej Komisji*, 13:68.

33. A dictionary published in 1969 translates *ludobójstwo* as *genocide*; see Jan Stanislawski, *Wielki Słownik Polsko-Angielski* (Warsaw: Panstwowe Wydawnictwo Wiedza Powszechna, 1969), 465.

34. Datner, Gumkowski, and Leszczynski, *Biuletyn Głównej Komisji*, 13:66.

35. See, for example, Artur Eisenbach, *Operation Reinhard: Mass Extermination of the Jewish Population in Poland* (Poznan: Instytut Zachodni, 1962); Edward Serwanski, *Obóz Zagłady w Chełmnie nad Nerem, 1941–1945* (Poznań: Wydawnictwo Poznańskie, 1964); Jan Sehn, *Obóz Koncentracyjny Oświęcim-Brzezinka (Auschwitz-Birkenau)* (Warsaw: Główna Komisija Badania Zbrodni Hitlerowskich w Polsce, Wydawnictwo Prawnicze, 1964), 119; Irena Lange, ed., *Oświęcim* (Warsaw: Zarząd Główny Związku Bojowników o Wolność i Demokrację, 1967), 8, 16–17.

As shown, the "tragic fate" of Polish Jews was discussed in public. The regime did not consider the subject taboo, unlike the Ribbentrop-Molotov Agreement, the Yalta Conference, or the Katyn Massacre, which censors vigilantly erased from all public media. Polish scholars, both Jews and Christians, studied the history of the Holocaust and the camps. Some school textbooks devoted sections to the fate of the Jews in Poland, indicating that Jews were treated differently from Poles.[36] Socialist Poland's policies in 1956–67 regarding the history of the Holocaust (named "eksterminacja ludności żydowskiej," "extermination of Jewish population," or "zagłada Żydów," "destruction of the Jews") thus differed markedly from those of the Soviet Union.[37] In 1961, the Jewish American organization B'nai B'rith reported on the Polish regime's attitude toward the Holocaust. The survey lauded the official policy of "emphasizing the evils of Nazism and anti-Semitism" and the efforts to "combat the imbedded traditions of anti-Semitism."[38] Through the eyes of scholars today, Polish historiography in the 1960s on the Holocaust seems limited in scope, ignoring the complexities of an occupied society, but it was on a par with its time. The study and commemoration of the murder of the Jews coincided with growing research and memorialization of the Polish national underground, the AK, forming parallel spheres of scholarship on World War II.

During the same period, Western Europeans and Americans increasingly embraced the idea that Jews had a separate experience during the war and that the Holocaust was a unique event. Movies, books, and the television broadcasts of the Eichmann trial in 1961 brought the Holocaust to ordinary households.[39] Abducted in Argentina by the Israeli Mossad, Adolf

---

36. See Henryk Sędziwy, *Historia dla klasy XI: od wielkiej socjalistycznej rewolucji październikowej do końca II wojny światowej* (Warsaw: Państwowe Zakłady Wydawnictw Szkolnych, 1967), 242–43; Marian Wojciechowski, *Historia dla Klasy VIII* (Warsaw: Państwowe Zakłady Wydawnictw Szkolnych, 1971), 114–15.

37. On the Soviet Union, see Harvey Asher, "The Soviet Union, the Holocaust, and Auschwitz," *Kritika: Explorations in Russian and Eurasian History* 4, no. 4 (2003): 886–912; Tarik Cyril Amar, "A Disturbed Silence: Discourse on the Holocaust in the Soviet West as an Anti-site of Memory," in *The Holocaust in the East: Local Perpetrators and Soviet Responses*, ed. Michael David-Fox, Peter Holquist, and Alexander M. Martin (Pittsburgh, PA: University of Pittsburgh Press, 2014), 158–83. For the Germanies, see Michael Meng, *Shattered Spaces: Encountering Jewish Ruins in Postwar Germany and Poland* (Cambridge, MA: Harvard University Press, 2011).

38. *Survey: A Background Study Prepared by B'nai B'rith International Council*, no. 5 (April 19, 1961).

39. Films (some of them shown in Poland at this time) included *Nuit et brouillard* (1955); *The Diary of Anne Frank* (1959); *Judgment at Nuremberg* (1961); and *The Pawnbroker* (1964). Books (none of them translated at this time into Polish) included Raul Hilberg, *The Destruction of the European Jews* (1961); Gerald Reitlinger, *The Final Solution: The Attempt to Exterminate the Jews of Europe, 1939–1945* (1961); Primo Levi, *Survival in Auschwitz: The Nazi Assault on Humanity* (1961); Elie Wiesel, *Night* (1960); and Isaac Zuckerman, *The Fighting Ghettos* (1962).

Eichmann, the Nazi deportation specialist, stood trial in Israel for crimes against humanity and against the Jewish people. The government of Israel decided to use the opportunity to render the Holocaust more personal, as dozens of survivors took the stand to tell their stories.[40] As people around the world listened to these painful testimonies, the concept of the Holocaust as a unique event in history, the central event of the war, began to take hold.

Kazimierz Kąkol, who would play an important role in anti-Zionist propaganda after March 1968, was the Polish journalist covering the Eichmann trial for the weekly *Prawo i Życie* (Law and life). The book based on his dispatches, *Eichmann's Road to Beit Ha'am*, was published in 1962. The book brought the story of the Jewish Holocaust to the non-Jewish Polish reader. Kąkol's work presented some of the themes that would plague the post–June 1967 campaign. While he strongly criticized the Israeli government's management of the trial, he did not deny the genocide against Jews or attempt to minimize it; instead, Kąkol attacked West German–Israeli relations, censuring the reparations agreement and the close relationship between the Federal Republic of Germany (FRG) and Israel. He saw the Eichmann trial through the lens of German-Israeli cooperation: to him, prosecuting Eichmann while ignoring war criminals living in the FRG resulted from a quiet agreement between Konrad Adenauer and David Ben-Gurion. The Israeli government, he believed, chose to protect Germany in exchange for arms. As for the Poles, Kąkol argued that the Nazis "prepared for the Poles the same fate as for the Jews; Poles were also outside the law." Following previous communist and Polish depictions of the war period, Kąkol paralleled Nazi plans for Jews and Poles, arguing the Poles would have been next, had the war continued. His account also emphasizes Polish help for Jews, and the latter's ingratitude. Although many of the witnesses who testified during Eichmann's trial owed their lives to Polish gentiles, argued Kąkol, the "extermination of Poles" found no place in the trial.[41]

The period 1956–68 gave rise to a narrative that is still central to Polish perceptions of the Holocaust, as it integrates the fate of Polish Jews into the story of Polish heroism in a particular way. In that time, both Polish and Jewish scholars published works dealing with the rescue of Jews. With the

---

40. On the Eichmann trial, see, for example, Gideon Hausner, *Justice in Jerusalem* (New York: Harper & Row, 1966); Hannah Arendt, *Eichmann in Jerusalem: A Report on the Banality of Evil* (New York: Viking, 1963); Hanna Yablonka, *The State of Israel vs. Adolf Eichmann*, trans. Ora Cummings with David Herman (New York: Schocken, 2004).

41. Kazimierz Kąkol, *Adolfa Eichmanna droga do Beit Haam* (Warsaw: Iskry, 1962), quote from page 276. Beit Ha'am was the hall in which Eichmann's trial took place.

lifting on the ban of the Home Army, the activities of Żegota (Rada Pomocy Żydom), the underground organization that attempted to save Jews and worked under the umbrella of the Home Army, became known to the general public and embraced by the regime. Books, films, and newspaper articles, in addition to the scholarly works, publicized stories of Poles risking their lives to hide Jews.[42] In this narrative, the specificity of the Holocaust could not be blurred: the German occupiers wanted to hunt and kill all Jews, and the few survivors owed their lives to Poles. Jews became a foil against which Poles measured their heroism and willingness to sacrifice, turning the Holocaust into background story and Jews into passive victims, in contrast to the active Poles. Rescue narratives stressed the dangers Polish rescuers faced, portraying them as equal to those of the Jews. Gomułka himself in his fifth-column speech explained to Israelis that "the only ones saved [from extermination] were those [Jews] whom the Poles concealed, at the risk of their own lives."[43]

The emerging rescuer narrative fit well with the contemporaneous state ideology that stressed the Polish national way to socialism and aimed to push out of the party all Jewish elements in favor of "patriotic" Poles. Interior Minister Mieczysław Moczar and the "partisan" faction in the ruling party wanted the state and the party cleansed of Jews and also wanted Jewish history to disappear from the pages of Polish history. Many in Moczar's circle, including Moczar, claimed to be former members of Poland's wartime resistance (i.e., partisans).[44] As the systematic murder of the Jews became a key issue in the history of World War II, not just in Poland but also in the West, voices within the party began to protest. They had grown tired of seeing commemorations of World War II "taken over" by Jews, while fictional and scholarly works, at home and in the West, omitted the torment of Poles during the war.[45] The

---

42. Władysław Bartoszewski, *Ten jest z Ojczyzny mojej. Polacy z pomocą Żydom 1939–1945*, oprac. wspólnie z Zofią Lewinówną (Krakow: Znak, 1967, 1969); Tatiana Berenstein and Adam Rutkowski, *Pomoc Żydom w Polsce 1939–1945* (Warsaw: Polonia, 1963); *Dzieło miłosierdzia chrześcijańskiego: Polskie duchowieństwo katolickie a Żydzi w latach okupacji hitlerowskiej*, Chrześcijańskie Stowarzyszenie Społeczne (Warsaw: Stowarzyszenie, 1968).

43. AAN 237/V/899, 85.

44. It has been claimed that an American journalist and operative in Poland coined the term in his report to the US embassy in Warsaw. The report is found in the Hoover Archives at Stanford University: "PZPR Factionalism and 'Partisans,'" the Hoover Institution Archives, Radio Free Europe/Radio Liberty Records, box 256, folder 14.

45. Works that appeared in the West at the time include Raul Hilberg, *The Destruction of the European Jews* (1961); Gerald Reitlinger, *The Final Solution: The Attempt to Exterminate the Jews of Europe, 1939–1945* (1961); Primo Levi, *Survival in Auschwitz: The Nazi Assault on Humanity* (1961); Elie Wiesel, *Night* (1960); Isaac Zuckerman, *The Fighting Ghettos* (1962). Films include *Nuit et brouillard* (1955); *The Diary of Anne Frank* (1959); *Judgment at Nuremberg* (1961); and *The Pawnbroker* (1964).

"partisans" worried that Zionist Jews worked purposefully to erase Polish sacrifice from the pages of history and that their role in defeating Germany would be forgotten. Once Gomułka indicated in June 1967 that the time had come to at last purge the Jews, officials from the Ministry of the Interior's highest ranks turned to that most painful thing, the memory of the war. Many of them were founders and members of the Związek Bojowników o Wolność i Demokrację (Society of Fighters for Freedom and Democracy, or ZBoWiD), Poland's World War II veterans' organization, and they were determined to make Polish suffering and heroism the one and only subject of national commemoration.[46] As today, so then, Polish politicians pressed scholars, artists, and intellectuals to become patriotic and embrace a view of World War II in which Jews were marginalized, passive victims and Poles played only a positive role, as either victims or saviors.

The Concentration Camp Entry in the Great General Encyclopedia

Adam Bromberg, director of the publishing house Państwowe Wydawnictwo Naukowe (PWN, National Scientific Publishers) conceived of the first Polish postwar socialist encyclopedia, to be called *Wielka Encyklopedia Powszechna* (The great general encyclopedia); work on the project began in the early 1960s.[47] The editor in chief was Leon Marszałek.[48] In 1965, Karol Kuryluk replaced Adam Bromberg as director of the PWN, but the change did not interfere with the work. The persons involved would be characterized later as "a bunch of revisionists and Jews," but at the time they were respected in party and academic circles.[49]

Janusz Gumkowski circulated drafts of his concentration camp entry among the editors and experts in the field. Outside of some corrections regarding the number of victims, none of his points was questioned.[50] In early versions, Gumkowski had offered the estimate of 4.7 million Jews

---

46. In the late 1950s ZBoWiD accepted many former fighters of the AK and became a nationalist organization, promoting the commemoration of Polish (non-Jewish) armed resistance to the Nazi occupation. See, for example, *ZBoWiD i pamięć drugiej wojny światowej 1949–1969*.

47. Jerzy Eisler, *Polski Rok 1968*, 158. For more about Bromberg's life, see Henryk Grynberg, *Memorbuch* (Warsaw: Wydawnictwo WAB, 2000).

48. AAN 237/XVI–414, 8–21.

49. Teresa Torańska, *"Them": Stalin's Polish Puppets*, trans. Agnieszka Kolakowska (New York: Harper & Row, 1987), 194; Eisler, *Polski Rok 1968*, 158–61.

50. AAN 237/XVI–413, 42–44, 70, 123–32.

murdered in the death camps alone; he had to increase the number to 5.7 million to agree with the entry for Auschwitz, according to which 3.5 million people perished in Birkenau alone, and added that 99 percent of the victims were Jews.[51] It was the official Polish claim that up to 4 million had died in the Auschwitz-Birkenau camp complex that led to an exaggeration of the number of Jewish victims, not a Jewish conspiracy.[52] As the former party leader Stefan Staszewski later commented, "For Moczar's group, to give the number of Jews who had been killed was almost a challenge flung at the Polish nation."[53] The entry realized their fears that the Jewish Holocaust would overshadow Polish victimhood. Moczar and his appointees in the Ministry of Internal Affairs launched an investigation into the heresies of the encyclopedia three weeks after Gomułka's fifth-column speech, which began the anti-Zionist campaign. In the atmosphere of crisis and fear around Poland's Jews, the appearance of such an entry reinforced the sense of threat to the Polish nation from the Jewish minority.

Three months earlier, in April, the Ministry of Internal Affairs had issued a report accusing Zionists and Israelis of anti-Polish slander. The simultaneous publication in the West of several works dealing with the fate of the Jews in Poland during World War II was not, according to the ministry, accidental. It was part of a Zionist ploy to destabilize communist countries, beginning in Poland. The communists behind these reports did not simply repeat prewar tropes about Jewish plots; in their communist conspiratorial imagination, coincidences did not exist. If their country had been cast in a negative light, a conspiracy was at work, a coordinated worldwide effort to implicate Poles in the murder of Jews. The secret report issued in April 1967 had concluded, "What all the works have in common is the false presentation of the situation in Poland during the occupation and after the liberation. Poles are presented as antisemites and as collaborators with the occupier in the extermination of the Jews."[54] A depiction that stood against the image of Poles as resisters and rescuers of Jews aroused

---

51. *Wielka Encyklopedia Powszechna* (Warsaw: Panstwowe Wydawnictwo Naukowe, 1966), 8:359.

52. The exact number of the victims of the Holocaust is unknown. *The Holocaust Encyclopedia* estimated that the Nazis massacred between 5.59 and 5.86 million Jews; of these, 3.5 million were murdered in extermination camps. Yad Vashem Shoah Resource Center, s.v. "extermination camps," accessed October 27, 2006, http://www1.yadvashem.org/odot_pdf/Microsoft%20Word%20-%206308.pdf. On the issue of the number of victims in Auschwitz, see Marek Kucia, *Auschwitz Jako Fakt Społeczny* (Krakow: Universitas, 2005), 148–62.

53. Torańska, *"Them,"* 194–95.

54. AIPN 1288.29, 20.

fear that Poland's sacrifices during the war would be deliberately obliterated by Jewish forces.

On July 4, 1967, Czesław Pilichowski, the director of the Central Commission for the Investigation of Hitlerite Crimes in Poland, sent the first official report on the concentration camp encyclopedia entry to Justice Minister Stanisław Walczak. In his report, Pilichowski pointed out a number of errors in the text and outlined specific criticisms that would consistently appear in internal reports and in the press. He could not accept the figures given for the number of Jewish and non-Jewish victims of the Nazis. Pilichowski thought that Jewish victims should not be counted separately and that scholars should not differentiate between those murdered in camps on Polish soil (the majority of death camps) and in the rest of Nazi-controlled Europe. He portrayed the division into concentration camps and death camps as a political scheme aimed at presenting Poles as antisemitic (since it reinforced the idea that the Nazis situated the death camps in Poland because Poles were antisemites); this was an anti-Polish Zionist plot.[55] How could one divide the dead according to nationality? Pilichowski praised the East German encyclopedia *Neues Meyers Lexicon*, which mentioned 11 million dead in camps all over Europe.[56] In his view, the editors of *Wielka Encyklopedia Powszechna* had not followed the Soviet line, that all victims were equal, and had distorted the truth as a result of their Zionist, or Jewish nationalist, inclinations. Pilichowski's letter was the opening shot in the campaign against the encyclopedia. A series of similar reports followed. On July 17, 1967, Colonel S. Kończewicz, director of the office of the minister of the interior and a longtime employee of the secret police, sent his own report to the heads of the PUWP.[57] He stated that 6.28 million Poles were killed in the war and that only 2.5 million of them were Jews. Taking a stronger position than Pilichowski, Kończewicz saw the entry as an insult to the Polish nation since it suggested that "the only victims of Hitlerite crimes in the death camps on Polish soil were Jews," and he accused those responsible for the encyclopedia entry of conspiracy to falsify history.[58]

The growing internal controversy over the encyclopedia demanded an official response: the presidium of the Central Commission for the

55. AAN 237/XVI–413, 6–7.

56. AAN 237/XVI–413, 7.

57. AAN 237/XVI–413, 12–14; Mirosław Piotrowski, *Ludzie Bezpieki w walce z narodem i Kościołem* (Warsaw: Klub Inteligencji Katolickiej, 1999), 356.

58. AAN 237/XVI–413, 13.

Investigation of Hitlerite Crimes in Poland was convened on July 19, 1967. Among the participants were the entry writer Gumkowski, Vice Minister of the Interior Kazimierz Światła, Vice Minister of Arts and Culture Kazimierz Rusinek, and Undersecretary of State Kazimierz Zawadzki.[59] Światła and Rusinek had strong connections with Moczar and the "partisans" group of hard-liners in the PUWP. Światła was Moczar's second-in-command in the Ministry of Internal Affairs, and Rusinek occupied the analogous role in the veterans' organization ZBoWiD, where Moczar was president.[60] The men of ZBoWiD led the attack and promoted national chauvinism in Polish historiography: they wanted more Polish misery and heroism and less Holocaust. A Polish encyclopedia that spoke of Jewish victims roused their fury and anxiety, as evident from the minutes of the meeting held on July 19. Rusinek wondered how an entry patently offensive to Polish victims had ever been published. Not only offensive, but also inaccurate: were not Mauthausen and Gusen, located outside of Poland, also death camps? Did they not have gas chambers? Gumkowski responded that the death camps and concentration camps were distinct, that everything he wrote was true; extermination camps were part of the "final solution," and 99 percent of their victims were Jews. He was referring to the camps that the Germans set up specifically for the murder of Jews and that did not serve any other purpose in the Nazi camp system. In the past he had never been censored for making similar statements. Apparently unshaken and not realizing that the rules of the game had changed, the scholar stuck to established historical facts. The head of the Central Commission, Pilichowski, told Gumkowski that he was wrong: all Nazi camps were death camps; the Jews did not receive special treatment and should not have been considered a national group—they should simply have been counted as Polish victims. Such errors fueled Federal Republic of Germany (FRG) propaganda and harmed the Polish state.[61] Pilichowski accused Gumkowski of acting in the interests of former Nazis, still living in West Germany.[62] His essay seemed calculated to help the FRG, as the Israelis were already doing—an idea that would soon surface in the press. Zionists, according to the theory set out by the Ministry of the Interior, sold themselves to the Germans for guns and

---

59. AAN 237/XVI–413, 136–49
60. Andrzej Paczkowski, *The Spring Will Be Ours: Poland and the Poles from Occupation to Freedom*, trans. Jane Cave (University Park: Pennsylvania State University Press, 2003), 300–306.
61. AAN 237/XVI–413, 136–49
62. AAN 237/XVI–413, 146.

used their victimhood against the Poles, depicting the latter as antisemitic collaborators in the murder of Jews. Interestingly, the high-ranking officials did not mention fascism or the internationalization of the victims, central terms from the 1950s, but instead dealt with Poles and unrecognized Polish martyrdom. The gathering ended with a promise to follow up on the matter and find those responsible for "falsified history."[63]

Rusinek, Walczak, and Zawadzki indeed continued to pursue the writers and editors responsible for the encyclopedia. At their request, Kuryluk, the director of the publishing house, provided a detailed report about those in charge of the entry: during an editorial meeting on May 4, 1966, the editors discussed the concentration camp entry. They read through the text, made some changes, and approved it; they saw nothing that would provoke a scandal. Kuryluk added that the encyclopedia staff was now writing a revised entry to be printed in a special supplement, work being carried out in collaboration with ZBoWiD, the Commission for the Investigation of Hitlerite Crimes, and the Commission for the Protection of Sites of Suffering and Martyrdom.[64] Kuryluk signaled to the party that he knew who was responsible for the mistakes and that he would make sure that they would not repeat them. The director's report was followed by a series of letters by various editors from the publishing house to the heads of the party, attempting to explain their position.[65]

The letter from encyclopedia's editor in chief, Leon Marszałek, was the most compelling. He tried to convince the PUWP's Department of Education that this matter was all a misunderstanding and that he was blameless. All along he had wanted someone else to write the entry; he would have liked to see Polish suffering emphasized; the affair hurt him personally, for he had spent time in "Hitlerite prisons." Marszałek went on to blame contemporaneous studies of the Nazi system—historians had confused the creators of the encyclopedia—and perhaps others needed to do new work on the topic.[66] Marszałek hoped that he could show the party that the entry was within the boundaries of academic discourse and that the Polish reader simply did not understand that the offensive sentences about the numbers of victims referred to death camps and not to the entire Hitlerite camp system. At that point, Marszałek still thought that the affair would be resolved if the party realized that the group working on the encyclopedia comprised only

63. AAN 237/XVI-413, 149.
64. AAN KC PZPR XVI 414, 10–12.
65. AAN KC PZPR XVI 414, 55–64.
66. AAN KC PZPR XVI 414, 55–58.

loyal Poles doing their jobs; he did not grasp that times had changed and that nothing short of an overhaul of the encyclopedia's "Zionist" staff would satisfy those concerned with the place of Poles in World War II narratives.

It was too late for explanations in the spirit of communist self-criticism. The Polish Ministry of Foreign Affairs had already circulated a report that portrayed *Wielka Encyklopedia Powszechna* as a Jewish project. While an encyclopedia was meant to be an "honest and objective [rzetelnym i obiektywnym]" source of information, *Wielka Encyklopedia Powszechna* was not. It was not what one expected from an "academic publisher in socialist Poland."[67] If this was a "Polish encyclopedia," why were there so many Jewish entries? From the encyclopedia, readers could learn about Bar Mitzvahs, the Kol Nidre prayer, Kabbalah, Hasidism, and the Bund, as well as famous Jewish figures such as David Friedlander, Moses Mendelssohn, Moshe Dayan, and David Ben-Gurion. Surely the creators of the encyclopedia were Zionists, nationalist Jews, who had infiltrated the state's publishing house and imposed their agenda, claimed the report.[68] Rusinek and Moczar's men in the press attacked the encyclopedia, while publicly amending its mistakes. Newspaper articles condemned the editors and once more denied that death camps served a different purpose from that of other camps in the Nazi system; local ZBoWiD branches sent letters of protest to the party, and at least one workers' demonstration was held in Warsaw.[69]

In her memoir, Ewa Kuryluk, daughter of Karol Kuryluk, gives us a glimpse of the mood of the period:

> In late September 1967, we were walking back from shopping on Mokotowski Street when on the corner of Ujazdowski Avenue we ran into a demonstration—"Że-Rań," "Meat Factories' Crews," "Clothing Industry Workers"—I read the signs loudly, mechanically. "Working Class Protest," "Zionist Conspiracy"—these I read quietly. "Death Camps"—this I mouthed silently. "Hands off Polish Suffering!" "Down with PWN!" A protest against the publishing house that you run? You turned pale, leaned against a wall, and bit your lip. "Away!" "Away!"—those at the front of the march arrived at Trzech Krzyży Square. "Conspiracy! Conspiracy!" they chanted next. "Scram! Scram!" At the gloomy end staggered a cripple—"To the Gas!" he waved a yellow sign, "To the Gas!"[70]

---

67. AAN KC PZPR XVI 413, 167–73.

68. AAN KC PZPR XVI 413, 171–73.

69. For example, Henryk Dobrowolski, "Mało znana karta z historii obozów zagłady," *Życie Literackie* 37, no. 815 (October 9, 1967): 12; Władysław Machejek, "Smutno mi, Boże," *Życie Literackie* 32, no. 810 (June 8, 1967): 16; KW PZPR 469, 92.

70. This passage comes from the memoir of the daughter of Karol Kuryluk, editor in chief of PWN: Ewa Kuryluk, *Goldi: apoteoza zwierzaczkowatości* (Warsaw: Twój Styl, 2004), 34–35. In December 1967, Karol Kuryluk passed away at the age of fifty-seven.

Following the ministerial investigations, a special party commission was formed to investigate the encyclopedia entry. On September 26, 1967, the members—among them Rusinek and Zawadzki—met with Gumkowski, Marszałek, and the other editors.[71] The questioning started with Gumkowski: one official asked whether the editors had significantly changed the article he had composed. Gumkowski replied that he had not been involved in the editing and therefore was not responsible for the final result. However, he stood by the definitions, saying, "Concentration camps, death camps—those are two different Hitlerite types, with different objectives; different kinds of crimes were committed in those camps."[72] These exchanges prompted a series of remarks. Rusinek evoked his role in the veterans' organization (ZBoWiD) and told the committee that the entry had outraged former concentration camp prisoners; they worried that their own sacrifice would be forgotten. Surely the idea that there were more Jewish than Polish victims was an insult to every Pole. It was, he insisted, a falsification of history that played into the hands of Poland's enemies.[73] Should not the encyclopedia say far more about the Nazi plans to exterminate thirty million Slavs?[74] The undersecretary of state, Zawadzki, continued on a similar note, insisting that the Germans falsely classified many of those murdered in the camps as Jews.[75]

In the face of these attacks, Gumkowski continued to stick to what he considered the facts: the existence of separate death camps was supported by broadly accepted research, and the Germans did have a special plan for the Jews. The more he said about the use of the gas chamber in Stutthof or about whether Jews transported to extermination camps could be considered prisoners, the clearer it became that he had no clear idea why he had been summoned. This interrogation was not about the discourse acceptable until then or what Gumkowski (and most historians) considered to be the facts; it was about pushing Jewish genocide out of public discussions and establishing a particular way of speaking about World War II. Gumkowski failed to comply with the officials' expectation to replicate the new party line concerning the war. The fate of Jews under Nazi occupation was irrelevant when presented outside of a Polish context—it simply did not belong

---

71. AAN 237/XVI-414, 338.
72. AAN 237/XVI-414, 75.
73. AAN 237/XVI-414, 77.
74. AAN 237/XVI-414.
75. AAN 237/XVI-414, 86–87.

in a Polish socialist encyclopedia. Rusinek told Gumkowski that he wanted to hear about Polish fatalities, not "99 percent Jews."[76]

After Gumkowski, the commission spoke with Marszałek, Biernacki, and Majzner, all editors at the publishing house. Marszałek and Biernacki expressed similar opinions to those of Gumkowski, pointing out that the entry was within the boundaries of accepted research. They also mentioned that the encyclopedia would in the near future include an entry on Hitlerite crimes in Poland that would provide readers with information about Polish deaths. All three complained about the press campaign against them and declared that they were not conspiring to falsify history.[77] Rusinek, Zawadzki, and Wróblewski were not listening. The minutes of the meeting showed that while those involved in the publication talked about historical facts, current research, and correctable mistakes in the language of socialist self-criticism, the comments and questions of the party officials belonged to a separate political-national discourse about national suffering and Polish uniqueness.

In its final report submitted to First Secretary Gomułka and senior party officials on October 11, 1967, the special commission demanded the sacking of those "responsible for the mistakes."[78] In particular, Gumkowski was to lose his position as special adviser to the minister of justice, Biernacki was to leave the publishing house, and Majzner was to be moved to a different job. Marszałek would receive only a reprimand. The committee also insisted on a reorganization of the publisher's editorial board and its Department of Dictionaries and Encyclopedias, which would involve the transfer and firing of several workers. The report demanded the replacement of the head of the relevant censorship divisions and two other staff members.[79] All of these people had demonstrated a marked lack of "political sensitivity."[80] In the purge of PWN, thirty-four workers lost their jobs and were removed from the party.[81] Two of the censors responsible for previous review and approval of the encyclopedia were fired as well.[82]

In addition to calling for heads to roll, the commission set out to correct the alleged mistake made in the encyclopedia. A revised entry to be

---

76. AAN 237/XVI–414, 101.
77. AAN 237/XVI–414, 109–31.
78. AAN 237/XVI–414, 341.
79. AAN 237/XVI–414, 342–44.
80. AAN 237/XVI–414, 342.
81. AIPN 01288/24, 79–84.
82. AIPN 01288/24, 48.

published in a supplement, previously mentioned, was insufficient. A book by legal expert Alfons Klafkowski, to appear within a few months, would set the record straight about the camps, and one of the major Polish weeklies would print an article refuting the entry. Finally, the special commission advised the Ministry of Justice to promote cooperation between the Central Commission for the Investigation of Hitlerite Crimes and Polish academics. The point of this last step was to monitor and curtail further academic research on the subject.[83]

Klafkowski, author of the party-approved monograph *Obozy Koncentracyjne Hitlerowskie* (Hitlerite concentration camps), was a legal scholar, former rector of Adam Mickiewicz University in Poznań, and a member of the Catholic progovernment organization PAX, which would take an active rule in the anti-Zionist campaign after March 1968.[84] In his attempt to correct the "one-sided presentation of the tragic fate of Europe's Jews," Klafkowski relied not on new materials but on legal arguments.[85] He claimed that according to international law the creation of concentration camps was the most heinous of war crimes—no distinction was made between such camps and death camps. Klafkowski quoted the Nuremberg verdict, which stated that confining people in concentration camps was "one of the most shameful means of terror toward the civilian population in the occupied countries."[86] *Obozy Koncentracyjne Hitlerowskie* provided the updated party line: the Germans built concentration camps all over occupied Europe, killing prisoners from all nationalities; they murdered over six million Polish citizens during the war, of whom three million were Jews; Jews may have been the first nation the Nazis wiped out, but Poles and Slavs would have suffered the same fate had the Germans won the war. Polish and Jewish suffering were presented side by side as equal tragedies.[87] The new narrative did not

83. AIPN 01288/24, 345–46.
84. Tadeusz Gadkowski and Jerzy Tyranowski, *Alfons Klafkowski: Prawnik Internacjonalista* (Poznań: Wydawnictwo Poznańskie, 2004), 33. PAX, a Catholic communist organization that absorbed former members of the AK and even the extreme right, played a leading role in the campaign, publishing an article condemning Zionists and warning of Zionist influence. On PAX and the anti-Zionist campaign in Poland, see Mikolaj Kunicki, "The Red and the Brown: Bolesław Piasecki, the Polish Communists, and the Anti-Zionist Campaign in Poland, 1967–1968," *East European Politics and Societies* 19, no. 2 (2005): 185–225; Mikolaj Kunicki, *Between the Red and the Brown: Nationalism, Catholicism, and Communism in Twentieth-Century Poland—The Politics of Bolesław Piasecki* (Columbus: Ohio University Press, 2012).
85. AAN KC 237/XVI–414, 339.
86. Alfons Klafkowski, *Obozy Koncentracyjne Hitlerowskie jako zagadnienie prawa międzynarodowego* (Warsaw: Państwowe Wydawnictwo Naukowe, 1968), 14.
87. Klafkowski, *Obozy Koncentracyjne Hitlerowskie*.

deny that the Germans murdered vast numbers of Jews—their persecution served the image of Poles as rescuers and active resisters—yet Jews became one group among many whom the Nazis targeted.

Bearing the same title as Klafkowski's book, "Obozy Koncentracyjne Hitlerowskie," an article by Rusinek himself, appeared in the widely read weekly *Polityka* on November 11, 1967. It set out the new view on the fate of Poland's Jews during World War II. Far more widely read than Klafkowski's scholarly monograph, this was one of the first articles that fully brought the encyclopedia affair, so far discussed mostly in the party, to the general public. Rusinek rejected the distinction between death camps and concentration camps, claiming that both were designed for mass killing. Western European scholars had made such a distinction, but a Polish encyclopedia should not blindly repeat Western scholarship. The Nazi system of camps was so complicated that one could not attribute a particular role to any one camp. In the end they all served one purpose—the killing of prisoners.

"The names and types of camps do not really matter. The slave-like working conditions in all camps and the starvation food rations [given] to all prisoners, regardless of their descent and nationality, sentenced the prisoners to death, whether immediately or slowly. Camps run according to Hitlerite policy were meant to function as a central instrument in the mass extermination of subdued and occupied nations."[88]

Rusinek did not deny that the Germans pursued the "final solution" or that they used some camps to murder the Jews. But he denied that the treatment of Jews differed significantly from the treatment of other nationalities, particularly Poles. When Rusinek spoke of mass murder, he named Poles first, then Soviets, then Jews.[89] In the piece, Rusinek claimed the special authority of a camp survivor. Captured by the Germans in 1939, Rusinek had been sent to Stutthof and later to Mauthausen, where he remained until the US Army liberated the camp in 1945. He led the attack on the encyclopedia not only as the vice minister of arts and culture and the secretary of the veterans' organization but also as a former prisoner of the camps. In his memoirs published in 1989, well after the events of 1967–68, Simon Wiesenthal, the famed "Nazi hunter," described meeting Rusinek at Mauthausen after the war—both were former prisoners. According to Wiesenthal, their paths crossed after the

88. Kazimierz Rusinek, "Hitlerowskie Obozy Koncentracyjne," *Polityka* 45, no. 558 (November 11, 1967): 3.

89. Rusinek, "Hitlerowskie": "Do kagtegorii akcji masowej zagłady należy akcja 'Endlosung'—tj. zagłady Żydów i osób pochodzenia żydowskiego w całej okupowanej Europie."

camp had been liberated: when Wiesenthal had recovered enough to leave the camp, he applied to Rusinek, who had become part of the camp's interim administration, for permission to leave. In response to Wiesenthal's request, Rusinek allegedly struck him simply because he was a Jew. This very incident, said Wiesenthal, showed him that antisemitism had not disappeared from Poland.[90] Later, Wiesenthal established and headed the Jewish Documentation Center in Vienna, achieving international renown as he helped bring hundreds of Nazi criminals to trial.[91] On June 19, 1967, Wiesenthal sent an open letter to the International Auschwitz Committee, the communist-dominated organization supervising the memorial site, denouncing the anti-Zionist campaign and telling the committee that the vast majority of the victims at Auschwitz had been Jews.[92] Twenty-two years after the defeat of Germany, two prominent victims of Nazi policies disagreed over the very question of victimhood. In the eyes of Rusinek and others mentioned here, highlighting the suffering of one group dismissed the persecution of the other. They feared that the world would forget their role and their sacrifice if the Holocaust took central stage in global memory of the war.

As Rusinek wrote in *Polityka, Kultura*, his insult at the implication that Jews had special status as victims is clear: "The Hitlerite drive to murder entire nations in occupied Europe was not limited to the final solution. The final solution was not an exception to the Hitlerite politics of extermination on conquered European lands. The number of those murdered in the final solution constituted about 30 percent of the victims of Hitlerism. That is the truth, and these are the facts. The entire Polish nation was to be exterminated. And the extermination of our nation was not limited to isolated camps: the entire country was a battleground, and there were millions of victims."[93]

Not coincidentally, Rusinek used the term *battleground*, emphasizing that Poles fought in a war rather than being passive victims in "isolated camps" like the Jews. In the "partisan" narrative, Poles fared worse than Jews since the Nazis turned Poland into a combat zone, hounding and hunting Poles, destroying not only their lives but also their homeland. Poland was once more "Christ among the nations."

---

90. Simon Wiesenthal, *Justice, not Vengeance* (New York: Grove Weidenfeld, 1989), 208.
91. Hella Pick, *Simon Wiesenthal: A Life in Search of Justice* (Boston: Northeastern University Press, 1996); Tom Segev, *Wiesenthal: Ha'Biographia* (Jerusalem: Keter Books, 2010), 238–41.
92. ANN 237/XIX-351, 2–5.
93. Rusinek, "Hitlerowskie," 3.

The Jewish Response

Surprised by the change in the regime's position toward the fate of Jews during the war, Poland's central Jewish organization tried to respond to the affair through its Yiddish-language organ, *Folks Sztyme*. But the censors erased paragraphs dealing with the Holocaust from "Przypomnienie—w dwadzieścia pięć lat później" (Remembrance, twenty-five years later), an article by Józef Korman published on November 25, 1967.

The deleted lines read as follows: "There are those who try to present the six million Jews murdered by the Germans as French, Belgians, and others—anything but Jews. They forget that the Hitlerite murderers had a diabolical plan, a final solution to the Jewish problem, a plan to exterminate the entire Jewish people. Those who count the victims of the *Endlosung* and estimate their part in the total number of Hitler's victims forget to add that one-third of the entire Jewish nation was exterminated."[94]

Against the critics of the encyclopedia, Korman insisted on the exceptional fate of the Jews during World War II and on the history of the war as he and his colleagues had written about it until then. This was the period when, in various locations, the narrative on the uniqueness of the Holocaust was born. But the boundaries of the discourse had changed, and a discussion of the "final solution" that did not gesture at the heroism and suffering of Poles was no longer tolerated; any hint of Jewish uniqueness was banned. The censors criticized Korman and other writers from *Folks Sztyme* "for generalizing, letting drop hints, and offering suggestions that could not be misunderstood [okazja do wielu ogólnikowych, aluzyjnych sformułowań i sugestii o jednoznacznym charakterze]."[95]

The censorship's Department of Press and Radio also deleted the following passage from an article in the Polish-language edition of *Folks Sztyme, Nasz Głos*: "I will say more. Sometimes one struggles to answer certain questions, for example, those related to publications in which the primary goal of Marxism—class analysis of problems, events, and human behavior—is forgotten; publications in which criticizing the 'Targowica line' in our nation's history quickly leads to erroneous and totally false

94. AAN, GUKPPiW 824, 89.
95. AAN, GUKPPiW 824, 89.

generalizations, forgetting that this line was not paramount throughout the history of Polish Jews."[96]

The author condemned the new party line and the "partisans" in the party for continuing nationalist-antisemitic traditions and abandoning the Marxist outlook in their criticism of Jews. Because of the affair, relations between the TSKŻ, the social-cultural association of Jews in Poland, and the Polish government further declined as the Jewish organization tried to resist an increasingly restrictive policy.[97]

The Aftershock of the Affair

The head of the censor's non-periodical department described 1967 as "a difficult year": his division came under close examination and had to censor many books dealing with World War II and the occupation. They canceled the publication of thirteen books and made extensive changes to forty-one publications, compared with four questionable books in 1966.[98] The censors now treaded carefully around the issues of Jewish-Polish relations, the German occupation, and resistance to that occupation. Grounds for censorship included presenting a "negative image of Poles" or emphasizing the genocide of the Jews. The Polish censors also edited some works rather than completely suppressing them. Depictions of Poles mistreating Jews or handing them over to the Germans were deleted. In general, the preferred topic in 1967 and 1968 was the sacrifice and struggle for the "biological preservation of the Polish people."[99]

One book that did not make it past the censors was *Egzamin* (Examination) by Tadeusz Słupecki. This novel told the story of a working-class Pole who did everything in her power to survive World War II. Among the horrors of the war, she witnessed the murder of Jewish prisoners at the hands of Germans, an experience that shook her out of her lifelong antisemitism. According to the censors, the theme of Polish antisemitism pervaded the novel; they cited this as a reason for suppressing the book.[100] Clearly the

96. AAN, GUKPPiW 885, 33. The reference to Targowica, the confederacy established under Russian protection in 1792, needs explanation: antisemites accused the Jews in Poland of supporting the pro-Russian line of the Targowica confederacy, whose inability to rule led to the final partition of Poland. Jerzy Lukowski and Hubert Zawadzki, *A Concise History of Poland* (Cambridge: Cambridge University Press, 2001), 102.

97. Anat Plocker, "Between Emigration and Silence: Jewish Reactions to the Anti-Zionist Campaign in Poland, 1967/68," *Simon Dubnow Institute Yearbook/Jahrbuch des Simon-Dubnow-Instituts* IX (2010).

98. AAN GUKPPiW 831, 137.

99. AAN GUKPPiW 831, 144.

100. AAN GUKPPiW 831, 144.

work did not suit the dominant narrative that presented Poles as instinctively defending Jews out of a sense of honor and a willingness to sacrifice for others. An academic work also ran into problems, the same sort of problems that assailed *Wielka Encyklopedia Powszechna.*[101] A. J. Kamiski's *Dookoła kolczastych drutów* (Around the barbed wire) was a commissioned work, originally intended as a sort of primer on Nazi Germany's anti-Polish crimes. But when the censors saw that Kamiski had divided the Hitlerite system into concentration camps and sites of mass murder, they deemed the essay unpatriotic and anti-Polish: "When discussing relations between prisoners or former prisoners of the camps, he quoted liberally from memoirs and accounts published in the West. These presented Poles in a bad light, emphasizing the alleged chauvinism, meanness, and lack of respect among Polish prisoners."[102] Once more, government officials considered the use of Western sources on the war as playing into the hands of a deliberate move to present Poles as antisemitic and malicious.

While other departments within the Bureau of Censorship informed publishers that they would be publishing fewer and shorter books in 1967, the Department of Film, Television, and Theater decided to shelve pictures about the Holocaust and World War II. Three movies from previous decades also raised concerns. The first movie was *Róża*, director Janusz Majewski's short film from 1962. Written by the well-known Polish Jewish poet Stanisław Wygodzki, it is the story of a man looking for the graves of relatives who had died during the war. Footage clearly showed that Poland's Jewish cemeteries were in ruins. Though it had won an award in a festival held in Kraków, *Róża* suddenly became unacceptable in 1967, as it focused exclusively on the fate of Jews and the condition of Jewish sites. The second movie was a short from 1961, written and directed by Edward Etler and entitled *Cmentarz Remu* (Remu Cemetery). The film, which dealt with the fate of the old Jewish quarter and the cemetery in Kraków, was deemed "too Jewish" by the censor since it showed a young Jewish girl deep in prayer. The censor also mentioned another movie by the same director, *Judaica*, released in 1966, about the dedication of a Jewish museum. Both films were found overly religious and overly Jewish, despite having been approved in the past.[103] In the Polish socialist homeland, there was little room for expressions of Jewish identity. The last and most important of the

101. AAN GUKPPiW 831, 144–45.
102. AAN GUKPPiW 831, 146.
103. AAN, GUKPPiW 846, 197–98.

banned pictures was *Pod Jednym Niebem* (Under the Same Sky), written by the journalist Bronisław Wiernik, directed by Kurt Weber, and narrated by the renowned poet Tadeusz Różewicz. The film, which was released in 1956 and which won the first prize for documentaries at the Karlovy Vary International Film Festival, juxtaposed the situation of the Jews in Poland during and after the war with the lives of Christian Poles in the same period. Catholics and Jews lived under the same sky but did not share the same fate, an idea that was new to Polish depictions of the war.[104] Made during de-Stalinization, *Pod Jednym Niebem* belonged to the time of new openness about Jewish topics in Poland. In 1967, representations of the war that distinguished between the fate of Jews and Poles and did not include Polish heroism were no longer tolerable, and the censors banned this important movie.[105] They reflected party members' concern that the Polish role in fighting the occupation and the persecution of Poles during World War II would be overlooked in international forums.

The encyclopedia affair not only changed what could be said about the Holocaust in Poland but ushered in a reevaluation of what had already been said, affecting historians, writers, and filmmakers. After a period of increasing debate on the future of socialism and the events of World War II, Polish communists wanted again to control public discourse. They believed that a "Zionist" entry in a Polish encyclopedia could have appeared only in troubled times for socialism. They saw Jews as excessively influencing Polish socialist culture and held them responsible for the maladies of communism. Moreover, these party members feared that a Jewish conspiracy was working behind the scenes to erase the memory of Polish suffering and heroism and to highlight the Holocaust. They believed that Jews, particularly Zionist Jews, used the memory of World War II for political gains in the international arena: they plotted with West Germany and the United States to undermine the communist regime and turn Poland from a country of heroes into a nation of Nazi collaborators. The encyclopedia served as proof of this "partisan" anxiety, and party officials acted to correct the situation and purge the system of "Zionist" influences.

From 1967 on, it became unacceptable in communist Poland to discuss the Holocaust openly or to mention in public the suffering of Jews without

---

104. For information on the Karlovy Vary Film Festival, see its official website at http://www.iffkv.cz/?m=32.

105. AAN, GUKPPiW 846, 197–98.

the heroism of Poles. When it came to World War II, the veterans' organization ZBoWiD (with the help of the Central Commission for the Investigation of Hitlerite Crimes in Poland) tried to control the construction of memory and the historiography. ZBoWiD, the social arm of the "partisan" faction, came to strongly influence the planning of monuments and museums, publications on the war, and public ceremonies. The period of discursive change gave birth to a myth of silence about the Holocaust in Poland: when Western visitors and scholars visited Poland in the late 1980s, they fell under the impression that from its inception the communist regime had stifled the memory of the Holocaust.

The view that Poles either rescued Jews or remained indifferent during the war persisted into the postcommunist era and retained a central position.[106] According to historian John Connelly, the war supplied Poles with "dramas of idealism, self-sacrifice and betrayal."[107] After decades of the silencing of certain aspects in the history of the German occupation, and despite the demands of the European Union to come to terms with the past, some in Poland "reacted with suspicion to the sudden concern with the fate of Jews during World War II," as the historian John-Paul Himka explains.[108] In the European context of Holocaust memorialization, Poland, as Dan Diner asserts, "developed [its] distinctive memory of victimhood, resulting ultimately in a dynamic rivalry with Jewish memory—[and] may find it difficult to come to terms with accepting the Jewish Holocaust as an all embracing foundational event."[109] The rescuer narrative left little room for Jewish suffering and no space for Polish collaboration and participation in the mass murder of Jews. Certain aspects of the Holocaust were not

---

106. For example, see the series "Kto ratuje jedno życie," which collects stories of rescue in different regions of Poland published by the Instytut Pamięci Narodowej, a state-funded institution. Paweł Knap, ed., *"Jak ci się uda uratować, pamiętaj": relacje "Sprawiedliwych" i o "Sprawiedliwych" z województwa zachodniopomorskiego* (Szczecin: Instytut Pamięci Narodowej—Komisja Ścigania Zbrodni przeciwko Narodowi Polskiemu, 2010); Ewa Kurek, *Dzieci żydowskie w klasztorach: udział żeńskich zgromadzeń zakonnych w akcji ratowania dzieci żydowskich w Polsce w latach 1939–1945* (Lublin: "Gaudium," 2004); Kazimierz Przybysz, *Gdy wieś ratowała życie* (Warsaw: Muzeum Historii Polskiego Ruchu Ludowego, 2001); Elżbieta Rączy, *Pomoc Polaków dla ludności żydowskiej na Rzeszowszczyźnie 1939–1945* (Rzeszów: Instytut Pamięci Narodowej, 2008).

107. John Connelly, "The Noble and the Base: Poland and the Holocaust," *Nation*, November 14, 2012, http://www.thenation.com/article/171262/noble-and-base-poland-and-holocaust.

108. John-Paul Himka, "Obstacles to the Integration of the Holocaust into Post-communist East European Historical Narratives," *Canadian Slavonic Papers/Revue Canadienne des Slavistes* 50, no. 3/4 (September–December 2008), 359–72.

109. Dan Diner, "Restitution and Memory: The Holocaust in European Political Cultures," *New German Critique* 90 (Autumn 2003): 36–44.

forgotten or silenced, but they rather served to strengthen the national myth. The perception of Poles as saviors of Jews and heroes of wartime Europe complemented the idea of "Christ among the nations," a central Polish national ethos. By stressing Polish martyrdom during World War II, both communist and postcommunist political myths affirmed these decades-long cultural perceptions of the role of Poland in history.

As 1967 neared its end, two contradictory tendencies emerged in Poland: while intellectuals, students, and professors called for more reforms, for the creation of a socialist regime "with a human face," the nationalist wing of the party's fear of Jewish conspiracies intensified and unleashed a far stronger attack against Poland's "subversive Jews." Just as the "partisans" saw publications about the Holocaust as part of a Zionist conspiracy against Poland, they perceived the reform movement as a Jewish-Zionist attempt to weaken communism. The next chapter will outline the rise of the movement to reform socialism in Poland, leading to the open clash between the reformers and the regime in March 1968.

4

WE, THE STUDENTS

The Party and the Opposition

WITH THE PARTING OF THE "MAN OF STEEL," the "Father of Nations," and Khrushchev's public denouncement of Stalin, communist intellectuals in the Soviet bloc began seeking in Marxism-Leninism new ways to practice socialism. Under Władysław Gomułka's leadership (1956–70), the Polish state "weakened the control over citizens to a higher degree than was done in other countries."[1] The socialist elite aimed to redefine the Polish path to socialism without destroying communism. As we saw in previous chapters, two visions of Polish communism emerged in the party. One camp wanted to infuse Polish socialism with nationalism. The so-called "partisans" imagined a strong, stable nation-state with a state-run socialist economic system and a powerful police mechanism. Among them there were those comrades like Mieczysław Moczar and Jerzy Putrament, who believed that Poland's geopolitical position mandated compliance with the Soviet Union. Since its western neighbor, the Federal Republic of Germany (FRG), did not recognize the Polish border and was "the descendent of Nazi Germany," they considered their eastern neighbor the only guardian of Poland's post-1945 boundaries. Like Roman Dmowski, the founder of the right-wing National Democratic Party (known as the Endecja), national communists were deeply anti-German, and like Dmowski during World War I, they believed an alliance with Russia would protect Polish interests.[2] The hard-liners softened the socialist rhetoric and played up their nationalism.

---

1. Andrzej Friszke, "The Polish October of 1956 from the Perspective of Its Fiftieth Anniversary," *Polish Quarterly of International Affairs* 3 (2006): 99–118.

2. T. David Curp, "The Revolution Betrayed: The Poznań Revolt and the Polish Road to Nationalist Socialism," *Polish Review* 51, no. 3/4 (2006): 307–24.

The so-called "revisionists," or rather reformists, on the other hand, wanted "socialism with a human face," meaning a policy of increased attention to civil rights that would not compromise the socialist economy. From the center of the communist elite, concurrently with intellectuals in neighboring Czechoslovakia, emerged a group that wanted greater personal freedoms and believed that socialism would triumph in an open market of ideas without need for coercion. One of the student leaders of 1968, Adam Michnik, son of Polish Jewish communist parents, described his position as a young communist in the 1960s: "Paradoxically, I belonged during the sixties to a small circle that didn't fear the Communists. I felt that Communist Poland was my Poland. So what should I be scared of? I believed then that a Communist was someone whose mission was to denounce injustice. So I did."[3] Michnik's circle was largely made up of intellectuals from Jewish homes, though as communists they did not strongly identify as Jews and their parents were generally nonpracticing. The younger members of the reformist group were part of the baby-boomer generation; they were born after World War II, had grown up in communist homes, and had attended socialist schools: "We were twenty years old when the People's Republic turned twenty years old," explained Barbara Toruńczyk.[4] The older members had converted to communism in the 1930s or during the war and now heeded Khrushchev's call for a return to a "true" Marxism-Leninism. After 1956, reformist intellectuals such as Zygmunt Bauman and philosopher Leszek Kołakowski militated for a return to pre-Stalinist Marxism—for them, Stalinism and terror had been aberrations, deviations from true socialism. From the late 1950s to 1968, these young academics publicly criticized Gomułka for his unwillingness to press ahead with further reforms to the regime, in spite of their high hopes of him. Gomułka had defaulted, so they said, on his promise to launch a new era in Polish socialism. By late 1967, official censorship of the press and the arts usually kept pace with resentment toward Gomułka and nipped in the bud attempts to protest the first secretary's policies. Then, in January 1968, a group of intellectuals protested the closure of Adam Mickiewicz's nineteenth-century play *Dziady* (Forefathers' Eve). Casting themselves as the champions of Polish national culture, the reformists insisted that heritage had to come before politics.

---

3. "Not Your Father's Communism: A Conversation," *Books & Culture* 5, no. 1 (January/February 1999): 18.

4. Piotr Osęka, *My Ludzie z Marca: Autoportret pokolenia '68* (Wołowiec: Wydawnictwo Czarne and ISP PAN, 2015), Barbara Toruńczyk quoted on page 31.

The regime, already engaged in campaigns against Zionism and the insidious influence of Western imperialism, saw the staging of the play as a public expression of anti-Russian (i.e., anti-Soviet) feelings and refused to tolerate any undermining of Polish socialism. Gomułka's government feared that the students and their very public protests would further weaken the regime. Moreover, they believed that the student opposition was part of the wide-reaching Zionist-American-West German conspiracy against Poland. So many of the intellectuals behind it and the students leading it had Jewish origins, and therefore were under the sway of Zionism.

The Promises and Disappointments of "the Polish October"

On October 21, 1956, the Central Committee elected Gomułka first secretary. In early November, Soviet forces overran Budapest, toppling a reformist Hungarian government and killing tens of thousands. In his new-old role as the head of communist Poland, Gomułka stood up to his commitments to Khrushchev: in 1956–57, he curtailed Polish reforms; in 1967, he adopted wholeheartedly the Soviet position on the war in the Middle East; and in 1968, he sent Polish troops into Prague alongside other Warsaw Pact counties to crush the reformist Czechoslovak government.[5]

Reform-minded party members, weary of Stalinism, wrongly pinned their hopes to Gomułka's return to power. Sustentative changes were made. Gomułka disbanded what was left of collective farms and authorized some private businesses. He released from prison the Polish primate, Cardinal Wyszyński; reintroduced religious instruction in public schools; allowed for a freer Catholic press; and even permitted some independent Catholics to run for the Sejm.[6] Gomułka also promised and delivered a return to Polish "family values"; female labor was scaled back, and conventional gender roles were exulted. As historian Malgorzata Fidelis explains, for Poles, "shop-floor hierarches were more than economic or social matters. They

---

5. Jerzy J. Wiatr, "Pokolenie '56," *Przegląd Humanistyczny* 5/6 (2006): 65–72; Mark Kramer, "The Soviet Union and the 1956 Crises in Hungary and Poland: Reassessments and New Findings," *Journal of Contemporary History* 33, no. 2 (1998): 163–214; Krzysztof Persak, "The Polish-Soviet Confrontation in 1956 and the Attempted Soviet Military Intervention in Poland," *Europe-Asia Studies* 58, no. 8 (2006): 1258–1310.

6. Gomułka's relationship with the church changed over the decade; for more on this, see Mikołaj Stanisław Kunicki, *Between the Brown and the Red: Nationalism, Catholicism, and Communism in Twentieth-Century Poland: The Politics of Bolesław Piasecki* (Columbus: Ohio University Press, 2012), 111–39.

were matters of national identity as well . . . women working in men's jobs would remain a powerful symbol of Soviet dominance."[7] In the same manner that Jews were no longer to be visible at the helm of the party, so women had to go back to their place in society. The reforms of 1956–57 had less to do with creating a more open, vibrant, and discussion-filled socialism and more with reverting to traditional Polish identities: Catholics, peasants, mothers, and fathers.

In terms of personal freedoms, the new government permitted the revival of a private sphere. Gomułka reorganized the Committee for Public Security, renaming it the Ministry of Internal Affairs, a government office that exists also in liberal democracies. But although the Security Services abandoned society-wide terror, reduced the number of their operatives, and scaled back their operations, they continued to monitor troublesome groups, including reformists, intellectuals, and church officials. Secret agents followed members' every move and recruited informants close to them. The threshold for persecution had changed: criticism of the government was considered a threat only if it came into the open and publicized. The Ministry of Internal Affairs set out mostly to gauge public opinion; it did not engage in mass repression or incarceration.[8] The Gomułka regime lessened its control of the cultural sphere. Artists, poets, and writers could abandon socialist realism, the only acceptable style under Stalinism, and explore new modes of representation. But their freedom was still restricted: though they did not have to produce odes to Stalin, intellectuals could not call for the replacement of the system of governance. Until the rise of the underground press in the 1970s, real oppositionists had almost no public voice in Poland, as most Polish intellectuals and artists active during the 1950s and 1960s were either party members or sympathetic in some way to socialism. Those who objected to any form of socialism could not take part in the discussion; their sole vehicle for publication was the émigré press.[9]

Yet a movement opposed to the current regime had been born. The dissident Adam Michnik claimed, much later, "Revisionism [i.e., reformism] was not a faction in the communist party or in the party apparatus. It was

---

7. Fidelis, *Women, Communism and Industrialization in Postwar Poland*, 203–37; quote from page 229.

8. Anthony Kemp-Welch, *Poland under Communism: A Cold War History* (Cambridge: Cambridge University Press, 2008), 93–145.

9. Andrzej Friszke, "Przystosowanie i opór. Rozważania nad postawami społecznymi, 1956–1970," in *Komunizm: Ideologia, System, Ludzie*, ed. Tomasz Szarota (Warsaw: Neriton, 2001), 139–55.

a style, a cultural group, a fashion."[10] Young socialist intellectuals, disappointed by the government's half-hearted measures, longed for true freedom of speech, press, and assembly—these were the "revisionists" whom Michnik had in mind. Gomułka was determined to silence the voices that demanded significant changes. He had reached an accord with Khrushchev and had drawn the lesson from the Soviet invasion of Hungary. Gomułka was a communist true believer who also understood the dangers of breaking with Moscow and who thought he was working in the best interests of Poland. To put an end to public debates, the government shut down the reformist student paper *Po Prostu* and tightened censorship of Polish newspapers and radio, although both had played a central part in Gomułka's return to power in October 1956. In private, intellectuals continued to meet and mutter.[11]

The reformists wished for the day when rank-and-file party members would have some influence over decision-making. In the party-state system that developed after Stalinism, the Central Committee sent resolutions to the party congress or to local party cells that in turn served as rubber stamps.[12] In Poland, young academics such as Jacek Kuroń, Karol Modzelewski, and Leszek Kołakowski objected to such voting gestures and believed socialism would benefit and evolve through open debates. They did not hope for a liberal democracy but rather for a better socialist state. Leszek Kołakowski's *Czym jest socjalizm?* (What is socialism?) symbolized the reformist spirit of the late 1950s. Kołakowski had hoped to publish it in *Po Prostu*, but the censors banned the short work, which then circulated in handwritten copies among intellectuals. Kołakowski opened with the words, "I will tell you what socialism is. But first I will tell you what it is not," referring to a society in which it is better not to think than to think, in which anyone could be arrested and no one could leave. Stalinism was not

10. Quoted in Anna Bikont and Joanna Szczęsna, *Lawina i kamienie: Pisarze wobec komunizmu* (Warsaw: Prószyński i S-ka, 2006), 277. "Rewizjonizm—nie był frakcją w partii komunistycznej czy aparacie partyjnym. Był stylem, formacją kulturalną, modą."

11. Krzysztof Persak, *Sprawa Henryka Hollanda* (Warsaw: PAN-ISP, 2006), 26–67; Konrad Rokicki, "Służba Bezpieczeństwa wobec inteligencji twórczej od Października '56 do Marca '68," *Pamięć i Sprawiedliwość* 2, no. 10 (2006): 167–82.

12. Alexei Yurchak, *Everything Was Forever, Until It Was No More: The Last Soviet Generation* (Princeton, NJ: Princeton University Press, 2006), 116–18. As Alexei Yurchak shows in his work on the Soviet Union, after Stalinism voting became a ritual, something one had to do to be part of the system. By voting, Communist Party members indicated that they were part of the "we," the Soviet public. Yurchak claimed that in the Soviet Union most party members accepted the new performative character of communist discourse.

socialism, said Kołakowski, but what *was* socialism? The answer, "Socialism is truly a good thing," is ironic and hopeful at the same time.[13] For many in the reformist group, socialism had been a fundamental article of faith until 1968. They formed discussion clubs, most significantly the Catholic Intelligentsia Club (Klub Inteligencji Katolickiej) and the Crooked Circle Club (Klub Krzywego Koła), named after the street where the meetings were held. Founded in 1955, the Crooked Circle had as members well-known intellectuals, writers, and university professors. Often, lively discussions followed lectures on politics and culture.[14] As Gomułka's reforms wavered, the club's organizers grew more determined to keep the spirit of the reforms of 1956 alive.[15] In February 1962, the authorities disbanded the Crooked Circle, claiming that a student had been attacked while leaving a meeting.[16] The end of the Crooked Circle and introduction of stricter censorship increased disgruntlement and disappointment among writers and intellectuals. They felt that Gomułka had betrayed them and the "promise of 1956." In 1964, thirty-four writers signed an open letter to President Cyrankiewicz protesting censorship and demanding that the government uphold constitutionally guaranteed freedom of speech. Radio Free Europe publicized the protest a few days later, drawing support for the Polish writers from intellectuals around the world. The party reacted with a letter of its own; six hundred writers endorsed it. The statement condemned the signatories of the "letter of the thirty-four" for "organizing a smear campaign against People's Poland." The regime also banned the works of those who had organized the protest, and the Ministry of Internal Affairs began monitoring them more closely.[17]

---

13. Kołakowski's text appears in Bikont and Szczęsna, *Lawina i kamienie*, 278.

14. Members included Tadeusz Kotarbiński, Adam Schaff, Władysław Bieńkowski, Maria Ossowska, and Stanisław Ossowski. Jan Józef Lipski, who would become a leading dissident, was the group's president.

15. Konrad Rokicki, "Służba Bezpieczeństwa wobec inteligencji twórczej," *Pamięć i Sprawiedliwość* 2, no. 10 (2006): 167–82; Jan Józef Lipski, *KOR: Komitet Obrony Robotników* (London: Aneks, 1983), 13.

16. Mieczysław F. Rakowski, *Dzienniki Polityczne, 1958–1962* (Warsaw: Iskry, 1998), 362. Most likely this was a repercussion from the conviction of the group's secretary, Anna Rudzińska, for working for *Kultura*, a Paris-based émigré journal.

17. Bikont and Szczęsna, *Lawina i kamienie*, 321–39. Lipski and the writers Antoni Słonimski and Paweł Hertz had collected signatures by sending the letter to authors around Poland, as Hertz worried that "a letter signed only by Jews and communists would make no difference." Among others, sociology professor Maria Ossowka and writers Paweł Jasienica, Adolf Rudnicki, Jerzy Andrzejewski, and Adam Ważyk agreed to sign. On March 14, 1964, Słonimski, a famed poet of Jewish descent, delivered the letter to the office of the council of ministers.

The government's harsh reaction to the writers' protest unleashed further unrest among intellectuals. One center of reformist activity was Warsaw University. As the historian John Connelly demonstrated in his work on the Sovietization of Eastern European universities, in Poland the communists failed to gain complete control over the professoriate and Polish professors maintained their sense of community and identity: their intellectual credentials, their membership in the *intelligentsia*, not their political affiliation, gave them the right to guide the Polish people.[18] During the 1960s, young professors and students, educated mostly in the post-1945 era, drew on past academic traditions in a doomed effort to reform the communist regime.

Two members of Warsaw University's junior faculty, Jacek Kuroń and Karol Modzelewski, ran the Związek Młodzieży Socjalistycznej (ZMS, the Socialist Youth Union) discussion club at the university, allowing participants to speak freely. However, the authorities felt that the open forum encouraged opposition to the regime, so they quickly removed the two academics from the club.[19] Following recent events, Kuroń and Modzelewski drafted a document evaluating the state of socialism in Poland and criticizing the party's practices. As Kuroń explained in his memoir, "It was necessary to conduct a thorough critique of the system from a Marxist position. . . . We were sure that workers in Poland, in that bureaucratic socialist system, were unreserved supporters of a socialism based on workers' democracy."[20] In November 1964, the party expelled the young academics.[21] The head of the Central Committee's Academic Department, Andrzej Werblan, called the Kuroń-Modzelewski plan an "anti-party libel."[22] But that was not the end of the story. In March 1965, Kuroń and Modzelewski presented their critique of Polish socialism to the heads of the party and the ZMS in an open letter. The Security Services arrested them and detained a few young students, including Adam Michnik and Seweryn Blumsztajn. It appeared that a conspiracy was afoot: the two academics and their friends had made copies of their letter, which they planned to distribute among

---

18. John Connelly, *Captive University: The Sovietization of East German, Czech and Polish Higher Education, 1945–1956* (Chapel Hill: University of North Carolina Press, 2000).

19. Lipski, *KOR*, 17; Andrzej Friszke, *Anatomia Buntu: Kuroń, Modzelwski i komandosi* (Kraków: Znak, 2010), 84–96, 131.

20. Jacek Kuroń, *Wiara i wina: do i od komunizmu* (Wrocław: Wydawnictwo Dolnośląskie, 1995), 205.

21. AAN 237/ XVI–409, 62–96.

22. Kuroń, *Wiara i wina*, 221–23; Friszke, *Anatomia Buntu*, 183–85.

Polish intellectuals and abroad.[23] The police managed to seize several copies, though not all: Jan Józef Lipski had managed to send one to the Paris émigré journal *Kultura*, which then published the open letter.[24]

The Ministry of Internal Affairs accused Kuroń and Modzelewski of "drawing up a document inciting a revolution to overthrow the government of the People's Republic of Poland."[25] In the open letter, they had indeed called the communist party a monopolistic and monolithic party that suppressed organized factions and competing political programs. Without true alternatives, elections were meaningless, and decisions were left to the party's elite. Kuroń and Modzelewski claimed that in such a system the working class had little influence on the socialist state and that the "the central political bureaucracy became a separate class."[26] The new bureaucratic class ruled Poland—"a bureaucratic class dictatorship"—by controlling the means of production and a coercion mechanism (i.e., the police and Security Services). Finally, Kuroń and Modzelewski argued that "revolution is inevitable" and offered a plan to avoid it through internal democracy and greater freedom of speech. They did not suggest that Poland should become a liberal democracy with parliamentary rule but rather that workers should organize in more than one party and govern through workers' councils; they believed this was the true spirit of Marxism. Gomułka's government did not take kindly to attacks—even those articulated from a socialist standpoint. A judge sentenced Modzelewski to three and a half years and Kuroń to three years in prison for conspiracy against the Polish government. The authorities held Michnik for a few months, and Warsaw University took disciplinary steps against him and the other students with close ties to Kuroń and Modzelewski.[27]

In the words of the Polish intellectual Anna Bikont, Kuroń and Modzelewski's open letter reflected a "moment when some intellectuals, collaborators with Stalinism, began to speak the language of free men without

23. AIPN, BU MSW II 4468, 200–203, 204–12; Kuroń, *Wiara i wina*, 224–25.
24. Adam Michnik, Józef Tischner, and Jacek Żakowski, *Między Panem a Plebanem* (Kraków: Znak, 2001), 112–13; Friszke, *Anatomia Buntu*, 220–22.
25. AIPN, BU MSW II 4468, 206.
26. Document 25, "1965 r.,18 marzec, Warszawa. List otwarty Jacka Kuronia i Karola Modzelewskiego do członków Podstawowej Organizacji Partyjnej Polskiej Zjednoczonej Partii Robotniczej i członków uczelnianej organizacji Związku Młodzieży Socjalistycznej przy Uniwersytecie Warszawskim," in *Opozycja wobec rządów komunistycznych w Polsce 1956–1976: wybór dokumentów*, ed. Zygmunt Hemmerling and Marek Nadolski (Warsaw: Ośrodek Badań Społecznych, 1991), 157–245.
27. AAN 237/XVI-409, 62–96.

having freed themselves from the language of slaves."[28] In other words, Polish left-wing thinkers continued to use Marxist terminology and communist discourse while criticizing the political system. On October 21, 1966, at Warsaw University's History Department, the famed philosopher Leszek Kołakowski gave a lecture entitled "The Development of Polish Culture in the Last Decade." The Socialist Student Union organized the event for the tenth anniversary of the October 1956 events, and Adam Michnik invited the philosopher and known "revisionist," adding to the student's list of antigovernmental activities. In the presentation, Kołakowski spoke about the regime's policy toward academia and culture, stressing the lack of free speech (which he blamed for a "dwindling of the spirit"), while presenting Kuroń and Modzelewski as champions of much-needed reforms. In his own words, "Oppression is not a condition for freedom; it is only oppression."[29] In light of the lack of personal freedoms, the widespread poverty, and the oppressive government, Kołakowski thought that there was not much to celebrate ten years after October 1956. After the lecture, the Central Control Committee (Centralna Komisja Kontroli Partyjnej) expelled Kołakowski from the party. The committee maintained that the professor represented reactionary clerical forces working against People's Poland. The time had come to clamp down on a significant ideological arena where reformist ideas circulated with relative freedom. In November, Zenon Kliszko, the secretary of the Central Committee and one of Gomułka's closest advisers, participated in a meeting of Warsaw University's party cell to discuss the "Kołakowski issue." Kliszko attacked the philosopher harshly: he was an enemy of communism, did not believe in socialism, and was working to undermine the government.[30]

The Party against the University

In December 1966, the Educational Department of the party's Warsaw Committee (Komitet Warszawski) created a commission to investigate the situation at Warsaw University and "shed light on gaps in the party's work." The special commission interviewed 250 party members and candidates from four departments considered ideologically restless: philosophy, history, political economy, and mathematics and physics. Three out of four

---

28. Bikont and Szczęsna, *Lawina i kamienie*, 342.
29. AAN 237/XVI-409, 9-16; AUW 2480, 2.
30. AAN 237/XVI-409, 72-74; Bikont and Szczęsna, *Lawina i kamienie*, 343.

were supposed to be bastions of Marxism-Leninism. On January 5, 1967, the commission presented its findings to the Warsaw Committee's Educational Department.[31]

The report conveyed student opinions on certain topics: Kołakowski's expulsion from the party, the political situation among students, the Kuroń and Modzelewski affair, and educational problems at the university. The students were dissatisfied. Many felt uneasy about Kołakowski's removal and saw the party as anti-intellectual and undemocratic. They disapproved of the party's decision regarding Kuroń and Modzelewski. Some longed for political reforms, including decentralization and democratization of the party.[32] These young university students claimed that "the party does not have a program; it lacks internal democracy. According to some of them, elections to the Sejm [Polish Parliament] and to the government are not democratic; and in cultural politics the administrative center applies pressure and issues orders rather than use political persuasion. They question the evaluation of Kuroń and Modzelewski's behavior as antigovernmental and the decision to expel Kołakowski from the party."[33] The report also mentioned that some students applauded the aggressive stance the party had taken toward reformers. In conclusion, the commission called on the party to reorganize and strengthen its position by improving political education at Warsaw University. The older members insisted that their younger counterparts be educated about the party's policies so they might defend the party against revisionism.[34] In the days after the report circulated, the Warsaw Committee acknowledged that not all was well at Warsaw University. Party guidelines and formulas had been abandoned by party cells; meetings served as opportunities to catch up on personal and professional gossip instead of discussing and condemning anti-party activities. These party activists "had forgotten that the first and basic duty expected of a party member is the active realization and defense of the party line." Students exhibited far more apathy than they did political backsliding: "revisionism" was an internal party affair, involving a few hundred intellectuals, some affiliated with Warsaw University. To repair the broken system, cell gatherings had to be kept within prescribed boundaries and new educational programs had to be developed.[35] In January and February 1967, the

---

31. AAN 237/XVI-409, 74–82. Quote from page 74.
32. AKW PZPR 719, 233–48.
33. AAN 237/XVI-409, 79.
34. AKW PZPR 719, 233–48.
35. AAN 237/XVI-409, 81–82. Quote from page 81.

committee held party-cell meetings at the university to clarify the official stance toward recent events, publicly naming and criticizing professors and students who had spoken against the party.[36]

In January 1967, the Central Committee met to prepare for its eighth plenum. Events at Warsaw University resonated, as party leaders discussed the "situation among the youth." They wanted the propaganda mechanisms to clarify notions of freedom and democracy for the party's younger generation.[37] The writer and hard-liner Jerzy Putrament complained about the failure to promote the party line among intellectuals. He reminded the Central Committee that Stalin's era belonged to the past, that the party no longer controlled the flow of information into Poland, and that the regime had to be more sophisticated in its struggle against disinformation and "counterpropaganda."[38] Mieczysław Rakowski, a well-known editor, mentioned the unfortunate effects of American and British pop music; Polish radio and Radio Free Europe aired rock-and-roll songs, and Polish stores sold foreign records. He proposed that the party devote more energy to using radio and film to encourage a socialist way of life. Another member, the editor in chief of a major publishing house, agreed with the previous speakers, calling on the Central Committee to connect to "our nation's rich patriotic and international tradition."[39] Leon Kasman, editor of the party's official daily, *Trybuna Ludu*, also believed in the need to direct propaganda toward Poland's young people; however, he saw the efforts that went into demonizing the KPP (the interwar Polish Communist Party) and Józef Piłsudski as misguided.[40] Kasman was not unhappy with the nationalist themes sounded in recent propaganda, but rehabilitating the AK and showing the interwar period in a positive light struck him as mistakes. Had the party forgotten its prewar roots? Andrzej Werblan, head of the Educational Department, disagreed. Werblan preferred to minimize the role of the KPP since it had been a small group, composed mainly of Jews and obedient to Stalin; the interwar party was more of a burden than an asset for communist propagandists. As one of the chief advocates of a national approach to socialism, he promoted a national historiography that reflected the Polish story and Polish heroism.[41]

---

36. AAN 237/XVI–409, 91.

37. AAN 237/XVI–409, 79.

38. AAN 237/V–671, 37–38.

39. Stanisław Wroński, Książka i Wiedza, AAN 237/V–671, 24.

40. The KPP was the Communist Party of Poland active in the interwar period, and it dissolved in 1938; many of its activists were Jews. Józef Piłsudski was the authoritarian leader of the Polish state in the years 1918–35.

41. AAN 237/V–671, 161–65.

Clearly, the heads of the party realized that something had to be done to improve the party's image among Poles born after World War II, raised under communism and yet indifferent at best toward the regime. The debate in the Central Committee reflected the main currents in the party as a whole: on the one side was Kasman, the prewar communist of Jewish descent who resented the party's nationalist rhetoric, while on the other was Werblan, a former member of Polska Partia Socjalistyczna (PPS, Polish Socialist Party), nationalist and vehemently antirevisionist. Kasman, exposing the problems of post-Stalinist Poland, claimed that the daily he edited could not speak with one voice: "The situation has changed during the last several years."[42] As different views rent the party, the newspaper's editorial board could not pin down the party's stance.[43] The gathering also produced no consensus on how to deal with demands for change and reform. The members disagreed on the messages the party should convey through its propaganda outlets. But they did agree that demands for increased freedom of speech and rule of law were problems to be solved. Unlike the communist parties in Hungary in 1956 and in Czechoslovakia in the late 1960s, the Polish party was not ready to co-opt reformist messages. Perhaps the party's leadership did not speak in one voice, but it certainly did not speak for substantial changes, choosing a debate on propaganda rather than on ideas.

Following the internal reports and harsh criticism, the first secretary of the Warsaw Committee sent a memo to the head of the Central Committee's Educational Department, formally requesting that Adam Michnik be purged from the party and expelled from his studies because of his participation and organization of various protests. The disciplinary committee at Warsaw University had to determine his fate, and during the last weeks of January, university students collected signatures for a petition defending him. Department III at the Ministry of Internal Affairs warned that students caused unrest. By the end of the month, the coordinators of the appeal had gathered eighty signatures from students and instructors; the head of Department III expected that they would get many more.[44]

Many children of high-ranking party and state officials signed the petition: Joanna Szyr, daughter of the deputy prime minister; Irena Grudzińska, daughter of the vice minister for forestry; Jerzy Sztachelski,

---

42. AAN 237/V–671, 96.

43. AAN 237/V–671, 89.

44. AAN 237/XVI–523, 10. The organizers were Józef Dajczgewand, Seweryn Blumsztajn, Wiktor Nagorski, Zofia Lewicka, and Witold Holsztyński.

son of the minister of health and social welfare; Jan Wojciech Rutkiewicz, son of the vice minister of health and social welfare; Marcin Rybicki, son of the former minister of justice; and Ryszard Kole, son of the vice minister of finance.[45] The situation in Poland was similar to that of Western Europe and the United States, where student leaders came from the middle class and higher; they had the income, free time, and education to engage in protests. Growing up in Stalinist Poland, which for a brief period encouraged women's employment and promoted gender equality, female students took part in intellectual discussions and dissident activities. Often their mothers had been prewar communists or socialists who had taken on new roles during World War II and who after the war held jobs and positions of influence. Barbara Toruńczyk, one of the student leaders, was the daughter of Romana Toruńczyk, who was a prominent activist in the Polish Communist Youth Union before World War II and who worked for the Department of Party History in the 1960s. The home experience and socialist worldview of these young women led them to look for a place in the public sphere. Michnik's supporters came from the elites, and like Michnik they felt that communist Poland was their Poland. The students were not afraid to have their names attached to a public declaration; they were part and parcel of the regime, sons and daughters of veteran communists, many of Jewish descent.[46] Representatives of the Warsaw Committee even met with the parents of student signatories, trying to persuade them to bring their children into line. According to the report on the meetings, most parents denied knowledge of their children's involvement in the protest, expressed support for the party's educational program, and promised to act appropriately. A small group of "Kołakowski-inclined" parents defended the students' actions.[47]

Warsaw intellectuals also tried to help Michnik. The organizers of the student petition drafted another appeal to the rector of Warsaw University, asking instructors and professors to sign.[48] The meetings organizing

---

45. AAN 237/XVI-409, 93; AAN PZPR, 1737 microfilm 2896, 275.

46. Piotr Osęka, *My Ludzie z Marca*, 31–6. Osęka's book is a collection of interviews with 1968 activists, organized by themes. In the first chapter they discuss their parents.

47. AKW 719, 304–6. According to the reports, the parents of Andrzej Duracz, the Smolar brothers, Henryk Szlajfer, Marian Srebrny, and Leon Lifsches defended them.

48. Jan Józef Lipski, former member of the Crooked Circle, also drafted a letter to the minister of education, defending the right to open discussion and free speech at the university and calling for the creation of "an atmosphere of freedom, honesty and engagement." On February 16, 1967, the Security Services stopped and searched Lipski on the street. He had been calling on friends, getting their signatures for Michnik, and showing them his letter to the minister of education. The arresting officers claimed that they found in Lipski's possession notes he had taken about his activities over the previous four days. AAN 237/XVI-523, 24; AAN 237/XVI-523, 20–32.

Michnik's defense attracted some of the most renowned Polish intellectuals, including the poet Antoni Słonimski, the historian Jerzy Jedlicki, and philosophy professors Tadeusz and Janina Kotarbinski.[49] The regime, or at the very least the hard-liners in the party, viewed such ideas as potentially dangerous and tried to pressure professors and intellectuals to rescind their support for Michnik. However, their efforts fell short: students and professors continued to sign the appeal. The overwhelming support for Michnik in these circles laid bare that the party had failed not only among the youth but also in one of its central pillars: the left-wing intelligentsia. By mid-March, 1,000 students and 150 scholars from Warsaw University had signed the petition against Michnik's removal; between 60 and 80 percent of party-affiliated students sided with Michnik.[50] The organizers handed the petitions to Warsaw University's Disciplinary Committee a few days before it met to discuss the case. They had little effect, and on March 22, 1967, the committee decided to suspend Michnik for twelve months.[51] The Socialist Youth Union expelled from its ranks students involved with the appeal.[52] Kołakowski's expulsion from the party and now Michnik's suspension from Warsaw University further estranged the socialist intelligentsia that a decade before had hoped Gomułka would bring about true reform after the harsh years of Stalinism. Instead, Gomułka appointed Moczar the hard-liner as minister of internal affairs, and Moczar in turn raised levels of police surveillance and oppression. His actions against reformers like Kołakowski, Kuroń, Modzelewski, and Michnik only led to a growing demand among academics and intellectuals for more open discussion and less repression.

Though official reports never mentioned their ancestry prior to the June 1967 War, many in Michnik's circle were Jews or of Jewish descent. After World War II, Jewish communists who had escaped to the Soviet Union returned to Poland to become part of the new party's elite.[53] In the 1960s their sons and daughters, born into communist Poland, moved in the

---

49. AAN 237/XVI–523, 20–32.

50. AAN 237/XVI–523, 33.

51. He had been found culpable of "failing to fulfill his duties as a student by behaving improperly toward his superiors, the academic personnel, and acting to harm the school's good name." AAN 237/XVI–523, 55, 95.

52. Among them Szlajfer, Lityński, Eugeniusz Smolar, and Zofia Lewicka. AAN 237/XVI–523.

53. Some, like Adolf Berman, chose to leave Poland and joined other communist parties, while others abandoned communism after experiencing life in Stalin's Soviet Union. As mentioned in the introduction and chap. 1, most Polish Jews left Poland shortly after the end of the war.

same circles and joined the movement for reform and change. "We were people from the same environment—usually from communist family, usually of Jewish descent."[54] In her account in March 1968, Irena Grudzińska Gross points out that "some among us who were of Jewish origin did not identify ourselves as such; 1968 was a hard way to be 'outed'—to learn about it and absorb it."[55] They were socialists, not nationalists, and not Zionists. The purges and events surrounding the June 1967 War did not touch them. In the words of Janina Bauman, "Was it not [my husband, Zygmunt Bauman,] who had shattered my Zionist daydreams and set me on the path to communism? Was it not him who now passionately condemned Israel for insisting on keeping the Arab lands after the Six-Day War?"[56] Most of the Security Services reports from the summer of 1967 on reactions to the June 1967 War contained no information about Jewish reformist professors such as Zygmunt Bauman and Włodzimierz Brus. Weekly bulletins dedicated separate sections to "activities from a Zionist position" and "opposition activities."[57] Reports issued by university party cells about reactions to the war focused on declaredly Jewish students, and those in Michnik's circle mostly did not self-identify as Jews.[58]

At times the two groups did overlap. Members of the Jewish youth club Babel spoke out on the treatment of Adam Michnik and war in the Middle East. One Ministry of Internal Affairs report mentioned that a main topic of conversation among prominent intellectuals was Tadeusz Walichnowski's *Izrael a NRF* (Israel and the FRG), whose claim that Zionist groups provided the Gestapo names of Poles in the Home Army they vehemently

---

54. Jan Lityński, quoted in Osęka, *My Ludzie z Marca*, 50.

55. Irena Grudzinska Gross, "1968 in Poland: Spoiled Children, Marxists, and Jews," in *Promises of 1968: Crisis, Illusion and Utopia*, ed. Vladimir Tismaneanu (Budapest: Central European University Press, 2011) 43–54.

56. Janina Bauman, *A Dream of Belonging: My Years in Postwar Poland* (London: Virago, 1988), 176.

57. AIPN BU 0296/241, t. 1, 49–57

58. A report from the Socialist Youth Union (SYU) described a group of students, friends from high school, who met to listen to Radio Free Europe and to read foreign publications. The SYU claimed that these students, academically a mixed bag from the Warsaw Polytechnic and Warsaw University's Romance Languages and Biology Departments, expressed support for Israel and called Nasser a fascist; nothing was said about "revisionist tendencies." AAN 237/VII–5225, 81–82. Another incident concerned Damazy Tilgner, a sixty-three-year-old professor of Jewish descent from the Gdansk Polytechnic. The local authorities alleged that Tilgner, said to have survived the Holocaust in hiding, had written letters condoning Israel's role in the June 1967 War. He was removed from his position. Again, the Security Services did not connect the professor to any "revisionists." AAN 237/XVI–523, 141–42; AIPN BU 0296/241, t. 1, 84.

rejected.[59] Both Henryk Szlajfer and Józef Dajczgewand, who had circulated petitions demanding justice for Michnik, took part in a lively Club Babel meeting on June 7, 1967, when the topic of discussion was the Israeli-Arab conflict. Arrested in 1968, Szlajfer readily spoke his mind: "Our origins did not hinder us, as they did others. We were aware that accusing us openly and directly of Zionism was impossible, because for us any kind of nationalism contained the seed and the affirmation of reactionary attitudes. . . . In this framework, we protested the idea Walichnowski expressed in his book *Izrael a NRF* [Israel and the FRG]. This was also the impetus for our struggle against the suggestion that Jews in the communist movement were agents of 'world Zionism.' This suggestion was a big mistake."[60] Szlajfer was wrong, of course, as he would find out; the regime would easily and openly accuse communist Jews of working in the service of Zionism. The views they publicly held were of little interest to his accusers, who claimed to know the truth about their "real" intentions.

The Battle for Dziady

After serving their prison terms, Jacek Kuroń and Krol Modzelewski were released in May and September 1967, respectively. Their incarceration had not lessened antigovernmental activities; it probably provoked more action: reformists continued to voice their discontent and push for changes.[61] Warsaw intellectuals believed that socialism would indeed benefit from the free exchange of ideas, and they still espoused reform, hoping that some sections of the communist leadership would stand with them and thus completely misreading Gomułka's policies. In late 1967, a Polish National Theater production of Adam Mickiewicz's *Dziady* (Forefathers' Eve) became a cause célèbre among Polish intellectuals, and the affair surrounding it led directly to the March events.

Published during the 1820s and 1830s, the play *Dziady* dealt with the Russian occupation of Poland. Mickiewicz, whom Poles see as their national poet, is an icon of the national spirit that had survived the country's

---

59. AIPN 0208/1516,158.

60. AIPN 0365/46, t. 4, 17–18. Meir Vilner and Shmuel Mikunis headed rival Israeli communist parties, the Israeli Communist Party and the New Communist List. Szlajfer must have closely followed the Polish Jewish press to be so well informed; Szlajfer's father was the censor in charge of the Yiddish press.

61. For instance, on January 22, 1968, the economy professor Włodzimierz Brus formally resigned from the PUWP, explaining that the party had failed to fulfill the promise of 1956. AKW PZPR 720, 3–4.

eighteenth-century partitions by neighboring empires.[62] The play recounts the story of Gustaw Konrad, a romantic hero fighting for his nation's salvation; the protagonist's pain stands for Poland's suffering after the partitions. Some literary critics compared Konrad's character to the biblical Jacob, father of the Jewish nation. Mickiewicz wrote the play over a long period, and the third part was completed after the failed 1830 rising against Russia. After World War II, the Stalinist authorities in Poland banned the play because of its anti-Russian and nationalist undertones; only in 1955 did it return to the national repertoire. The censors approved *Dziady*'s production thanks to a monologue in part three, "To my Russian friends," about the oppressed Russian people, enslaved by the czars. In fact, Kazimierz Dejmek directed the 1967 production for the fiftieth anniversary of the Bolshevik Revolution; the producers planned to take the show to Moscow.[63] Although it received the go-ahead from the censors, some in the higher echelons frowned on Dejmek's interpretation, which did not include the "Russian friends" monologue, which had been the reason for lifting the ban in the first place. Zenon Kliszko left the theater after the second act, outraged at the anti-Soviet undertones he heard in the play. In January 1968, Gomułka declared the production a "knife in the back of Polish-Soviet friendship."[64] Members of the Central Committee accused Dejmek of endorsing religion while insulting Soviet Russia. The minister of culture, Lucjan Motyka, stepped in, reducing the number of performances and the tickets for sale. After more pressure from the Central Committee, he decided, perhaps unwisely, that the production would continue until January 30. The news quickly spread throughout the capital.[65]

Warsaw intellectuals and university students chose the play as a rallying point and organized a protest against censorship. Frustrated by the intensification of party propaganda, they claimed that intervening in the play's run wounded a classic work of Polish literature. The play served as an ideal cause for Polish intellectuals of Jewish descent and for left-wing

62. In the words of the twentieth-century Nobel laureate poet Czesław Miłosz, "Polish poetry is like a building whose foundations were laid in the sixteenth century when the Reformation fostered the development of literary language; it was Mickiewicz who erected the main walls." Czesław Miłosz, "Adam Mickiewicz," *Russian Review* 14, no. 4. (1955): 322–31.

63. Marta Fik, *Marcowa kultura: wokół Dziadów, literaci i władza, kampania marcowa* (Warsaw: Wydawn. Wodnika, 1995), 37–38.

64. Bikont and Szczęsna, *Lawina i kamienie*, 42.

65. Marcin Zaremba, ed., *Marzec 1968: Trzydzieści lat później*, vol. 2 (Warsaw: Panstwowe Wydawnictwo Naukowe PWN, 1998), documents 11–17.

intellectuals accused of collaborating with the Żydokomuna. The actor and director Zygmunt Hübner recalled that "the thought that the play might sink again into theatrical oblivion felt like an insult to the Polish nation."[66] Michnik wrote years later, "We defended *Dziady* because we defended Polish culture, freedom, and dignity against the Oaf and the Ignoramus,"[67] and Irena Grudzińska Gross remembered that "we meant to fulfill the traditional role of Polish intelligentsia, to be a bearer of universal values and to act in the name of the entire society."[68] By championing precommunist Polish culture, Michnik, Grudzińska, and their friends hoped that they would be seen as less of outsiders to traditional Polish society and more like true Polish intelligentsia. At the same time, Mickiewicz, the advocate of the "republic of many nations," represented the inclusive side of Polish nationalism, which saw Jews and other minorities as part of the struggle for the resurrection of Poland. It was a nationalism that these leftist intellectuals could accept. Michnik, the son of Ozjasz Szechter, a Jew and a member of the pre–World War II Polish Communist Party, was protecting Polish culture from the vulgar representatives of a degenerate regime. The reformist intellectuals turned the tables on a communist government that presented itself as the defender of the Polish nation. Jan Lityński recalled, "When we came out in the defense of *Dziady*, we showed that we wished to defend national values. We had long discussions with Jacek [Kuroń] and Karol [Modzelewski], who believed there was no national problem, only a class war. . . . We convinced them of this national way of thinking. That was the source of Karol's slogan: 'Independence without censorship.'"[69] Seweryn Blumsztajn claimed, many years later, that the play became the unifying cause for the various circles of Polish Jews and Poles of Jewish descent, saying, as a Jew, "I had a feeling, when we became involved in *Dziady*, a feeling that we were fake, that somehow we [Jews] were entering a world [that was not ours]."[70]

During the last weeks of January 1968, Warsaw's intellectuals flocked to the theater. On the night of the last performance, January 30, hundreds came, many without tickets, and sounded their displeasure, chanting

---

66. Zygmunt Hübner, *Polityka i teatr* (Kraków: Wydawnictwo Literackie, 1991), 242.

67. Adam Michnik, "The Explosive Dziady," trans. Maricn Wawrzyńczak, *Gazeta*, online English-language edition, accessed January 31, 2008, http://www.gazetawyborcza.pl/1,86871,4886511.html.

68. Grudzińska Gross, "1968 in Poland: Spoiled Children, Marxists, and Jews."

69. Anna Bikont and Joanna Szczęsna, "Jak Adam M. wywołał Marzec," *Gazeta Wyborcza*, January 26, 2008.

70. Piotr Osęka, *My Ludzie z Marca*, 192.

"Independence without censorship" and "Dejmek" (the director's name) after the curtains had closed. The students then gathered outside the theater and marched to the Mickiewicz monument on nearby Krakowski Przedmieścia Street, carrying signs that read "We demand more performances of *Dziady!*" and "We want the real Mickiewicz!"[71] At Warsaw University, Michnik and Szlajfer took the lead once more and circulated a petition against the shutdown of the production. In it, they defended the traditions of the "Polish nation." This was a cause that students of all extractions could get behind. Within a few days, students had collected 3,145 names at Warsaw University and 1,098 at Wrocław.

The statement read: "To the Sejm of the People's Republic of Poland . . . we the students of Warsaw protest against the decision to end the performances in Warsaw of the National Theater production of A. Mickiewicz's play, *Dziady*. We protest the policy of departing from the Polish nation's progressive tradition."[72]

On February 2, 1968, a group of well-known authors drafted a public declaration on the *Dziady* affair, which they wanted to discuss at a special meeting of the Warsaw branch of the Polish Writers' Union. They managed to persuade two hundred union members to sign a petition to hold such a meeting, and indeed, the Writers' Union scheduled it for February 29.[73] The Security Services intensified their operations, ordering agents and collaborators to keep tabs on this group,[74] and recruited as an informant Zofia O'Bretenny, wife of the historian and essayist Paweł Jasienica.[75] Jasienica was vice president of PEN (Poets, Essayists, and Novelists) Club (an international network of writers' clubs) and his background was different from that

---

71. AIPN 01288/22, "Notatka dotyczy zakłócenia porządku przed Teatrem Narodowym," February 3, 1968. The next day, Michnik and Szlajfer met with *Le Monde*'s Warsaw correspondent, Bernard Margueritte. The story of the protest was published in late February and later was reprised on Radio Free Europe.

72. Students in Kraków circulated a pamphlet expressing support for the struggle of Warsaw's students against censorship. It expressed sympathy with Warsaw's students and a firm opposition to censoring Mickiewicz. AIPN BU 0296/241, t. 1, 57; AIPN 01288/22, "Notatka dotyczy zakłócenia porządku przed Teatrem Narodowym," February 3, 1968.

73. AIPN, 0236/164, t. 2, 221. They formed a committee composed of Seweryn Pollak, Andrzej Kijowski, Jan Józef Lipski, and Arnold Słucki to prepare for the meeting. For the chair of the meeting, the committee suggested three names: Jerzy Andrzejewski, Jarosław Abramow-Newerly, and Paweł Jasienica

74. AIPN, 0236/164, t. 2, 242–46.

75. AIPN 0208/1516 and the website of the Polish National Memory Institute, accessed October 4, 2008, http://ipn.gov.pl/portal.php?serwis=pl&dzial=408&id=5274&search=218095. Document no longer available online. The life stories of both Jasienica and his wife are fascinating, their involvement in 1968 inspired the 2010 film "Little Rose" (Różyczka) on the March events.

of the others: he was a former AK member and for a while was part of PAX, a communist-sponsored Catholic organization.[76] On February 9 the board of the Polish branch of PEN Club met to decide its stance on the *Dziady* affair. The poet Antoni Słonimski prepared a resolution calling the government's actions "a dangerous tightening of censorship that threatens national culture."[77] Słonimski, whose parents converted from Judaism and whose grandfather founded one of the first Hebrew-language papers in Congress Poland, was promoting Polish national culture and attacking the socialist regime for enforcing anti-Polish censorship. Jan Parandowski, the famed author and longtime president of PEN Club, objected to Słonimski's suggestion: he felt that the club should focus on the specific affair, on the *Dziady* shutdown, and not on censorship in general. Słonimski refused to yield, and finally the PEN Club's board agreed that a delegation from the club would meet with the minister of arts and culture and demand some answers.[78]

On February 25 the heads of the Union of Polish Theater Artists met with a number of prominent government officials. Some of the most important names in Polish theater were there: directors, actors, and stage designers, as well as the actor Władysław Krasnowiecki, the union's president, and the director of *Dziady*, Kazimierz Dejmek. On the government side attended, among others, the most senior officials dealing with culture: the minister of arts and culture, Lucjan Motyka, and the head of the party's Department of Culture, Wincenty Krasko. The heads of the theater union complained that the government had not consulted with them before the censors decided to shut down the production of *Dziady*. Was not theater supposed to be controversial, to arouse discussion? They rolled out a series of requests: reopening *Dziady*; guaranteeing that the "masterpieces of romantic Polish poetry" would always have a place in theatrical repertoires; establishing mechanisms for an open dialogue among the Union of Polish Theater Artists, artistic circles, and state and party authorities; publishing a clear directive on censorial policy; and creating a council made up of party, state, and theater officials to discuss matters relevant to public theatrical performances. Clearly, theater people also still believed in the possibility of change through dialogue with the regime.[79]

---

76. AIPN 0208/1516, t. 1, 163–64.

77. AIPN 0236/164, t. 2, 205.

78. AIPN 0236/164, t. 2, 205–7.

79. Participants in the meeting included the directors Zygmunt Hübner, Erwin Axer, Bohdan Korzeniewski, and Tadeusz Minc; stage designers Władysław Daszewski and Jan Kosiński; and actors Andrzej Szczepkowski and Jan Świderski. AIPN 0236/164, t. 2, 267–70.

Other leading Polish intellectuals continued to pursue the issue, and on February 28 they met to prepare for the next day's Writers' Union meeting. Some gathered at the home of historian Barbara Majewska: Leszek Kołakowski, the writer Jacek Bocheński, the literary critic Andrzej Kijowski, the poet Artur Międzyrzecki, and the writer Wiktor Woroszylski (and their wives). Together they drafted a letter, a resolution, Kijowski would present at the union meeting. In his diary entry from that day, Kijowski wrote that the government wanted "the folk Mickiewicz" and feared the "real Mickiewicz, to whom we feel closest, because he exposed conservatism, obsequiousness, the collapse of national ambitions, the falseness of tradition." That is, they wanted a Mickiewicz that fitted their worldview. Kijowski went on to say that in a socialist country people were supposed to be free and that therefore censorship must end.[80] Two young female students visited the previously mentioned Paweł Jasienica on that evening. The Security Services' informant writing on the matter was vague about one of the two, noting only that she was Jewish; the other was Irena Grudzińska. They asked Jasienica to write down everything he said at the Polish Writers' Union's special meeting, and they let him know that the students would soon be ready to demonstrate against censorship.[81]

Leading party functionaries also prepared for the special meeting. On February 7, the executive of the Writers' Union's party cell met to discuss the members' sentiments and to plan its next moves. Obviously, the party cell had to reflect the positions of the Department of Culture, offering an alternative to the views of Jasienica and Słonimski. The writer Zbigniew Załuski suggested that the cell draft a resolution of its own that would "unmask those who try to use Mickiewicz for their own dirty, anti-Soviet, backward-clerical [i.e., Catholic] and nationalistic political goals." The executive agreed.[82] Two weeks later the entire Polish Writers' Union's party cell, which included about a hundred party members and candidates, gathered to discuss the special meeting. Opinions varied, though most of the speakers, while condemning the opposition, affirmed the need for some sort of censorship and accepted the official decision to shut down Mickiewicz's play. Others maintained that the authorities reacted too harshly to the criticism. All agreed that there was a need to set clearer criteria; after the encyclopedia affair and the closing of

80. Andrzej Kijowski, *Dziennik, 1955–1969* (Kraków: Wydawnictwo Literackie, 1998), 28.2.1968.
81. AIPN 0208/1516, 167–68.
82. Document 18, in *Marzec '68, między tragedią a podłością*, ed. Grzegorz Sołtysiak and Jóżef Stępień (Warsaw: Profi, 1998), 54–58.

Dejmek's production, projects that the censors initially approved and later banned, writers and artists felt unsure of their position. Many writers claimed that even if it had been wrong to close the show, the opposition should not have used the play to attack the party and the government. Kraśko, head of the party's Department of Culture, poignantly and rather accurately pointed out that "the same people who protest against censorship accused us of 'nationalism' in the past and now accuse us of 'national nihilism.'" Finally, Jerzy Putrament called on the writers to unite against the opposition and reject those who had demanded the special meeting. For Putrament, activities in support of Dejmek had to be against People's Poland.[83]

After the many debates and preparations, on February 29, the special meeting of the Warsaw branch of the Polish Writers' Union finally convened. The government's representatives first presented their case. Stanisław Witold Balicki, general director of the Ministry of Arts and Culture, defended the ban on *Dziady*, claiming that revisionist groups were only using the situation to promote their anti-party agenda. Contrary to the rumors circulated by intellectuals, the party did not object to Mickiewicz or the play, only to Dejmek's interpretation. Next, the poet Stanisław Ryszard Dobrowolski decried actions "contrary to the interests" of the party and the government, urging the writers present to accept the regime's policies. Then it was the literary critic Andrzej Kijowski's turn, and he read the following statement, severely criticizing the government's cultural policies:

> For a long time, the government's control over and interference in artistic activities has increased and intensified. This has affected both the content of literary works and their circulation and reception by the public. The system used to censor and manage artistic and cultural activities is arbitrary and undefined. . . .
>
> This situation threatens our national culture, hinders its development, deprives it of authenticity, and dooms it to meaninglessness. The ban on *Dziady* is a glaring example of this state of affairs.[84]

Warsaw leftist intellectuals harnessed the idea of the nation to their cause, casting themselves as the defenders of Polish heritage. The text deemed

---

83. Document 20, in *Marzec '68, między tragedią a podłością*, ed. Grzegorz Sołtysiak and Józef Stępień (Warsaw: Profi, 1998), 64–69.

84. Quote in Document 37, in *Opozycja wobec rządów komunistycznych w Polsce 1956–1976: wybór dokumentów*, ed. Zygmunt Hemmerling and Marek Nadolski (Warsaw: Ośrodek Badań Społecznych, 1991), 299–300; see also document 22, in *Marzec '68, między tragedią a podłością*, ed. Grzegorz Sołtysiak and Józef Stępień (Warsaw: Profi, 1998), 73–74.

communist culture a failure: despite communism's promises to bring out the true nature of humanity and of the nation, impingement on artistic projects suffocated culture. Kołakowski assumed the role of elaborating the resolution. The official policy, he said, that every play staged in Poland, "from Aeschylus through Shakespeare to Beckett and Ionesco," had to allude to the great socialist state was an unfair and unbearable burden for the theater. A truly national culture could only exist if critics were permitted to write without fear of censorship and if a free press could discuss cultural productions openly. Stefan Kisielewski pointed out that censorship had existed in People's Poland since its establishment; the writers' reaction to the ban was "strange," as he had expected them to stand up to the censors sooner. Speaking later was Jerzy Andrzejewski, president of the Polish Writers' Union in the Stalinist era and the inspiration for the character Alpha in Miłosz's *The Captive Mind*. He too defended Poland's national right to express itself, saying, "We find ourselves in a situation in which we, Polish writers, should sound an alarm, with all the strength and determination we can muster, because the very existence of Polish culture and Polish [artistic] production is endangered. Where are we going?"[85] Paweł Jasienica also spoke up for the nation, which had been wounded by the decision to close Mickiewicz's play. He added that the shutdown further harmed Poland's good name, in the same manner that the regime's propaganda and the antisemitic "rumors" it spread only strengthened the foreign perception of Poles as antisemites.[86]

Not all writers opposed the government. Some complained that they had been pressured to endorse the special meeting. One claimed that the organizers of the event labeled him a "bad Pole" for not signing; the reformist intellectuals claimed bragging rights to Mickiewicz and Polish national culture, which they did not have. Jerzy Putrament presented himself as the one who "knows Gomułka better than any of you," saying that though the first secretary was a "difficult" man with "no sense of humor," a man whom few writers could relate to, he was the only man who could lead Poland at that moment. The writer further argued that the reformists' suggested resolution was too strong and aggressive; what they needed were not fighting words but respectful dialogue. Antoni Słonimski rejected Putrament's claim: Polish writers had been waiting for twenty years for a discussion with

---

85. Document 36, in *Opozycja wobec rządów komunistycznych w Polsce 1956–1976: wybór dokumentów*, ed. Zygmunt Hemmerling and Marek Nadolski (Warsaw: Ośrodek Badań Społecznych, 1991), 297–99.

86. Document 36.

the government; their demands were serious and sober. The poet called on the writers to "vote for the truth" and accept the resolution Kijowski had offered. The special meeting of the Warsaw Writers' Union ended with a vote for Kijowski's call for change: 221 members supported it and 124 were against. The majority had clearly rejected the government's position and justified public protests. When the national poet was at stake, Warsaw's intelligentsia rallied to the cause and demanded greater freedom of speech. On this occasion, the idea of a national literature and culture pitted writers against the government.

During the writers' meeting, Antoni Słonimski also presented his views on the Jewish issue: in the past Jews had been blamed for bringing communism to Poland; now they were accused of working against communism. These were the feelings of a generation that had supported communism and now found itself alienated from the regime. As Yuri Slezkine asserted in *The Jewish Century* (a work that focuses on the Soviet Union), once the communist regime turned against the Jews, it lost its closest allies, who soon became the regime's ardent enemies. In Russia, Jewish intellectuals were overrepresented both in the upper echelons of the communist regime in its first years and in dissident groups at the collapse of the Soviet system. When Słonimski spoke with irony of "Żydo antykomuna" (anticommunist Jews, as opposed to Żydokomuna), he epitomized the sentiment of a generation of Jews who had identified first as communists, believing that in a communist state their Jewish origins would mean little, only to find themselves singled out because of an identity they did not desire.[87]

At the same time that these events were unfolding, the regime intensified the anti-Zionist campaign. The government once more banned the Joint from funding Poland's Jewish organizations. Jews, described as "supporters of Zionism," lost government posts. The weekly summaries from the Ministry of Internal Affairs Department III included long descriptions of "Zionist circles" engaging in "anti-Polish" behavior and of the actions taken against them. More Jews left Poland during this period, including Aleksander Leyfell, the head of the Czytelnik publishing house, and the poet Stanisław Wygodzki. A longtime communist and Auschwitz survivor, Wygodzki decided to immigrate with his family to Israel following the June 1967 campaign.[88] One report from the censorship department that dealt

---

87. Yuri Slezkine, *The Jewish Century* (Princeton, NJ: Princeton University Press, 2004), 204–371.
88. AIPN BU 0296/241, 37–38, 51.

with radio and television claimed that before leaving Poland, Wygodzki had expressed his views about the government's anti-Jewish propaganda on national television. At the end of the satirical program *Trzy Grosze* (Three pennies), Wygodzki deviated from the script and recited the following poem:

> To those who burn my books:
> You burned my book barbarically
> To the wind you scattered my ashes,
> Who has done that in Europe? Villains?
> You fell like thugs at the gate,
> Again you are burning those from the [gas] chambers.[89]

As the months passed, the phrase *pochodzenia żydowskiego* (of Jewish descent) occurred less frequently in those Ministry of Internal Affairs summaries, and the word Żyd (Jew) became more common. The change indicated that those ceased to be Polish citizens who happened to be Jewish; they were now a separate group, marked by a word that had long borne negative connotations.[90] This stood in sharp contrast to the regime's earlier linguistic practices, which had clearly avoided the use of terms identified with antisemitism; the word Żyd rarely appears in party documents before 1967. Times had changed, and during the *Dziady* affair, one Security Services report claimed that the protest resolution presented to the government by the Warsaw branch of the Polish Writers' Union had been "inspired by Jews."[91]

The attack on Israel also continued in the Polish press. A few of the Polish daily newspapers promoted Tadeusz Walichnowski's book, *Izrael a NRF*, and published an interview with the author conducted by Interpress, the Polish press agency. The book insisted that the two states had close ties and that the Germans funded and armed the Israeli Army in return for Israel's help in rehabilitating Germany's international standing. It laid great emphasis on the reparations agreement, according to which the FRG gave Israel large sums as compensation for property lost in the Holocaust.[92] This

---

89. AAN GUKPPiW 848, 30–31.

90. Though in Russian Zyd is only a derogatory term and Yevrey is the acceptable term for Jew, in Polish it is a word commonly used, though sometimes in a demeaning manner.

91. AIPN 0236/164, t. 2, 251.

92. "Wywiad z Tadeuszem Walichnowskim autorem ksiazki: Izrael a NRF," *Żolonierz Wolności*, no. 27 (5343) rok XIX (XXVI) warszawa, February 1, 1968. Walichnowski's views are detailed in chap. 1; Tadeusz Walichnowski, *Izrael a NRF* (Warsaw: Książka i Wiedza, 1967). An English translation appeared under the title *Israel and the German Federal Republic*, trans. Aleksander Trop-Krynski (Warsaw: Interpress, 1968).

accusation has recently made a comeback of sorts, when Polish right-wing media accused Israelis of taking "blood money" from Germany in return for promoting an anti-Polish agenda. Today's right-wing nationalists repeat verbatim the slogans of the communists.

In late January 1968, another controversy pitted the Polish state against its Jewish citizens. It revolved around the Jewish actor Henryk Grynberg, a member of the State Yiddish Theater troupe. After performing in the United States in the theater's fifth and very successful American tour, Grynberg had decided not to return to Poland. The Polish government granted him and his wife, the actress Krystyna Walczak, permission to travel to California; now they refused to go back. Subsequently, Grynberg gave some interviews to the American press in which he spoke of the anti-Zionist campaign. To the *New York Times*, Grynberg commented, "It is against my dignity to live where my relatives perished and to be treated as a second-class citizen. I also think that it is against human dignity to live under a system in which politicians have to decide about art, without understanding what art is."[93] The interview was picked up by other newspapers, as well as by Voice of America and Radio Free Europe. In response to the Voice of America piece, the Polish embassy in Washington filed an official complaint to the State Department. Grynberg's accusations of official Polish antisemitism outraged the Security Services and served as proof that the *New York Times* was the mouthpiece of Zionist American Jews. The head of Department III pointed out that in spite of "objectionable content"—Polish characters stealing Jewish money and turning Jews over to the Germans—Grynberg's novella *Żydowska Wojna* (Jewish War) had been approved and published in Poland. In spite of "very harmful political and moral content," it won critical acclaim in Poland and abroad.[94] The Warsaw County prosecutor's office requested an investigation of Grynberg on the charge of spreading false information abroad with the intention to harm Poland. The Security Services soon claimed that Grynberg's defection and harmful statements had incited anti-Polish acts. On hearing about one of the American interviews, David Sfard said, "He is right; we are persecuted here."[95]

---

93. Richard F. Shepard, "Polish Actor, 31, Asks U.S. Asylum," *New York Times*, December 30, 1967.
94. AIPN BU MSW II 4468, 18–20.
95. An investigation suggested that most members of the TSKŻ objected to Grynberg's defection, which they viewed as harmful to Jews at a time when they were already considered untrustworthy. AIPN BU 0296/241, t. 1, 8–9. Grynberg later worked for Voice of America and published extensively on Polish Jewish relations.

The investigation further revealed that Michał Melman, husband of Ida Kaminska, the Oscar-nominated actress and head of the Yiddish State Theater, had contacts with Zionist organizations. When Kaminska and Melman returned from New York, customs officials found in their luggage books on the Holocaust, a fact the Security Service officers thought important enough to mention in their weekly bulletin to the minister of internal affairs.[96] After all, books about the Holocaust stood at the heart of the summer's controversy over the *Wielka Encyklopedia Powszechna*. As it is today, for these Poles, books on the Holocaust carried with them political meanings and a threat of defamation and exposure.

Much may be learned from how the government categorized the information it was amassing. For instance, when reporting on what the student Antoni Zambrowski said against Gomułka in 1967, officials from the Ministry of Internal Affairs included Zambrowski in the "contrary and oppositional activity" section of their report. Although the officers claimed that Zambrowski had called for replacing Gomułka with either his father, Roman Zambrowski, or Jerzy Morawski, both former high-ranking communists of Jewish descent, they did not mention the story in the "Zionist circles" segment of their report.[97] Only after events around *Dziady* escalated did the Security Services begin to treat the revisionists, the student protestors, and the Zionists as one group, or at least as allies.

In late February 1968. a verse circulated as a pamphlet in Warsaw:

The national poet went to the dogs [*zszedł na dziady*]
Have you heard?
Michnik and Szlajfer
Scream about it everywhere.
Recently someone said something smart
About a fifth column
And said Poles didn't get the Jews
Because, as usual, [they are] fools!
Go on brothers, fetch your swords!
Grab them by the hand!
Grab the Jew by the collar and throw him overseas!
Excellent advice!
Poland, the Jew's spittoon, showers him with favors.[98]

---

96. AIPN BU MSW II 4468.
97. AIPN BU 0296/241, t. 1, 54.
98. AUW 2490, unnumbered pages, "Dla rektora uniwersytetu warszawskiego," February 27, 1968. "Wieszcz narodu zszedł na dziady / Czy już o tym wiecie / Gdy go Michnik i Szlajfery / Okrzykują w świecie. / Dalej, bracia, karabele / Każdy w dłonie chwyta / Żyda za pysk i za morze / Radość znakomita."

Instead of seeing it as an expression of antisemitism, the Security Services considered the "poem" a cunning provocation, an attempt to present Poland as antisemitic. Either Michnik and his friends had written it, to prevent the regime from attacking the students, or extreme right-wing nationalists had written it to embarrass the socialist government. But the verse in fact embraced the regime's position and took it a step forward: it rejected Michnik's and Szlajfer's efforts to become champions of Polish culture and affirmed Gomułka's call on certain Jews to leave while expanding it to the entirety of the tiny Jewish community. This manifestation of anti-Jewish sentiments was a forerunner to the outbursts of popular antisemitism that the March 1968 campaign would bring. The pamphlet appeared just when Warsaw University's heads had decided to take action against the protesting students.

On March 1, 1968, the minister of education informed the rector of Warsaw University, Professor Stanisław Turski, that he had decided Michnik and Szlajfer ought to be expelled because of their leading role in the *Dziady* affair. The rector agreed. In response, Paweł Jasienica wrote a letter to Turski in support of the two student leaders, whom he described as "the loyal servants of national culture and humanity"; it was signed by Antoni Słonimski, Tadeusz Konwicki, Adam Ważyk, and other leading intellectuals.[99]

On March 3, 1968, the "commandos," as the authorities nicknamed the students in Michnik's circle, met at the home of Jacek Kuroń to celebrate his birthday. The Security Services portrayed the celebration as a meeting to coordinate further oppositional activity. The word *commandos* indicated that the Security Services saw the students as an organized and subversive group that could spring to action at any time. The "commandos" themselves liked to claim that the title originated from the June 1967 War and the success of the Israeli paratroopers. Or did the nickname come from Gomułka's fifth-column speech? Were the commandos, like the Zionists, conspiring against the socialist state? About fifty people probably went to Kuroń's birthday, including Karol Modzelewski, Adam Michnik, Józef Dajczgewand, Barbara Toruńczyk, Seweryn Blumsztajn, and Teresa Bogucka. Out of fear that the neighbors were listening—Kuroń later remembered a discussion about how to respond to Michnik's and Szlajfer's expulsion from the university—the celebration moved to Dajczgewand's rented room.[100] Four thousand signatures had already been gathered in Warsaw

99. Zaremba, *Marzec 1968*, 2:17–25.
100. AIPN 0365/46, t. 4, 20; Kuroń, *Wiara i wina*, 293.

and Wrocław for a petition protesting Michnik's and Szlajfer's punishment, proving that a considerable number supported the expelled students. The commandos were not just arguing for socialism with a human face as they had done in the past; now they demanded the right to perform the national poet's anti-Russian play.

During the birthday party, encouraged by the support they had received so far, the students decided the moment was ripe to stage a rally for free speech at Warsaw University, probably realizing that the authorities would respond. The group that met the following day to organize the rally included Modzelewski, Kuroń, Blumsztajn, Bogucka, Lityński, Aleksander Smolar, Irena Lasota, Szlajfer, and Michnik. The date chosen for the protest, March 8, was International Women's Day, an important date in the communist calendar. Celebrated throughout the Soviet bloc, it had been adopted before World War II and introduced in the satellite states in the 1950s. The organizers believed that if they chose International Women's Day, the female members of the group could organize the rally without attracting much attention.[101] Relegating certain tasks to women and believing they could operate below the radar of the Security Services was a technique adopted from the Polish underground state and one that would be used again in the 1980s when the *Solidarity* movement went into hiding.[102]

Sensing that something was up, on March 6 the Security Services arrested Michnik and Szlajfer. The two were quickly released, only to be arrested again on March 8. On the night of March 7, Lasota and Bogucka followed the plan and hid in the history building at Warsaw University while the Security Services arrested some of the leading male members of their group, including Blumsztajn, Szlajfer, Lityński, Modzelewski, and Kuroń. Clearly, the student leadership suspected that the authorities knew about their plans. The rector issued a warning: students were not to demonstrate.[103] They paid no attention. The Security Services stood ready to act if students began to gather in front of the history building. On March 8 the police and the students clashed violently, with many arrested. The next chapter relates in detail the subsequent events of March 1968 and the culmination of the anti-Zionist campaign.

---

101. Kuroń, *Wiara i wina*, 294.

102. Shana Penn, *Solidarity's Secret: The Women Who Defeated Communism in Poland* (Ann Arbor: University of Michigan Press, 2005).

103. AIPN 01288/23, *Wykaz osób zatrzymanych w okresie 8–10.III.1968*, March 11, 1968; AUW 2486, 7.

5

"TO WARSAW STUDENTS"

Relaunching the Anti-Zionist Campaign

ON MARCH 8, AT NOON, HUNDREDS OF WARSAW University students gathered outside the history building to rally against the expulsion of Adam Michnik and Henryk Szlajfer, perhaps hoping that the police would respect the sanctity of academic freedom. Reservists from the Citizens' Militia (Ochotnicza Rezerwa Milicji Obywatelskiej, ORMO) soon stormed the campus, dispersing the demonstration and beating the students. Though the authorities arrested the leaders, protests soon spread to the major Polish universities: the Warsaw Polytechnic, the Jagiellonian University in Kraków, the University of Wrocław, and the University of Łódź. The government publicly countered the protests with a propaganda campaign; newspapers accused Zionist Jews of organizing the demonstrations at Warsaw University as part of a plan to destroy Polish socialism. Not only had Polish Jews supported Israel in the recent war, despite the position of the Soviet Union and the Polish government, but they now incited unrest among students and workers. Many in the party viewed the student demonstrations as further proof of Jewish disloyalty and subversion—a cause for more fear and anxiety about the Jewish menace. They believed that peace would be restored only if the Jews were purged from the party, fired from their jobs, and driven out of Poland.

State media promoted an essentialist discourse, presenting Poles as inherently loyal to the nation and its government, and Jews as responsible for the past and present ails of socialism. Despite the racial undertones, the definition of Jew included not only those born to Jewish families but also Poles who supported "Jewish agendas" and "Jewish" politics. Anyone who objected to the regime, resisted, and protested became a "Jew," someone outside the body of the nation, a threat and a danger. Gomułka demanded loyalty to *communist Poland* or *People's Poland*, not to the Polish nation alone—the nation was bound up with socialism and complete loyalty to the party. This was a way of organizing the world: since the communist regime represented the true will of the nation, those who were against it must be foreign and alien. And the most familiar stranger in Poland was "the Jew."

Two days before the start of protests, on March 6, 1968, an art historian working at Zachęta Gallery in Warsaw wrote to a friend in London, "For the first time in forty years, a special general meeting of the Writers' Union and a resolution regarding *Dziady* and censorship. Some repressions at Warsaw University. . . . I'm pleased to report that the 'resistance movement' [*Ruch oporu*] is gathering strength."[1] The letter was one of hundreds the Security Services seized that month. The historian's words reflected the spirit of the students. They wanted the government to follow the example of neighboring Czechoslovakia, which had unofficially abolished censorship in early March and was marching on the road to reform.[2] One of the architects of the March 8 rally wrote to a friend, "The date, time, and place of the rally are known only to the narrow group of organizers."[3] But she was wrong: Paweł Jasienica's wife was keeping the Security Services informed.[4] Before the rally began, the police arrested several of the leaders, including Seweryn Blumsztajn, Henryk Szlajfer, Jan Lityński, Karol Modzelewski, and Jacek Kuroń. The arrests pointed to the direction the regime was taking.[5]

Many of the participants in the Warsaw University demonstrations later commented that they had been surprised by the government's harsh reaction.[6] Perhaps the students were naive; perhaps it was a narrative adopted by the student movement: that of the innocent youth attacked by "Oafs and the Ignoramuses."[7] Since October 1956, Gomułka had refused attempts to further reform his regime, and when Gomułka met in February 1968 with Alexander Dubček, the new reformist first secretary of the

1. AIPN BU MSW II 5239, *Notatka Służbowa, 11.III. 1968, Dyrektor Biura W MSW*.

2. Joseph Rothschild and Nancy M. Wingfield, *Return to Diversity: A Political History of East Central Europe since World War II*, 3rd ed. (New York: Oxford University Press, 2000), 169–70. The law abolishing censorship was officially passed in June.

3. AIPN BU MSW II 5239, *Notatka Służbowa, 6.III. 1968, Dyrektor Biura W MSW*.

4. AIPN 0208/1516, 170. This was despite warnings by Modzelewski that the regime would react punitively.

5. AIPN 01288/23, *Wykaz osób zatrzymanych w okresie 8–10.III.1968*, March 11, 1968.

6. Osęka, *My Ludzie z Marca*, 206.

7. Adam Michnik, "The Explosive Dziady," trans. Maricn Wawrzyńczak, *Gazeta*, online English-language edition, accessed January 31, 2008, http://www.gazetawyborcza.pl/1,86871,4886511.html.

Czechoslovak Communist Party, he warned him that "in such times [of change], anti-socialist elements are most active."[8] Speaking at the plenum of his party's Central Committee, Gomułka reminded listeners that "anti-socialist forces" had taken advantage of de-Stalinization to promote "social democracy" and "revisionism" and that they might try to do so again.[9] Clearly, the first secretary saw events across the border as dangerous and threatening to the communist regime and had no intention of reopening the discussion on reform.

Then came student demonstrations, the March events, trying to force the issue of reform on Gomułka. On March 8, the students gathered in front of the history building and announced that they had drawn up a petition demanding the reinstatement of Michnik and Szlajfer as students. They then sang the Polish national anthem and the "Internationale," both songs that regularly opened party meetings.[10] The students chanted, "No bread without freedom!" referring to Gomułka's conviction that as the economy improved demands for reform would diminish. According to the Security Services' report, students began behaving "aggressively": they marched to the rector's office, where they demanded to meet with the rector and for the rector to ask the police, waiting at the campus gates, to retreat. The interim rector, Professor Zygmunt Rybicki, appeared at the balcony and implored the students to disperse. Upon their refusal, a company of uniformed Citizens' Militiamen, reinforced by three hundred men from the Militia Reserves (ORMO) in civilian dress, was called in. Officially, the members of the reserves were worker activists who volunteered their time; they answered to local branches of the Security Services.[11] While the reservists entered the campus, the uniformed Citizens' Militia (Milicja Obywatelska, the regular police) remained outside the university's gates for most of the day.[12] Disembarking from buses marked "vacation," the Militia Reserves advanced on demonstrators while wielding clubs. The students ran, but

8. Pawel Machcewicz, "'Do diabła z suwerennością' Władysław Gomułka wobec praskiej wiosny," in *Wokół praskiej wiosny: Polska i Czechosłowacja w 1968 roku*, ed. Łukasz Kamiński (Warsaw: Instytut Pamięci Narodowej, 2004), 60.

9. Pawel Machcewicz, "'Do diabła z suwerennością' Władysław Gomułka wobec praskiej wiosny," in *Wokół praskiej wiosny: Polska i Czechosłowacja w 1968 roku*, ed. Łukasz Kamiński (Warsaw: Instytut Pamięci Narodowej, 2004), 60.

10. The national anthem begins: "Jeszcze Polska nie zginęła, Kiedy my żyjemy." AIPN 01439/82, 17–19.

11. Paweł Piotrowski, ed., *Apart Bezpieczeństwa w Polsce, Kadra kierownicza*, vol.2, *1957–1975* (Warsaw: Instytut Pamięci Narodowej, 2006), 21–31.

12. AIPN 01439/82, 99.

not everyone managed to escape the police's truncheons. The demonstrators spilled out the university gates, pursued by reservists; film footage taken by the Security Services shows students and bystanders scurrying down Krakowskie Przedmieście, one of Warsaw's main streets, dodging into churches and stores for shelter. Letters written about that day describe the policemen beating everyone in sight, including young women, an act considered particularly offensive in Polish society. Some protesters began chanting: "Gestapo!" "Roundup!" "SS men!" "Hitlerites!" None thought to call the police "Stalinists," "Russians," or even "KGB." Two decades after the end of World War II, for Poles the memory of the war remained alive and the police hunting down civilians evoked images of the German occupation and Nazi brutality. Moreover, the organizers of the rally, raised under communism, were the sons and daughters of party members; for them the enemies were fascists and Nazis, as had been the case before and during the war.

Letters intercepted by Section W of the Security Services gave detailed descriptions of the rally from the point of view of the locals and the participants:

> In the meantime, the secret agents [*tajniacy*] began brutally dispersing the crowd, beating and kicking those on the ground, hitting girls in the face. It is difficult to write about what happened.
>
> Yesterday, I personally became convinced of the efficiency of the plainclothes branch of the Citizens' Militia, as well as of the splendidly attired members of the Citizens' Militia Reserves, who entered Warsaw University in workers' jackets to stop the antigovernment rally.
>
> They beat everyone on the street, including unarmed and innocent people. During the rally they beat two girls with clubs until they bled.[13]
>
> They blocked the gates of the university and beat everyone in sight: women, people who fell on the ground. A few people were trampled . . . a few were taken to the hospital.
>
> They used clubs to hit people in the face, and not only students, but also academic workers. I don't think that it bothered them to beat women on International Women's Day.
>
> I realized that what happened at the university was a massacre. . . . The most difficult thing for me was that they beat a pregnant woman in the stomach.[14]

---

13. AIPN 0746/7, *Notatka Służbowa, 10.III.1968*, 5–10. The report did not include the names of those who had written the letters.

14. AIPN 0746/7, *Notatka Służbowa, 10.III.1968*, 11–16. The report did not include the names of those who had written the letters.

The violence and the rumors that a student had been beaten to death did not deter the students but rather increased their determination.[15] The police reported that during that day, March 8, disturbances broke out around Warsaw's city center: at Krakowskie Przedmieście, the Academy of Fine Arts, the education offices, the Central Committee building, on Marszałkowska Street and Grójecka Street, in Konstytucja Square, and at Jedności Robotniczej Square.[16] Official reports claimed that the gathering at Warsaw University was "wild" and that students chanted antigovernment slogans, such as "Down with communism!" and "Down with the Gestapo!" The police accounts described the Citizens' Militia reservists as workers who wanted to negotiate with the students but found themselves obliged to resort to violence. The police detained fifty-four people. All but a few were soon released; Adam Michnik, Irena Lasota, Barbara Toruńczyk, Wiktor Górecki, and Wiktor Nagorski joined Kuroń, Modzelewski, Lityński, Szlajfer, and the others already in jail.[17]

The next morning's newspapers ran articles depicting the demonstrators as spoiled youths, the sons and daughters of the Stalinist elites. This infuriated the students, who were particularly enraged by a piece in *Życie Warszawy* entitled "Who Does It Serve?," which portrayed them as "a group of troublemakers" who did not have to worry about the "real needs and problems of our society" since they had never wanted for anything.[18] Angry letters to *Życie Warszawy* complained about the paper's slanted depiction: what it reported was "far from the truth," and there was no mention of "the brutal behavior of the Citizens' Militia." The daily also received about 120 phone calls protesting its coverage of the demonstration.[19] About five hundred demonstrators gathered outside the offices of *Życie Warszawy*, and several others met outside the Socialist Youth Union daily, *Sztandar Młodych* (The youth standard), which had printed a similar article.[20]

Official reactions to the student protest inspired many others to act. On March 9, throughout Warsaw, students carried signs and wrote graffiti

---

15. The Polish historian Jerzy Eisler thoroughly researched the rumor that a student or students had been killed; he found no conclusive evidence. Eisler, *Polski Rok 1968*, 255–60.

16. AIPN 01439/82, 17–19.

17. AIPN 01288/23, *Wykaz osób zatrzymanych w okresie 8–10.III.1968*, March 11, 1968.

18. "Komu to służy?" *Życie Warszawy*, March 9, 1968, "Na Uniwersytecie Warszawskim co pewien czas daje znać o sobie grupka awanturników, wywodząca się z kręgów bananowej młodzieży, której obce są troski materialne, prawdziwe warunki życia i potrzeby naszego społeczeństwa."

19. Document 1, in *Marzec '68: między tragedia a podłością*, ed. Grzegorz Sołtysiak and Jożef Stępień (Warsaw: Profi, 1998), 183–84.

20. AIPN 0746/7, *Notatka Służbowa, 11.III.1968, wydzialu W.*

declaring "We want *Dziady*." Police found similar slogans on a wall outside the Soviet embassy. At Plac Jedności Robotniczej, near the Warsaw Polytechnic, were fifteen hundred students. Another large group rallied around Warsaw University. The Citizens' Militia and the reservists violently dispersed the demonstrations after the minister of internal affairs, backed by Józef Kępa, Warsaw's party head, ordered the police to stop them at any cost. The Ministry of Internal Affairs later reported that 2,245 officers participated in the day's operations, a testimony to the concern the protests raised. In one memorable scene, protesters tried to hide from tear gas and water guns in the Church of the Holy Cross on Krakowskie Przedmieście Street. Carrying clubs, the police aggressively chased the demonstrators out of the church. The day was just as dramatic and as violent as March 8; only late at night did the police report, "All is calm."[21] On Sunday, March 10, things grew quieter.[22] However, a gathering of about a hundred students near one of Warsaw University's dormitories attracted the attention of the authorities. The protesters burned newspapers, chanting, "The press lies!"— a slogan sounded all over Warsaw.[23]

On March 9, the regime arraigned the first wave of arrested students. After speedy trials, three students received six-month sentences and one a four-month sentence; their crime: antigovernment activities. Irena Lasota, whom the Security Services saw as one of the organizers and who was singled out for her "ironic" replies under questioning, was sentenced to two months in prison.[24] The courts remanded many others, leaving them in jail for the duration of the March events. The police arrested seventy-seven people on that day alone, March 9, including Aleksander Smolar, son of *Folks Sztyme* editor Hersh Smolar.[25]

Newspapers began referring to demonstrators as "banana youths," a slur that implied that they had been spoiled and were wealthy enough to buy bananas, a rare commodity in 1960s Poland, and therefore came from elite families. In pamphlets circulated on March 10, students provided their version of the events. One leaflet addressed Catholics, informing them that

---

21. AIPN 01288/22, 101–10.

22. The Security Services arrested only four people in Warsaw, two of whom were the student Henryk Rubinstein and the economist Marian (Waldemar) Kuczyński. AIPN 01288/22.

23. AIPN BU MSW II 964, 13.

24. Nagorski, Szkoda, and Malarecki received six months and Maciej Dybowski four. AIPN BU MSW II 6657, 8–15.

25. AIPN 01288/23, *Wykaz osób zatrzymanych w okresie 8–10 III.68 w związku z zajściami na terenie Warszawy, 11.III.1968.*

although the rally of March 8 had been conducted peacefully, the Citizens' Militia had viciously attacked the students, killing one of them. Another pamphlet, entitled "Black Friday at the University," was directed to workers: it described the rally as larger and quieter than reported and stressed police brutality.[26] In yet another leaflet, students from Warsaw stated that their demands came "out of concern for the building socialism in Poland, out of concern for social unity in the struggle against attempts to stifle democracy in our homeland." The leaflet concluded, "We are not banana youths or hooligans; we are fighting for the right to study in a democratic and autonomous environment!!! Our goal is democracy and socialism."[27] The use of the term *democracy* here is not in the Western-liberal sense but rather in the socialist meaning: internal party democracy and participation of the working class in the decision-making process, as laid out in the Kuroń-Modzelewski open letter. Over the following weekend, young academics and student activists organized another wave of demonstrations and continued distributing pamphlets around Poland.

The authorities countered the students' claims with the assistance of the universities' administration. The heads of Warsaw's institutes of higher education failed their students, who had hoped for the sort of support their counterparts received in Czechoslovakia. The vice rector of Warsaw University, Ludwik Bazyłow, wrote an open letter to the youth, calling the protestors "a small group," troublemakers that "most of Warsaw's students avoid." He begged the students not to take part in any more illegal demonstrations and expressed the hope that classes would resume on Monday.[28] Dionizy Smoleński, the rector of Warsaw Polytechnic, called on students to preserve the peace, to shun illegal demonstrations and rallies, which were organized, he explained, by a small group with its own agenda.[29] A public letter from one of the party cells to Warsaw Polytechnic's students went further, identifying the leaders as the children of high-ranking communist officials, mostly of Jewish descent. The letter named Henryk Szlajfer, Aleksander Smolar, Wiktor Górecki, Irena Grudzińska, and "another Club Babel member, Dajczgewand." One protestor, a non-Jewish Pole, was quoted as saying, "Israel has the same right to Jerusalem as Poland has to the Western territories [gained by Poland at the end of World War II]." To

---

26. *Czarny piątek na Uniwersytecie!!!* AIPN 0296/99.
27. AIPN 01288/22, 141.
28. *Do Studentów Uniwersytetu Warszawskiego*, 10 III 1968r., AIPN 0296/99.
29. *Do Studentów Politechniki Warszawskiej*, Prof. D. Smoleński, 10.III.1968r., AIPN 0296/99.

join the protesters was folly, the pamphlet further explained, since they were intent on driving a wedge between workers and the intelligentsia.[30] At that point the Ministry of Internal Affairs still believed that the protests could be limited to Warsaw and would not spread to other cities.[31]

Yet on March 11, in Kraków, students from the Jagiellonian University fittingly assembled by the Adam Mickiewicz monument at the main city square and marched to the university, singing "March, Poland, March, Our Brave Nation" (Marsz, marsz Polonia, nasz dzielny narodzie), a well-known nineteenth-century patriotic anthem. The students split into two groups: the first rallied in front of university buildings, and the other met with the university rector, Mieczysław Klimaszewski. After inconclusive negotiations, the students decided to hold a rally that evening.[32] They also approved a resolution on recent events, expressing solidarity with their colleagues in Warsaw and demanding that the government uphold the constitution. Further, they asked for the release and reinstatement of students and faculty and for access to the media to explain their point of view on events.[33] At seven o'clock that evening, five thousand Krakówiaks gathered once more at the central square. They too sang the Polish national anthem and the "Internationale" and chanted slogans in support of Warsaw's students, democracy, and Czechoslovakia. The police broke up the rally and arrested about twenty protesters.[34] In Lublin a similar scene occurred, as about two thousand students from the Maria Curie-Skłodowska University, the Catholic University, and various high schools gathered. About half of the demonstrators marched toward the offices of the Lublin Central Committee and shouted slogans in support of the students in Warsaw and of *Dziady*. The Citizens' Militia stopped them before they managed to walk very far and violently broke up the protest, arresting thirty-nine demonstrators, most of them from the Catholic University.[35]

---

30. The Western Lands is a territory the Allies granted to Poland from Germany after World War II. *Do Studentów Politechniki Warszawskiej*, 10.III. 1968r., AIPN 0296/99.

31. AAN KC PZPR 1737 Biuletyn Wewnętrzny nr. 60/64.

32. Document 93, in *Marzec 1968 w Krakowie w dokumentach*, ed. Kwiek Julian (Kraków: Ksiegarnia Akademicka: Fundacja Centrum Dokumentacji Czynu Niepodległościowego, 2005). "Marsz, marsz Polonia, nasz dzielny narodzie" is taken from the "Marsz Polonii" (March Poland).

33. Document 2, in *Marzec 1968 w Krakowie w dokumentach*, ed. Kwiek Julian.

34. Documents 94–96, in *Marzec 1968 w Krakowie w dokumentach*, ed. Kwiek Julian.

35. AIPN BU MSW II 964, 17; Małgorzata Choma-Jusińska, "Lublin," in *Oblicza Marca 1968*, ed. Konrad Rokicki and Sławomir Stępień (Warsaw: Instytut Pamięci Narodowej, Komisja Ścigania Zbrodni przeciwko Narodowi Polskiemu, 2004).

A committee of professors, under instructions from the rector of Warsaw University, met with students in the university's main auditorium on March 11. The vice rector, Bazyłow, repeated the message of his open letter: most students, according to his knowledge, sought to distance themselves from the "group of troublemakers," sentiments that the university's faculty applauded. The professors' committee took the floor next and expressed solidarity with students in general but not with the demonstrators. Then students stepped forward, wanting to know who had summoned the Citizens' Militia, on whose authority it had entered the university campus, and whether members of the militia had beaten protesters to death. And they had demands: the reinstatement of expelled students, the immediate release of jailed protestors, the reopening of Dejmek's production of *Dziady*, compensation for the students harmed during the clampdown, the relaxation of censorship, honest reporting of recent events, and official condemnation of antisemitism. Bazyłow tried to answer some of the questions. He insisted that no one was killed on March 8: the university had tracked down the young women alleged to have been killed, and they were doing well. But the atmosphere in the auditorium, he complained, made real dialogue between students and the administration impossible. The students also used the occasion to pass a resolution that "protested against the violation of the Constitution and of human rights by the Security Services, the Citizens' Militia, and their 'troops.'"[36] Addressed to the government and university authorities, the resolution included the list of demands expressed at the meeting—they would be repeated countless times by university students throughout Poland. Given the "violations of the Constitution," "brutal actions of the plainclothes militia," "intervention by the Security Services in university affairs," and media representation of student protesters as "banana youths," the student leaders wanted the government to find and punish those responsible for the violent suppression of the protest. They also demanded academic freedom. Three thousand students voted for the resolution and decided to hold another rally on the next day.[37]

Several philosophy and sociology professors at Warsaw University drafted an appeal to the academic senate and the rector.[38] The letter

---

36. AIPN BU MSW II 4468, 43–47.

37. Document 39, in *Opozycja wobec rządów komunistycznych w Polsce 1956–1976: wybór dokumentów*, ed. Zygmunt Hemmerling and Marek Nadolski (Warsaw: Ośrodek Badań Społecznych, 1991), 301–3.

38. Later the Security Services named Bronisław Baczko, Stefan Morawski, Nina Assorodobraj, and Jerzy Szacki as the instigators. AIPN 01288/22, 219.

described March 8 as an "attack on students and academic workers" and protested "this act of violence." The professors expressed support for the student's resolution while condemning antisemitism and the press's attempts to "drive a wedge between the working class and the students."[39] The statement repeated some of the students' demands and suggested that the university hold a meeting with faculty and students. The following day, the entire faculty of the Philosophy and Sociology Departments met to discuss the statement and decided to pass it to the university senate. The Physics and Political Science Departments adopted the same position.[40]

Very few politicians stood by the students. The five Sejm members (Poland's parliament) representing the Znak Catholic faction decided to confront Prime Minister Józef Cyrankiewicz. Founded in 1956, Znak was one of three Catholic groups represented in the parliament; it had an influential weekly and a publishing house and ran the Catholic Intelligentsia Club. By sending questions to the prime minister, the Znak members, Stanisław Stomma, Konstanty Łubieński, Tadeusz Mazowiecki, Jerzy Zawieyski, and Janusz Zabłocki, employed a legitimate, albeit rarely exploited, protocol. They posed two questions:

1. What does the government plan to do to stop the Citizens' Militia's violent actions against academic youths and to determine who is responsible?
2. What does the government intend to do to answer the questions that the youths posed, and that concern public opinion more broadly, on the topics of civil democratic freedoms and the government's cultural politics?

They criticized the press's presentation of the events of March 8, they faulted the militia for entering the university, and they challenged the claim that student demonstrations had been antisocialist.[41] There was no significant difference between the Catholic representatives' questions and the demands of the students and professors. Intellectuals used similar formulations in public letters and speeches.

On March 9, Security Services bulletins already linked Jews or Jewish origins to the protesting students. Reports named as leaders mainly

39. Document 40, in *Opozycja wobec rządów komunistycznych w Polsce 1956–1976: wybór dokumentów*, ed. Zygmunt Hemmerling and Marek Nadolski (Warsaw: Ośrodek Badań Społecznych, 1991), 304–5.

40. *Protokół z Rady Wydziału Filozoficznego dnia 12.III.1968r.*, AIPN 0296/99, vol. 1; *Stanowisko pracowników naukowych IFT, IFD oraz Katedry MMF w sprawie ostatnich zajść*, AIPN 0296/99, vol. 1.

41. Tadeusz Mazowiecki went on to become the first prime minister of democratic Poland. Document 40, in *Opozycja wobec rządów komunistycznych w Polsce 1956–1976: wybór dokumentów*, ed. Zygmunt Hemmerling and Marek Nadolski (Warsaw: Osrodek Badan Spolecznych, 1991), 305–6.

those with obviously Jewish names, such as Rubinstein, Weintraub, Goldberg, and Smolar: they were the "troublemakers" and "hooligans" working against the party and the best interests of Poland.[42] In the spirit of the summer of 1967, the regime pointed to Jews leading and participating in the March 8 demonstrations, to Jews spreading rumors about a dead student protester, and to Jews from Warsaw University conspiring with students at other universities around the country.[43] An arrest report of one of the protesters, Katarzyna Werfel, the daughter of the Stalinist ideologue Roman Werfel, mentioned her contacts with Israel and her "Zionist views."[44] By March 13, the authorities had begun singling out Jewish professors as well. At Warsaw University, Stefan Morawski, Zygmunt Bauman, Bolesław Baczko, Krzysztof Pomian, Roman Zimand, and Leszek Kołakowski stood out in the reports. As not all of them had Jewish origins, the Security Services noted that the dissenting group of professors "had at its center academic workers of Jewish descent."[45] If they held "Zionist" views or followed a hidden "Jewish" agenda, non-Jews were included in the "Jewish circles" that the Security Services designated. Being Jewish, therefore, was not merely a matter of ancestry but also of politics: critics of the regime were considered Zionists and "honorary" Jews.

Sons and daughters of party members of Jewish origins who had high-ranking positions in the Stalinist period immediately fell under suspicion; in the ministry's eyes, they had multiple motivations for working against the regime. The ministry's reports accused Antoni Zambrowski, son of the prominent Stalinist Roman Zambrowski, of circulating the rumors that a student was killed on March 8.[46] In 1956, the party's Central Committee had chosen Roman Zambrowski as first secretary, only to opt for Edward Ochab after pressure from Moscow. Zambrowski the elder, embittered and cast aside, or so the officials claimed, wanted to undermine the party's authority, and his son acted in his name. According to them, Antoni led the group of

---

42. AAN KC PZPR 1737, Biuletyn Wewnętrzny nr. 59a/63.

43. AIPN 01288/22, 78–83.AAN KC PZPR 1737 Biuletyn Wewnętrzny nr. 60/64. On March 10, officers identified Henryk Rubinstein, who had taken an active part in the March 8 rally, as one of the "commandos" from Warsaw University trying to forge links with students at the Warsaw Polytechnic. A summary from the same day remarked that sociology students Jan Gross and Jerzy Działłowicki traveled to Kraków and met with students at the Jagiellonian University. The officers speculated that Gross must "undoubtedly have tried to get Kraków's students to demonstrate." AIPN 01288/22, 101, 127, 218.

44. AIPN BU MSW II 6657, 8–15.

45. AIPN BU MSW II 6657, 219.

46. AAN KC PZPR 1737, Biuletyn Wewnętrzy nr. 59a/63; AIPN 01288/22, 78–83.

Jewish students who instigated events at Warsaw University and who saw themselves as a military unit—it was Zambrowski who had referred to his fellow activists as "commandos."[47] On March 12, Antoni was arrested.[48]

As they had done in the wake of the June 1967 War, the Security Services now reported that the general population supported the government's stance, while Zionist Jews were stirring up trouble.[49] Officials described citizens of Jewish descent as "terrorizing" anyone who criticized the students. In one incident, they claimed, a lecturer at the Central School for Planning publicly slapped a student who had denounced the recent protests.[50] A Jewish employee of the Ministry of Agriculture accused the authorities of behaving like "Gestapo officers."[51] A Department II bulletin portrayed workers at the State Academic Publishing House as divided along national lines: Jews supported the protesters, while non-Jews "were satisfied with official attempts to unmask the Zionist conspiracy." The report praised a worker who "had expressed her anti-Zionist views, even to the Jews who controlled the publishing house"; this outspoken woman dared to hope for the eradication of "the Jewish roots of evil [*źródło zła*] in Poland."[52] Many in the rank and file of the state bureaucracy could now show tolerance for and even applaud public expressions of anti-Jewish sentiment and openly antisemitic language—such as referring to Jews as the "root of evil," a phrase taken from the interwar lexicon. Though most high-ranking party officials avoided explicit and overt antisemitism (many did not hold such views), officers of the Ministry of Internal Affairs had fewer qualms about using racially loaded language.

Press outlets also expressed a hard-liner position, rejecting all suggestions for reform and viciously attacking the protestors, particularly those of Jewish descent. On March 11, *Trybuna Ludu* published an article on the demonstrations maintaining that though the call for the reinstatement of Szlajfer and Michnik had some outspoken supporters among the students, most students objected to the rally and wanted nothing better than to attend classes. This vocal minority "could not harm the good reputation of our academic youths."[53] Only a fraction of students participated,

47. AAN KC PZPR 1737, Biuletyn Wewnętrzny nr. 60/64.
48. AIPN 01288/22, 78–83, 212.
49. AAN KC PZPR 1737, 44.
50. AIPN 01288/22, 210.
51. AIPN 01288/22, 235–36.
52. AIPN BU MSW II 4051, 64–65.
53. *Trybuna Ludu*, November 3, 1968.

and their behavior led to the violence because they attacked "worker activists" and started "brawls," forcing the Citizens' Militia to intervene. Among the "ringleaders" named were Michnik, Dajczgewand, Szlajfer, and Werfel. Almost all of them were of Jewish descent, a fact not mentioned but well-known to the readers, mostly from their Jewish-sounding names. *Trybuna Ludu* further claimed that many in Warsaw wondered what kind of parent would allow such behavior, especially when these parents held key positions. Or was it the case, as the author hinted, that the parents shared their children's views?[54]

A notorious and more inciting article, "To Warsaw's Students," was published in *Słowo Powszechne* on the same day, March 11. *Słowo Powszechne* was the daily newspaper published by PAX, a small procommunist Catholic organization founded after World War II by Bolesław Piasecki, a prewar fascist whose antisemitic view were well-known. The daily served as the ideal vessel for views that the minister of internal affairs promoted but that the party's overall leadership might see as too extreme.[55] The article, unsigned but apparently written by the editor, Witold Jankowski, named the organizers of the protests at Warsaw University, stressing their Jewish ancestry, and claimed that Jewish Stalinists stood behind them.[56] The piece began with the allegation that Israel and the Federal Republic of Germany (FRG) had formed an alliance aimed at shifting the blame for the Holocaust from Germany to Poland. Moreover, Israel and the FRG worked to undermine the authority of Gomułka, "the most important international politician in Poland." The "Polish Zionists," Jewish members of the party, could not bear to see Gomułka succeed and hoped to install in Poland a less patriotic, more pro-German government. Just as the Stalinist "deviation" originated with the Jewish members of the Communist Party, now the very same members aligned themselves with "the anti-Polish politics of the FRG."[57] The article named the leading students and their parents, including Roman Zambrowski's son Antoni and Roman Werfel's daughter Katarzyna as well as Grudzińska, Michnik, Szlajfer, and Dajczgewand. These provocateurs had faltered when faced with the "natural" connection

54. *Trybuna Ludu*, November 3, 1968.

55. Kunicki, "The Red and the Brown." PAX willingly collaborated with the communist regime and was regarded as a puppet organization. Before the war, Piasecki headed the ONR-Falanga, an extreme right-wing party inspired by other European fascist parties.

56. Kunicki, *Between the Brown and the Red*, 153.

57. *Słowo Powszechne*, November 3, 1968.

of Polish youths to cultural traditions of democracy and patriotism that allowed most students to resist the provocation.The piece juxtaposed "true" Poles, who were Catholic, and the Jews, who once more conspired against Poland and had no part in the Polish socialist nation.

A significant attack on reformist intellectuals came from *Kurier Polski*. Written by Ryszard Gontarz, a former Security Services officer and known member of the partisan faction of the party, the article entitled "Instigators" [*Inspiratorzy*] articulated the views of the Ministry of Internal Affairs.[58] In painstaking detail, Gontarz waged personal attacks against opposition activists. He began with a question: How could it be that Warsaw's students, "known for their patriotism,"[59] would join street rallies against the government? The answer was that behind events stood Leszek Kołakowski, Andrzej Kijowski, Stefan Kisielewski, Jerzy Andrzejewski, Paweł Jasienica, and Antoni Słonimski, prominent Warsaw intellectuals. These were the men who, at the special meeting of the Warsaw branch of the Polish Writers' Union, defended Michnik and Grudzińska, the "daughter of the vice minister of forestry," and encouraged youths to attack the government. Gontarz then dropped a bombshell: Jasienica, a well-respected journalist and historian, had been born Lech Beynar and had good reason to change his name. In 1944, Beynar (Jasienica) had deserted the Polish Army and joined a "bandit unit" in the Białystok region that killed peasants and burned villages. Gontarz claimed that after the war the police had arrested every member of the "bandit unit" and that everyone except for Beynar (Jasienica) stayed in jail—insinuating that he had informed on his comrades. *Bandit unit* in communist Polish discourse referred to anticommunist partisans, and in this case the article also hinted that Jasienica had been a *Volksdeutsche*, a Pole of German descent, often synonymous with collaborator. Later, continued the article, Beynar (Jasienica) had become part of a group that "subscribed to the Israeli-FRG propaganda that slanders our government and people, describing us as antisemites." Gontarz then presented a history of the "Michnik group," beginning in 1962, and of the "Contradiction Seekers Club" (Klub Poszukiwaczy Sprzeczności) that the student leaders had formed as high schoolers. He maintained that since the Jewish-revisionist professors had failed in their attempt to inspire revolt among high school students in general, they took "banana revisionism" to Club Babel. That

58. AIPN BU 01753/13, Gontarz Ryszard.
59. *Kurier Polski*, December 12, 1968.

group fostered the "spirit of Jewish chauvinism": at the Club Babel summer camp, he wrote, young people proudly wore Stars of David and sang, "We are going to Sinai, we are going to Gaza, and we will be Jews. Moshe Dayan showed us how to win." Young Jews influenced by Jasienica, Kisielewski, and others were solely responsible for the latest attacks on the government and the party and for the disturbance of the peace. Since Gontarz's accused were obviously not all Jews, he labeled them "honorary Jews," and their leader was a *Volksdeutsche*.[60]

These newspaper articles presented student leaders as a foreign element, alienated from the general student body, a privileged and predominantly, if not entirely, Jewish group. The press demarcated the lines between "those under attack" and "the attackers," between loyal Poles and Jews, who should be feared for their connections with former Stalinists and with West Germany. In this spirit, Józef Kępa, the first secretary of the Warsaw Party Committee, addressed "events at Warsaw University." On March 11, he conveyed to party activists the views of First Secretary Gomułka: bluntly stated, the student leadership comprised nothing more than spoiled children of prominent Jewish party members. The provocateurs—he mentioned Michnik, Szlajfer, and Dajczgewand, linking them to Club Babel—had in mind the downfall of People's Poland. They falsely accused Poles of antisemitism; for these Jews, any criticism of individual Jews or Israel had to be antisemitism. However, the party was determined to stem all forms of nationalism and racism, and it would not allow Zionist propaganda to influence Poland's institutions of higher learning or its youth. In any case, most students had shunned the demonstrations. Kępa promised his listeners that the party would not tolerate any further disturbances in the capital. The boundaries of the socialist nation were delineated.[61]

In the days after Kępa's speech and the appearance of "To Warsaw's Students" in *Słowo Powszechne*, Security Services reports documented many instances of Jewish indignation and anger, but "the general population

60. *Kurier Polski*, December 12, 1968. The day after the article appeared, Gontarz complained of threatening telephone calls and alluded to the fate of the son of Bolesław Piasecki. In 1957, the fifteen-year-old Bohdan Piasecki was kidnapped and murdered; the police never found the perpetrators, but Piasecki and others blamed the Jews. By mentioning the murder, Gontarz evoked fears of Jewish Stalinists, who had in the past acted against a Polish nationalist and would perhaps do so again. He echoed the suspicions of the Ministry of Internal Affairs concerning such former leading members of the party as Zambrowski and Berman. AIPN 01288/22, 216; Piotr Zychowicz, "Mordercy Bohdana uchodzą," *Rzeczpospolita*, October 12, 2007, http://www.rp.pl/artykul/75790.html.
61. Józef Kępa, "Co się kryje za ulicznymi awanturami?" *Trybuna Ludu*, March 12, 1968.

saw the situation differently." Ordinary people realized who stood behind recent events: most students saw that they "had fallen victim to political intrigues, that the expulsion of Michnik and Szlajfer from Warsaw University was a pretext for provoking disturbances."[62] Only Jews like Roman Karst, a professor of German literature, complained that the publication of "To Warsaw's Students" in a national newspaper "testifies to the existence of antisemitism . . . preparing public sentiment for an anti-Jewish pogrom." The Security Services report estimated that about half of the seventy participants at a meeting of the literary PEN Club were Jewish; the informants classified them according to nationality. During the meeting, the "alarmist" (Jewish) writer Józef Hen had shouted, "Turn on the crematoria's ovens!"[63] Informants at the Jewish Historical Institute in Warsaw heard the historians Artur Eisenbach and Adam Rutkowski say that Kępa's speech was "a great scandal and an endorsement of antisemitism." Three other prominent Jews complained that Kępa had adopted "Hitlerite" methods, including blaming parents for the crimes of their children.[64] Journalists in key positions were also heard speaking out for the demonstrating students: an editor for *Życie Gospodarcze* expressed solidarity with the students; an editor for the weekly *Świat* spread rumors about the brutal behavior of the Citizens' Militia; another from *Głos Pracy* claimed that Gomułka was exploiting the situation to unleash antisemitism.[65] Many Jews expressed growing concern that public opinion had turned against them, that the government's implicit endorsement of antisemitism would lead to violence. Polish Jews felt that two decades after the Holocaust, they again had to confront a racial vocabulary, which portrayed them as essentially different and threatening. Moreover, any concern about antisemitism was understood as slander of the party and the state and proof of Jewish disloyalty.

Members from Club Babel, the young generation of the TSKŻ, including Marek Web, Ernest Lederman, and Natan Tenenbum, seeking to show that the protests did not originate at Club Babel, proposed a formal rebuttal to the allegations detailed in "To Warsaw's Students." The TSKŻ committee in charge of the Jewish press believed that no censor would allow for

62. AAN KC PZPR 1737, Załącznik do biul. Wewn. Nr 62/68, Ministerstwo Spraw Wewnętrznych Gabinet Ministra.

63. AIPN 01288/22, 164–65.

64. AIPN 01288/22, 217–18.

65. AAN KC PZPR 1737, Załącznik do biul. Wewn. Nr 62/68, Ministerstwo Spraw Wewnętrznych Gabinet Ministra.

the publication of such a letter, but the activists wrote a strongly worded response anyway. In an early draft, the young Jews argued that the author of "To Warsaw's Students" used the word Zionists in much the same way that the fascist right had used Żydokomuna. Such words could lead to violence, as they had in the past. At the end of the draft, they wrote, "On the eve of the twenty-fifth anniversary of the Warsaw ghetto uprising, we fellow citizens and heirs to the traditions of the *Jewish Fighting Organization* declare: We are not obliged to remain passive, indeed we will not remain passive, when we are confronted with the deceitful anti-Jewish tricks of the gentlemen from *Słowo Powszechne* and the politicians who stand on their shoulders."[66]

Like everyone in the public sphere in Poland at the time, Jewish youth referred to World War II, presenting themselves as the successors of the Jewish wartime resistance, rejecting the image of the acquiescent Jew. On March 13, they formally applied for permission to publish a denial of connections between Club Babel and the organizers of the March demonstrations. Recent efforts to lump all Jews together, they asserted, were reprehensible, and the editors of *Słowo Powszechne* had failed in their ethical duty to stem antisemitic tendencies. Rather, they published an article reminiscent of the Obóz Zjednoczenia Narodowego (OZN) and Obóz Narodowo-Radykalny (ONR), right-wing fascist movements that enjoyed some success in Poland before World War II and to which some of the editors of the daily belonged. The activists were barred from publishing the letter.[67]

When the central board of the TSKŻ met on March 12, members expressed similar outrage over the suggestion of a link between events in the Middle East and student unrest in Warsaw, and between Club Babel and the opposition. As Leopold Domb, the president of the TSKŻ, and other members asserted, the Jewish *communist* association was devoted to opposing Zionism, not to promoting it. The Yiddish daily *Folks-Sztyme* had run several articles about "Israeli aggression" after the June 1967 War; Club Babel hosted lectures against the "nationalist influences of Zionism"; and the association had on several occasions strongly condemned Israel's "aggression." Domb expressed incredulity at the lapses of censors who approved the article in *Słowo Powszechne*: "It used violent slogans, the sort of thing the Falanga-ONR used to incite pogroms."[68] After all, the former

---

66. AIPN 0296/99, vol. 1, *Oświadczenia Prezydium Zarządu Głównego TSKŻ*.

67. AIPN BU MSW II 831, 8–7; AIPN 0296/99, vol. 1, *list do redackji, Tajny odpis*.

68. AIPN 0296/99, vol. 1, 30.

head of the Falanga-ONR was now behind the publication. The TSKŻ was fighting the wrong enemy: Piasecki and his band of "former" fascists had seized on the moment and understood where the wind was blowing, but they were not in charge. At the meeting, the central board of TSKŻ agreed that it would ask the party for permission to respond in the press to allegations it viewed as inaccurate, inflammatory, and antisemitic and that it would request meetings with officials from the Ministry of Internal Affairs and the Central Committee to clarify the situation. The heads of the Jewish organization had expected that by playing by the rules of the game they would signal to party leaders that this was not a Zionist group. But at that moment the government was already taking steps to rein in the TSKŻ: censors no longer accepted articles or books in Yiddish, demanding that they be translated into Polish first; the veterans' association ZBoWiD gradually took over the commemoration of the twenty-fifth anniversary of the Warsaw Ghetto Uprising; the Ministry of Education shut down the Jewish school in Łódź and hoped to close the one in Wrocław; finally, teaching Yiddish was no longer allowed.[69] Such restrictions on Jewish language and education had no precedence in communist Poland (until then, the Jewish system had faced the same limitations as the Polish one). Fears of "Jewish nationalism" led the government to take steps to curb Jewish independent activity and essentially put an end to the cultural autonomy Yiddish institutions had enjoyed.

March 12 was also a day of protests around Poland. At Warsaw Polytechnic, about four thousand students met in the main auditorium to approve a resolution addressed to the Sejm and the Central Committee. They demanded the release of all arrested students, a formal announcement in the press that articles about the student protests had been deceitful, the reinstatement of faculty members fired for supporting the students, a guarantee that the police would not enter the campus or the dormitories, and a proper investigation to determine who was responsible for police violence. Finally, the students demanded that the press publish their declaration. Were they not dedicated to building "socialism in a democratic homeland"? The Warsaw Polytechnic statement also referred to the anti-Zionist campaign: the students declared that they had nothing to do with Zionism or anti-Zionism.[70] Their sole goal was to improve socialism in Poland: expanding

---

69. AIPN 0296/99, vol. 1, 30–34.
70. AIPN 01439/82, 52; AK AO IV.43.12.

the scope of democratic practices, making a commitment to open debates, and allowing for inclusion of nonparty members in the decision-making processes. The Polish students' understanding of democracy at that time was socialist: they had not set their sights on creating a pluralist or liberal regime.[71] When students from the Philosophy Department at Prague's Karl University wrote a letter of support to their colleagues from Warsaw University, they told their Polish friends that they shared similar goals: "Your aspirations and ours are united in the struggle to apply democratic principles to public and political life. We salute your efforts to apply the ideas of humanism, democracy, and personal freedom."[72]

At Warsaw's Central Planning School, about three thousand students gathered the morning of March 12 and drafted their own declaration to the Sejm. Like the polytechnic students, they underlined their desire to help advance socialism in Poland and to improve cooperation between workers and the intelligentsia. In addition, they wanted the incarcerated students freed, the militia investigated, police violence stopped, and the press censured for falsely reporting on the events. Lastly, they called on students at other schools to hold peaceful rallies and avoid conflict with the militia. These students too declared that they had nothing to do with Zionism, that the press lied—they were working for socialism, not against it.[73] During the meeting, one student presented the draft of an open letter to the Student Union that more closely represented the party's stance. It blamed former Stalinists for instigating student protests, rejected "the resolution of the *World Rabbinical Assembly* [*światowe zgromadzenie rabinów*]" as having "nothing in common with academic youths," and faulted the Student Union for supporting the organizers of the rallies. The Department II officer who drew up the report on this gathering was puzzled by the comment on the World Rabbinical Assembly, a term outside of communist discourse meant to indicate that a cabal of Jews were behind the wave of protest. Probably, it originated from the anti-Jewish stereotype that Jews had a central organization that coordinated Jewish malevolent activities, the Elders of Zion, and from the actual Jewish assembly (the Council of Four Lands) that organized Jewish life in pre-partition Poland.[74] The student speaking against the

71. Igal Halfin, *Intimate Enemies: Demonizing the Bolshevik Opposition, 1918–1928* (Pittsburgh, PA: University of Pittsburgh Press, 2007), 24–25, 240–44.

72. Praha, 12.III.1968, Do wszystkich studentów warszawskich, AIPN 0296/99, vol. 1.

73. AIPN BU MSW II 6051, 67–69.

74. Document 7, in *Marzec '68: między tragedia a podłością*, ed. Grzegorz Sołtysiak and Jożef Stępień, 199–202.

protests combined traditional antisemitic ideas with a communist vocabulary, exemplifying a growing current beyond just party circles.

Students kept busy in other cities too as the protests spread beyond Poland's main universities. In a country with a long history of clandestine activity, activists hurried to print leaflets and spread the news about what had happened in Warsaw. They publicized their demands, encouraging others to take action. Radio Free Europe also broadcast the activists' declarations. Students at other universities quickly organized and created similar lists of demands from their local university authorities and party cells.

On March 12, in Łódź, about a thousand students participated in an afternoon meeting at the university's library. They came from academic institutions across the city, including the university, the famed Łódź Film School, and the Łódź Polytechnic; the Security Services noted that the Łódź Film School students pushed for the most extreme agenda. The organizers invited participants to take part in another rally that would be held in a week.[75]

On the same day, in the Lower Silesian city of Wrocław, students also held street rallies in support of their colleagues in Warsaw. Protesters from Wrocław University and the Wrocław Polytechnic carried banners criticizing the press and praising the students in the capital; they marched to the main hall of the polytechnic, where the rector and vice rector exchanged thoughts on recent events with student representatives, who offered various resolutions. That afternoon, at a gathering at Wrocław University, students agreed on a resolution.[76]

In Poznań, about a thousand demonstrators met at the Mickiewicz monument near the Adam Mickiewicz University and chanted slogans supporting jailed students, calling on the government to adopt "the Czech model." A representative from the university invited the demonstrators to participate at an assembly at the university that evening. The gathering was well attended, and after some loud discussion, the students marched to the party's County Committee building, shouting more antigovernment slogans.[77]

In the port city of Gdańsk, four thousand people came to the Gdańsk Polytechnic's auditorium and approved a resolution that expressed solidarity with Warsaw's students, demanded less stringent censorship, and

75. Document 2, AK AO IV.43.23-Łódź; Document 8, in *Marzec '68: między tragedia a podłością*, ed. Grzegorz Sołtysiak and Jozef Stępień, 203–9.

76. Document 8, in *Marzec '68: między tragedią a podłością*, ed. Grzegorz Sołtysiak and Jozef Stępień, 203–9.

77. AAN KC PZPR 1737, 32. 12.III.1968, Informacja Wydziału Organizacyjnego KC PZPR, in Zaremba, *Marzec 1968*, 2:61–63.

condemned the Citizens' Militia.[78] That evening, the longtime minister of foreign affairs, Adam Rapacki, gave a speech on international policy at a local student club. In office since 1956, Rapacki was not part of the partisan group, and he objected behind the scenes to the anti-Zionist campaign; he had not come to Gdańsk to present the government's position on recent events. The meeting itself was quiet, but outside, about a thousand people protested the government's recent actions. They burned newspapers, sang songs, and shouted slogans such as "Down with Moczar!"; "We want freedom of speech!"; and "We demand the truth!"[79]

In Kraków, a group of university rectors appealed to local students not to participate in any upcoming protests. Characterizing those who had joined demonstrations as an alienated minority, the rectors lauded the good behavior of Kraków's students and pleaded with them: "We deeply believe that in the city of Kraków, the cradle of Polish culture and scholarship, academic youths will appreciate our friendly advice and will take the steps that the rest of society will see as proof of your maturity."[80] The Security Services reported that on March 12 a group of students from Warsaw traveled to Kraków to help organize a rally to be held the next day.[81]

After five days of demonstration and discussion, the representative committee elected at Warsaw Polytechnic prepared a new list of demands in response to the press's portrayal of the protesters as troublemakers, decadent youths, and Zionists. When the polytechnic's senate and the rector's office organized an official meeting to discuss the situation on March 13, the committee, which included delegates from all the departments, presented the new resolution. Among its sixteen points, they insisted that all civic liberties (*swobody obywatelskie*) specified in the Polish Constitution, including freedom of speech and creative freedom, be upheld; that sympathetic professors not be disciplined; that all forms of antisemitic, anti-Soviet, and anti-Zionist provocation cease; and that full immunity be extended to participants in the rallies.[82] A sense of national momentum had exhilarated the students, who were now proposing unprecedented reforms. Warsaw

78. AIPN 0746/15, 77–78; documents 3–4, AK AO IV.43.22-Gdansk.
79. AIPN BU MSW II 964, 33; AAN KC PZPR, 1737, 33; 12.III.1968, Informacja Wydziału Organizacyjnego KC PZPR, in Zaremba, *Marzec 1968*, 2:61–63.
80. Document 8, in *Marzec '68: między tragedia a podłością*, ed. Grzegorz Sołtysiak and Jożef Stępień, 203–9.
81. AIPN 01288/22, 157.
82. Notatka Służbowa, dnia 13.III.1968r, AIPN 0296/99, vol. 1.

University's senate assigned a special commission to examine recent events: in its recommendations, it called on the authorities to create conditions for an open dialogue between professors and students. Stating that they worked, not for the regime, but rather for the university, the members of the senate sent a clear message to the students that they would support their cause.[83]

In Kraków, street demonstrations and clashes with the Citizens' Militia continued. On the morning of March 13, about two thousand students from the city's universities came together at the Jagiellonian University, carrying signs calling for student-worker solidarity and expressing support for Warsaw's students. A hastily elected interuniversity committee then drafted a resolution and called for a sit-in at the universities. In addition to the demands and claims that had become quite standard at the time, they argued that the desire to develop socialism in Poland drove the protests; no one stood behind their activities; they had done everything of their own free will.[84] The demonstrators then split into two groups: one marched toward the city's main square, where they encountered the Citizens' Militia, while the second protested by the Collegium Novum, chanting slogans against the authorities. Despite the rector's promise, the Citizens' Militia entered the premises of Jagiellonian University, beating and arresting students. They went from room to room, striking and dragging protesters. Militiamen used clubs and tear gas, chasing many down the city's main streets. Later, the militia claimed that students had thrown stones and metal; two militiamen were reportedly wounded. Twenty-one "top-level activists" were arrested. That evening, the rector sent an official complaint against the militia, noting his promise to the students that the police would not enter the university.[85]

In Poznań, about two thousand students met again by the Mickiewicz monument. Carrying signs reading "The press lies," "We support the students of Warsaw, Kraków, and Wrocław," and "Students have the same goals as workers," they shouted, "Down with the clubs!"; "Everyone is with us!"; and

83. Warszawa dnia 13.III.1968 roku, Komunikat Komisji Senatu UW, AIPN 0296/99.

84. 13.III.1968r., Rezolucja uczestników wiecu studenckiego w Krakowie, in Zaremba, *Marzec 1968*, 2:86–87; Ryszard Terkecki, "Kraków," in *Oblicza Marca 1968*, ed. Konrad Rokicki and Sławomir Stępień (Warsaw: Instytut Pamięci Narodowej, Komisja Ścigania Zbrodni przeciwko Narodowi Polskiemu, 2004), 138–39.

85. AAN KC PZPR 1737, 34; documents 100, 102, in Kwiek Julian, ed., *Marzec 1968 w Karkowie w dokumentach.*

"Democracy!" They also sang the "Internationale" and the Polish national hymn. When a group of militiamen asked the students to disperse, they refused, and the men with clubs forcefully broke up the demonstration. They arrested 116 protesters, the majority of whom were released the next day.[86] In Gdańsk, about three thousand students from the Tri-Cities area (Gdańsk, Gdynia, and Sopot) participated in a rally at the local polytechnic and elected a student delegation charged with visiting local factories and persuading workers to join the demonstrations.[87] Government reports from Gdańsk emphasized the presence of Jews protesting or cheering on the students.[88] The local branch of the Security Services reported that among Gdańsk Polytechnic students there was a "well-known group of Jewish descent" that "stood out" since it had "plenty" of money to spend on parties and drinking.[89]

On March 14, at the High School of Agriculture (Szkoła Główna Gospodarstwa Wiejskiego) in Warsaw, three thousand people demonstrated, including members of the school's senate and many faculty members. At the end of three "quiet and peaceful" hours, the students passed a resolution that they had prepared in advance and that requested the release of all students from jail, accurate reporting in the press, and formal assurances from the government that it would respect the autonomy of the universities. In addition, the students protested attempts to drive a wedge between workers and students and declared that they were for "socialism and democracy."[90] At many of Wrocław's institutes of higher education, students got together and discussed the resolutions passed the previous day (March 13). They decided to start a forty-eight-hours sit-in that night, and a large group of protesters marched to the polytechnic and tried to get to the city center, only to be confronted and attacked by the Citizens' Militia.[91] In Szczecin, about

---

86. AAN KC PZPR 1737, Ministerstwo Spraw Wewnętrznych Gabinet Ministra, Załącznik do biul. wewn. nr. 63/68.

87. AIPN 0746/15, 7, 17; part 2, document 11, in *Marzec '68: między tragedia a podłością*, ed. Grzegorz Sołtysiak and Józef Stępień (Warsaw: Profi, 1998), 218–22.

88. Ministerstwo Spraw Wewnętrznych Gabinet Ministra, Załącznik do biul.wewn. nr. 63/68 AAN KC PZPR 1737. For instance, a report filed with the Ministry of Internal Affairs claimed that a junior faculty member at the Normal School, Anna Kunert, publicly expressed "satisfaction" about the protests, which she viewed as part of a "justified" struggle with the government; a worker at the State Farms Administration, Stanisław Modzelewski, someone "known for his Zionist outlook," also backed the demonstrators.

89. AIPN 0746/15, 7.

90. 13–14 marca 1968r. Informacja Wydziału Organizacyjnego KC PZPR, in Zaremba, *Marzec 1968*, 2:89–90.

91. 14 marca 1968r., Informacja Wydziału Organizacyjnego KC PZPR, in Zaremba, *Marzec 1968*, 95–96.

three hundred people gathered by the Adam Mickiewicz memorial, burned the day's newspapers, and shouted slogans; they too faced the Citizens' Militia. Later that day (March 14), a group of five hundred students from the city's polytechnic and the medical school assembled at the polytechnic. The rector tried to calm them, but they shouted him down with cries of "We want the truth!"; "The press lies!"; and "We are with the workers!" The rally carried on late into the night. The local Security Services staff "determined that eighteen people stood out for their hostile attitude, of whom six were of Jewish descent."[92] They were not arrested, but the Security Services began to draw up lists of Szczecin residents considered troublesome. In Toruń on the same day, at Mikolaj Kopernik University, about eight hundred students gathered, as did the rector, the deans, and party officials. Some students "gave hostile and demagogical shouts," including, "We support Warsaw's students!"; "Autonomy for academia!"; "Why do the police beat students?"; and "Socialism without clubs!" Such shouts, according to the author of the party's report, demonstrated that the students had not the slightest idea what is meant by *Zionism* and *antisemitism*.[93]

In spite of the increasingly venomous propaganda campaign, the arrests, and the beatings, students boycotted classes and thronged to rallies. With the spread of protests to major cities, the Ministry of Internal Affairs decided to strengthen Citizens' Militia forces around the country. From Warsaw the militia's central command dispatched 800 militiamen to Kraków, 130 to Gdańsk, and 80 to Poznań.[94] The ministry also reported that the local Volunteer Reserves of the Citizens' Militia (ORMO) gathered in large numbers to help restore law and order; in Kraków, for instance, about 6,500 men were recruited to participate in the extraordinary policing action.[95]

As part of the attack on protestors, the Socialist Youth Union branch at Warsaw University circulated a plea to students on March 12. The Youth Union knew perfectly well, it said, that many of the participants in the street demonstrations were "hooligans" and "criminals"; regular students did not

---

92. 14 marca 1968r., Sytuacja w środowisku akademickim Szczecina, part 2, document 15, in *Marzec '68: między tragedia a podłością*, ed. Grzegorz Sołtysiak and Jóżef Stępień (Warsaw: Profi, 1998), 232–34.

93. AIPN 01288/22, 258; 14 marca 1968r., Informacja Wydziału Organizacyjnego KC PZPR, in Zaremba, *Marzec 1968*, 2:97.

94. Ministerstwo Spraw Wewnętrznych Gabinet Ministra, Załącznik do biul.wewn. nr. 62/68, AAN KC PZPR, 1737.

95. Part 2, document 12, in *Marzec '68: między tragedia a podłością*, ed. Grzegorz Sołtysiak and Jóżef Stępień (Warsaw: Profi, 1998), 223–24.

smash windows or break into stores. They had to refuse to hear the organizers of the rallies, "who are responsible for the sad consequences of the latest events."[96] In an appeal to "Polish Youths" published in *Trybuna Ludu*, the veterans' organization ZBoWiD similarly reflected on recent events. Who, asked the veterans, was in a better position to evaluate the country's direction than the partisans, former members of underground movements and former concentration camp prisoners, who had risked all to defeat Hitler? The authority of the war still held strong in Poland, and ZBoWiD never missed an opportunity to emphasize that point. According to the organization, the students of 1968 had much to learn from the youth of the 1940s, who had made true sacrifices for the nation. Above all, students ought to avoid the example of a small number of peers who were working in the service of Zionism, a foreign ideology "most active in the slanderous campaign against People's Poland and socialism."[97] The by-now familiar enemy appeared: "those known for years for their national nihilism," Zionist malcontents who brought together all the "oppositional circles." The veterans urged the students to reject the reform movement and rely on their good education to avoid any "mistakes." Finally, ZBoWiD called on the students to behave in the "spirit of our nation's beautiful and progressive traditions, and our struggle for freedom, independence and socialism."[98] Once more, the lines were drawn between the nation and the other, the nihilist, Jewish enemies and the innocent Polish students, misled by those conspiring against them.

On the same days as antigovernment protests, the party apparatus organized counterrallies in factories and offices throughout the country, in which worker representatives harshly criticized the students and expressed support for the regime. In the Poznań area, the speakers demanded that the authorities prosecute not only those who organized and attended "extreme disturbances" (*ekscesy awanturnicze*) but also their parents.[99] In Kraków factories, party cells held similar gatherings and passed resolutions expressing outrage at the students' behavior. The Kraków County Party Committee counted about fifty such rallies, in which three hundred thousand workers

---

96. AIPN, 012/2811, t. 2, 35.

97. *Trybuna Ludu*, March 13, 1968. Mieczysław Moczar, the minister of internal affairs, was the president of ZBoWiD, and the ministry could easily have dictated the statement.

98. *Trybuna Ludu*, March 13, 1968.

99. 12. III. 1968, Informacja Wydziału Organizacyjnego KC PZPR, in Zaremba, *Marzec 1968*, 2:61–63.

participated.[100] Party cells also wrote letters and resolutions in support of the party. In Warsaw, several factories adopted motions endorsing Józef Kępa, the influential local party secretary. One such motion demanded that the media be "cleansed" of "elements" that worked for "hostile forces" of "ideological diversion." Another called on Warsaw University to fire Kołakowski, Brus, and others who consorted with Poland's enemies.[101] A factory in Rzeszów passed a resolution urging the party to "destroy the groups of Zionists who pursue antisocialist programs ... and are more sympathetic to the politics of Israel's [Moshe] Dayan than to building socialism in our country."[102]

The government also arranged a mass rally in Katowice on March 14. Press releases spoke of a hundred thousand party members gathered in Feliks Dzierżyński Square to listen to the heads of the Katowice Party Committee. Many carried signs in support of the government, with slogans such as "Śląsk (Silesia) is always loyal to the party," "Work—Study—Peace," "Long live the People's government," "Cleanse the party of Zionists," and "Fire Zionists from their jobs." During the public meeting, Edward Gierek, a well-known party leader, the first secretary of the Katowice Party Committee (in December 1970 he would replace Gomułka as first secretary), gave a lengthy speech broadcast on the radio and television. Gierek reached out to Poland's workers, praising them as the foundation of the party's "strength and mind." Throughout his speech, he used the word *nation*, pointing to Poland's "revolutionary history" of struggle for "Polishness." The socialist government presented itself as the successor of the tradition of preserving the Polish nation under foreign rule. Gierek also spoke of the upcoming party convention, where the "millions of members of the Polish family" would decide how to continue building socialism. Katowice's working class, said Gierek, had been "outraged" at the news of the "deplorable" events at Warsaw University. Most young people had nothing to do with the recent events; most were grateful for what they had been given and "behaved in a dignified manner." Ingrates amounted to a small minority of "troublemakers" and "political adventurers" exploiting the naivete of the

100. Part 2, document 8, in *Marzec '68: między tragedia a podłością*, ed. Grzegorz Sołtysiak and Józef Stępień, 203–9.

101. 14–16 marca 1968r., Informacja Wydziału Organizacyjnego KC PZPR, Aktualna sytuacja w Warszawie, in Zaremba, *Marzec 1968*, 2:121.

102. 15–16 marca 1968r., Informacja Wydziału Organizacyjnego KC PZPR, in Zaremba, *Marzec 1968*, 2:126.

majority to ignite the riots. They had been joined by gangs of "hooligans" from the margins of society who reveled at any chance to participate in brawls. As it turned out, the troublemakers found themselves ostracized by the majority of students. The division Gierek sketched implied a fundamental antipathy between Jews—his language referring to the organizers of the protests implied "Jew" repeatedly—and the good Catholic working class of Poland. Gierek asked next who was behind the agitators, who wanted to harm relations with the Soviet Union, arouse social unrest, and undermine the nation. His answer: Roman Zambrowski, Stanisław Staszewski, Słonimski, Kisielewski, and Jasienica; four out of the five were Jews. To advance their anti-Polish goals, argued Gierek, they were trying to turn young people against "their country and their nation." Why? For the sake of "obscurantism," "political ignorance," and "social backwardness" and, most importantly, "to control souls [*sięgać po rząd dusz*]." For such people, Mickiewicz was only a pretext. They were the "dirty froth that rose to the tops of the waves of the October events eleven years ago and has yet to be fully removed from the current of our lives."[103] This was the language of communism that had been used since Lenin's era. Being in opposition did not mean holding different political views; it meant either suffering from a lack of class consciousness that could be corrected through education or having an irredeemable soul possessed by harmful intentions. The opposition was accused of trying to control the souls of workers.[104] The local party secretary then linked the protesters to "revisionists": they wanted Poland to break away from the socialist camp and return to capitalism, a move that would destroy "the future and hope." Such "reactionary, hostile" politics tempted some, the sort of people the local Citizens' Militia had apprehended that very day: students from Warsaw on their way to the Katowice area. As to all of the falsehoods spoken about the party and antisemitism, this was simply slander: the party would never discriminate against citizens because of their origins and would always combat racism. Gierek next called on the youths to remember their homeland and to come to its "defense." He also expressed solidarity with Warsaw's workers, who had stood firm against "the organizers of anti-Polish rallies," and he saluted Gomułka, the leader of the party. He concluded, "Long live our wonderful nation—the Polish nation!" The message was clear: to keep the (mostly Jewish) opposition

---

103. *Trybuna Ludu*, March 15, 1968.
104. This issue has been studied for the Soviet Union by Igal Halfin; see Halfin, *Intimate Enemies*.

from stealing souls, influencing the naive and the weak, the working class had to go on the offensive.[105]

The party's leading newspapers took it on themselves to explain Zionist ideology to the Polish masses. On March 15, "after many requests from readers," the party's chief organ, *Trybuna Ludu*, had printed a long essay entitled "What Is Zionism?" From Theodor Herzl's *Jewish State* to Britain's Balfour Declaration, the early history of Zionism was presented as a conspiracy of world Jewry. Zionists worked to deepen the identity of people of Jewish descent and "inhibit the process of assimilation" so that all Jews would immigrate to Israel. Thus, the article explained, Zionists both provoked antisemitism and received the support of antisemites. The article reminded its readers that communists had criticized Zionism from the beginning, seeing it as a "nationalist and racist" ideology that broke with the working class and served its exploiters. Now, two decades after Israel was established, Zionists had finally realized they could not bring all the Jews to Israel and changed their strategy. By agitating and fueling nationalism and religious fanaticism in Jewish circles, they were able to collect, "as is generally known," vast sums of money from American Jews. These funds permitted Israel to develop expansionist goals: American and Western imperialists, warned the article in *Trybuna Ludu*, wanted to use the Middle East as a way to obtain Arab oil and as a "launching pad" for an attack against the Soviet Union and other socialist countries; Poland was in fact already under attack. Finally, the newspaper asserted that Zionists called anyone who dared attack them antisemites. Clearly and simply, the party organ outlined recent Jewish history and Zionist ideology in a manner that linked Zionism to recent events in Poland. Time and again the article referred to the wealth of Jews, their ability to organize, and their inability to accept criticism, anti-Jewish tropes much used since the beginning of the century.[106]

As the press and party campaign against the protests grew louder, so did the determination and the number of protesters, who wanted their voices to be heard. The brutality of the militia also helped boost protests. In Warsaw and Wrocław, students staged sit-ins at the universities. Resolution after resolution demanded the publication of the "truth about the events" and a thorough investigation into the behavior of the Citizens'

---

105. *Trybuna Ludu*, March 15, 1968
106. "Co to jest Syjonizm," *Trybuna Ludu*, March 15, 1968.

Militia. Though the government gave no indication that it would negotiate, let alone accede to student demands, the reformist government of neighboring Czechoslovakia gave protesters hope. The Polish Security Services intercepted enthusiastic letters from Czech students to their Polish counterparts. In a letter from the agricultural college in Prague to the students of Warsaw and Kraków, Czech and Slovak youth expressed their "concern" about the brutal treatment of protestors and mentioned that they understood that Polish students wanted to "democratize socialism rather than topple it."[107]

Unrest continued around Poland's major cities. In Kraków, on March 15, a group of three thousand students gathered to decide on their next moves. Students and professors addressed the crowd, and in the end the protestors decided to return home quietly. The local party officials reported that the students "decided not to strike and rally because of their trust in the party." It may well be that after the Citizens' Militia entered the dorms and dragged students out, protesters preferred not to clash with police again.[108] In Gdańsk, the future cradle of the solidarity movement, at around two o'clock that afternoon, a crowd of about four thousand gathered by the Gdańsk Polytechnic and the Baltic Opera Building. The protestors—university and high school students and workers—shouted anti-party slogans and burned newspapers. Claiming that the group was blocking traffic, the Citizens' Militia decided to intervene and attacked with clubs and tear gas; the demonstrators reacted with cries of "Gestapo! Gestapo!" Three thousand uniformed and plainclothes militiamen participated in the action. In all, the Security Services estimated that up to twenty thousand people took part in the demonstration.[109] In Katowice, just a day after the progovernment rally at which local party secretary Gierek had spoken, a few hundred protesters rallied in the city's main square. Students burned newspapers and shouted, "The press lies!"; "The government lies!"; and "Freedom of the press!" Skirmishes between the militia and the demonstrators lasted all afternoon, ending only at eight o'clock that night. All told, 223 people were arrested, of

---

107. AIPN BU MSW II 964, 43, 46, 53; AIPN BU MSW II 5239, 33.

108. AIPN 01288/22, 260; Documents 115–22, in *Marzec 1968 w Krakowie w dokumentach*, ed. Kwiek Julian (Kraków: Ksiegarnia Akademicka: Fundacja Centrum Dokumentacji Czynu Niepodległościowego, 2005); 15 marca 1968r., Załącznik do Biuletynu Wewnętrznego MSW, in Zaremba, *Marzec 1968*, 2:112–13.

109. AIPN BU MSW II 5239, 36; AIPN 0746/15, 27, 80–81; AIPN 01288/22, 265; AIPN 01288/22, Kronika Wydarzen od 30.I do 15.III; 1968r., Informacja Wydziału Organizacyjnego KC PZPR, in Zaremba, *Marzec 1968*, 2:116–17.

whom only 23 were students; the majority were workers, contrary to the government's assertions that students took the lead in the events. In fact, what brought demonstrators together was generation; born during or after the war, in the United States they would be considered baby boomers.[110]

Warsaw's students decided to organize a strike: they would not attend classes, and some of them would occupy the university's buildings. On the afternoon of March 15, about a thousand students gathered at the main hall of Warsaw University. When the rector appeared and asked them to "quietly" return to their studies, they replied by shouting "Rector, resign!"[111] Yet it was the beginning of the end of the student protest movement. After the violence and mass arrests, the exhausted students started to realize they were fighting a losing battle. The sit-in organized by Wrocław students ended when they understood that the university's heads were not going to support them; in a leaflet, the leaders of the protest thanked the people of the region for their "moral and material support."[112] On March 18, students in Kraków also finished their sit-in and announced that they would return to classes. They claimed that the strike had proved their unity and their strength, and they ended their declaration with the words "Long live Poland. Long live the union with the intelligentsia. Long live the Constitution."[113] In the capital, about fifteen hundred students gathered at Warsaw University's main auditorium to discuss further steps.

After a rather long public silence, First Secretary Gomułka finally announced he would give a speech to party activists on March 19. In the period before the speech, the TSKŻ still hoped to continue its normal operations, despite government pressure and large budget cuts. The anti-Zionist campaign, which intensified daily, worried many Jews in Poland, even though they felt that they had nothing to do with Zionism. As described above, during the meeting of the central board of TZKŻ on March 13,

---

110. AIPN Ka 07–240, t.1, 64–65; AIPN Ka 223–7, 67; AIPN 01288/22, Kronika Wydarzen od 30.I do 15.III; Jarosław Neja, "Katowice i województwo katowickie," in *Oblicza Marca 1968*
ed. Konrad Rokicki and Sławomir Stępień (Warsaw: Instytut Pamięci Narodowej, Komisja Ścigania Zbrodni przeciwko Narodowi Polskiemu, 2004), 99–100. In another example, one anonymous student from Warsaw claimed in a letter that "the workers of FSO and Rosa Luxemburg [a car factory and a light bulb factory] collected thirty thousand zloty to help students pay fines." AIPN BU MSW II 5239, 28, 34–35.

111. AIPN 01288/22, 264–65.

112. 15–16 marca 1968r., Dalsze informacje KW o sytuacji wśród studentów i nastrojach, in Zaremba, *Marzec 1968*, 2:131–32.

113. 16–18 marca 1968r., Sytuacja w srodowisku akademickim Krakowa, in Zaremba, *Marzec 1968*, 2:146–147.

members of the organization expressed anger at insinuations that there was any connection between events in the Middle East and the current student unrest in Warsaw, between Club Babel and the reformist opposition. Domb, the president of the TSKŻ, expressed fury at the antisemitic article in *Słowo Powszechne* and amazement that it had not been censored.[114] On March 17, at a meeting of the Katowice TSKŻ club, he still urged activists to carry on as usual until the storm passed. Domb assured them that he would answer allegations that the group was a Zionist stronghold, and he once more communicated his outrage at the identification of student protesters with Club Babel: "Someone like, for example, Aleksander Smolar, [Hirsh] Smolar's older son, had absolutely nothing to do with the TSKŻ—never! . . . Michnik, one of the organizers of that club in the old city . . . had nothing to do with either Club Babel or with the association."[115] Several people at the meeting urged the association's leaders to clarify to the public the difference between a Zionist and a Jew and to assure the public that Jews as Jews were not to blame for recent events. One asked, with evident frustration, "How could a party member also be a Zionist?"[116] Zionism was a political, not an ethnic, identification. Despite everything that had happened, many still believed that the situation could be cleared up, that it was all a misunderstanding.

An anti-Jewish purge was already in full swing: officials in party and state administration had lost their positions and their party membership during the preceding weeks. A few days after the first demonstrations, Roman Zambrowski was removed from the party, and later the government fired vice ministers Jan Grudzinski, Jan Górecki, and Fryderyk Topolski, fathers of the arrested student leaders Irena Grudzinska, Wictor Górecki, and Krzysztof Topolski, all of Jewish descent. The first dismissals sent a clear sign to the protesters that their parents would also pay the price for their behavior and that Jews would be singled out.[117] In this case the fathers paid for the sins of the sons.

On March 19, Gomułka at last presented his official interpretation of recent events. He began his exposé to party activists by assuring them that the "entire country" stood against the "illegal" actions of the students.[118]

---

114. AIPN BU MSW II 6658, 30–34.
115. AIPN BU MSW II 831, 2.
116. AIPN BU MSW II 831, 2–5.
117. Eisler, *Rok '68*, 570–71.
118. ANN 237/V- 903, 158–99. Gomułka's speech is widely available online, for example: https://www.mpolska24.pl/post/4240/przemowienie-na-spotkaniu-z-warszawskim-aktywem-partyjnym-wygloszone-19-marca-1968.

"Using facts and documents," he set out to describe the genesis of the movement, beginning with the special meeting of the Warsaw branch of the Polish Writers' Union. Gomułka cited the writers' statement, which included a demand for the reopening of *Dziady*. He went on to say that Mickiewicz's play had not been censored in the postwar era, that it in fact had been printed in hundreds of thousands of copies and staged seventeen times, including a television production. Gomułka was careful not to attack the Polish hero Mickiewicz or his work, blaming instead the director and the leading actors of the banned production, who, he said, had transformed the play. The first secretary described how the audience had cheered after certain lines calling for Polish liberation from the "hands of Moscow." Surely the party could not allow the staging of a play reshaped from "anti-tsarist" to "anti-Soviet" and "could not close its eyes" to performances that became "political demonstrations" against the regime. Gomułka reminded his audience that the Soviet Army had helped liberate Poland from the German occupation and that Poland's alliance with the Soviet Union was the cornerstone of "the safety, independence, and development of Poland." Mickiewicz appreciated this important connection; he was a "true internationalist and patriot." But Dejmek's production harmed Soviet-Polish relations. And on the day the production closed, the "openly hostile political demonstration" moved from the theater to the streets. Gomułka went on to explain just who "stood behind" the special meeting of the Writers' Union and the protests surrounding *Dziady*. How could anyone criticize a government that had spent billions of zlotys on culture? One critic was Paweł Jasienica. According to Gomułka, the secret interests and motivations of Jasienica and his friends explained the resolution of the Warsaw branch of the Polish Writers' Union. Gomułka openly accused Jasienica of informing on his companions to the Stalinist regime in return for his freedom after the authorities captured him and his fellow "bandits" in 1945. Jasienica had been trained in "clandestine work" against People's Poland; he knew how to turn young people against the party and use "patriotism" against the regime. The first secretary also claimed that Jasienica was responsible for the student petition in support of *Dziady*, a tool used to scare other students into participating in further protests.

The next chapter in Gomułka's narrative opened with a birthday party: "A group of students, mainly of Jewish descent and known for their revisionism,"[119] met at the home of Jacek Kuroń. Under the cover of a party,

---

119. ANN 237/V- 903, 158–99.

they planned the rally held on March 8. When fifteen hundred students gathered to protest the treatment of Michnik and Szlajfer, the Warsaw party leadership had to mobilize the Citizens' Militia, which was met with "provocative shouts" and physical violence. Malevolent rumors of a student's death were meant to turn students against the police. Gomułka went on to claim that these intellectuals "learned nothing from history" and "do not understand what is right for Poland." Men like Jasienica, Kisielewski, and Słonimski, the spirit and the instigators of recent demonstrations, put the country at risk and were mostly Jews and revisionist academics. At the same time, claimed the first secretary, the majority of Poland's intelligentsia had remained loyal to the party and to socialism, and he called on the majority to speak up for the government.

Finally, as he neared the end of his speech, Gomułka broached the issue of Jews. "Students of Jewish descent or nationality took an active role in the recent events," he said. This was relevant because Zionism, or Jewish nationalism, endangered Polish socialism "like other nationalisms and reactionary movements." And one could not forget June 1967, when many Polish Jews had wanted "to go to Israel and participate in the war against the Arabs." These "nationalist Jews . . . identified not with Poland but with Israel," and "if one resented them it was a reaction of communists to nationalists—which nationality did not matter." Eventually, the "Jewish Jews" would leave Poland: "The borders are open to anyone who does not want to be a citizen," announced Gomułka.[120]

But not all of the country's Jews were "Jewish Jews"; there was also the type represented by Słonimski, the poet who authored an article on his Jewish identity published in 1924, during a very different period for Jews in Poland. In the piece Gomułka quoted, Słonimski described feeling like "neither a Jew nor a Pole," gazing enviously at Jewish scouts and young Polish soldiers fighting for a cause (clearly, Słonimski could not find a place for himself in a nationalizing world). And Gomułka continued, "We have citizens in our country who feel neither Jewish nor Polish . . . and while we cannot condemn them for that," they should not work in fields "that require complete devotion to the nation." The first secretary of the Polish communist party was at the same time against nationalism and in favor of devotion to the nation. In his view, only a truly faithful Pole—not a Polish Jew with a unique identity—could be trusted to be loyal to socialism and to Poland. In the end, Polish citizens would be judged by "their attitude to socialism and

---

120. ANN 237/V- 903, 158–99.

to the main concerns of our nation," and "loyalty to the homeland, People's Poland," was the main criteria. It may appear that Gomułka had contradicted himself, demanding "national affirmation" while rejecting nationalism, yet his views were in accordance with late communist ideology that combined local national symbols with homegrown communism. Gomułka demanded loyalty to *communist Poland* or *People's Poland*. He indicated that cosmopolitan Jews had taken a leading role in recent protests and were responsible for the mayhem of the previous weeks. During Stalin's era, cosmopolitans were already considered the worst of the group since they could not commit to a point of view, to a nationality—neither Jewish nor Polish—they were rootless and therefore dangerous. Gomułka had no intention of carrying out any reforms or engaging in a dialogue with the protesters. The party would meet only with "lawful" representatives of the students, and it would address only resolutions made in "legal rallies that the rector approved." The time had come for students to return to their studies. In the last part of his speech, Gomułka thanked the workers for supporting their government, accentuating differences between the intelligentsia and the working class. The reformers, "the reactionaries," had circulated lies, but the proletariat stood shoulder to shoulder with the party, as it always had.[121]

In the days after the speech, party cells in factories, offices, and villages sent letters to Comrade Wiesław, expressing their unfailing support for the party and condemning the student demonstrators and the "bankrupt politicians" who led them. In the tradition of the People's Republics, most of the letters were identical, following a certain blueprint. Such letters were part of the party's mechanism for dealing with conflict; through them the rank and file of the party expressed support for the leadership and the proletariat demonstrated its loyalty to the party. In the case of the March demonstrations, in which the younger generation of workers participated, these letters were indispensable. One of the letters the first secretary received was from the State Car Transportation Office in Oświęcim. After they had condemned the "troublemaking politicians" and the "Zionist and revisionist circles" that had attempted to harm Poland, the authors of the letter added a few words about the nearby Nazi camp that had been liberated two dozen years earlier:

> The older ones among us, who remember the bourgeois government of the interwar era, who remember the poverty in the cities and villages, unemployment, lack of opportunity to study in high schools and universities, the political decision to

ally with imperialism, and what came of this policy, the outbreak of World War II provoked by German fascism—we, the united staff of a socialist enterprise, the State Car Transportation Office, from a place where four million people were exterminated, condemn the troublemaking politicians guilty of working against the just path charted by the Polish United Workers' Party, against the People's government, and against the alliance with the Soviet Union.[122]

This passage gives the entire narrative: Polish communists had brought a new age of prosperity, security, and progress to Poland; only an alliance with the Soviets helped maintain Poland's existence after the era of genocide. Following two world wars, this sort of reassurance was precious.

Many more resolutions in the same vein arrived in Gomułka's office over the next few days.[123] Most mentioned "hardworking students" from the working class and the peasantry who had a chance to study thanks to communism. Many letters asked the students to return to universities and "permit peaceful work to continue in our socialist homeland."[124] All demanded a purge of the party and state administration. Thus, organized pressure from the party's rank and file appeared to trigger the purge of Jews and intellectuals after Gomułka's speech.

Despite the onslaught on student leaders and the complete rejection of reform by the party leadership, protests continued. In Warsaw, Kraków, Łódź, and Wrocław, many classes were suspended. The student leadership in Warsaw responded to Gomułka's speech in pamphlets circulated in the capital on March 21.[125] One read:

> The official description of the instigators of recent events, according to which unidentified, bankrupt politicians recruited young people and influenced their minds, is primitive, false, and demagogical. . . . Thanks to our deep awareness of a responsibility toward the noblest civic ideals, toward the unforgettable tradition of student struggles for justice and truth, toward saving the honor of the students of the People's Republic of Poland, toward society and history, we are quite determined to remain firm throughout this dramatic period. . . . We demand the restoration of our good name; we demand the punishment of those responsible for the militia's brutal violence on March 8 and 9 and after. . . . In our struggle we are not alone. . . . People of good will are with us. . . . Long Live Poland! Long Live Socialism! Long live the rule of law and democracy. History will be with us.[126]

122. AAN 237/V-749, 135–36.
123. AAN 237/V-749, 33, 41.
124. AAN 237/V-749, 52.
125. AIPN 0296/99, 4:97.
126. *Odezwa do obywateli Polskiej Rzeczpospoliy Ludowej*, 21.III.68, AIPN 0296/99, vol. 1.

The students now cast themselves as rebels—just like Mickiewicz, whom the Russians exiled from his native Polish-Lithuanian lands—and as the successors of those who had risen up against occupying armies, taking up a distinctly Polish and patriotic discourse.

Despite the arrests of the first tier of the student leadership, new organizers emerged, and for some time the protests continued. On March 21, rallies were held at the universities and polytechnics in Warsaw, Wrocław, and Łódź, with leaders calling for a thirty-six-hour strike. At Warsaw Polytechnic, strikers hung large signs from the main building expressing solidarity with the working class, explaining the students' position, and asking for the community's help. The students took hold of offices, controlled the entrances to the universities, brought food from outside, and refused to back down. On March 22, a crowd of about four thousand students convened in the school's main hall. The organizers announced that they had received some support from the community and declared they would continue the protests. That afternoon, about seven thousand students also demonstrated by the polytechnic building on Noakowski Street. Around Warsaw University, groups gathered, shouting slogans such as "Socialism does not include batons," "Hands off the professors," and "Freedom is not a privilege; it's a right." The Citizens' Militia broke up the gatherings, arresting several protesters.[127]

Two days later, the students at Warsaw University and Warsaw Polytechnic chose a new "interinstitutional committee" to coordinate protests. Again, drawing on the Polish conspiratorial past, the students formed a secret council. The committee hoped to organize a statewide student demonstration on April 22, followed by a big rally in Warsaw on May 1. The Security Services reported that the leaders created a coordination body with student representatives from Poland's main cities; they met in Wrocław on March 25.[128] Among them was Leon Sfard, son of the TSKŻ vice president and a third-year student at Warsaw University who represented his department, Physics and Mathematics, on the university's student committee. Years later, Sfard remembered that one of the other students suggested that he step down, since as a Jew he would attract the attention of the regime, which had been "horribly" sprouting anti-Jewish slogans. He did not, and he felt that his Polish identity came under attack.[129]

127. AIPN MSW c.s.k sygn 126/17e, k. 46, 39–64.
128. AIPN 01288/25, MSW Department II, *notatka*, Warszawa dnia 28 marca 1968 roku.
129. Piotr Osęka, *My Ludzie z Marca*, 325.

The committees did not operate for long, and on March 26 and 27, the Citizens' Militia arrested the vast majority of student leaders throughout the country. Among the fifteen the police picked up in Warsaw was Leon Sfard. During the arrests, the militia apprehended several documents, including resolutions passed in universities, various pamphlets explaining recent events, a petition to the Sejm, and correspondence between the students. Along with a typewriter, paper, and other supplies needed for printing, the authorities had all the proof they needed of a conspiracy.[130]

The last gasp of the Polish student movement of 1968 was the rally held at Warsaw University on March 28, which drew about twelve hundred participants. A "Declaration of the Student Movement" insisted that protests would continue and that the reform movement was not finished. In a section entitled "Law and Human Rights," the reformists called on the regime to uphold the Polish Constitution and give the Sejm real powers. The manifesto ended with the words "A Poland that is socialist, democratic, and orderly is what we all desire!"[131] The last wave of arrests, with an intensification of the press campaign against Jews and purges of anyone connected to student leaders, led to the end of protest activities. A few more pamphlets were seized, but mass activities ceased. The students had failed to gain public allies within the regime, and they were never able to push their reformist agenda beyond declarations and lists. The students did not succeed in forming an alliance with either workers or the Catholic Church. Despite the church's antagonism toward the socialist regime and the participation of many young workers in rallies, the student leadership fell short in its attempts to bring older workers or the worker leadership into a joint struggle against the regime, as had happened in neighboring Czechoslovakia.

The ruling communist party never displayed any inclination to negotiate with the students; instead, it attacked their leaders and presented them as spoiled cosmopolitan/Zionist Jews and their activities as a threat to Poland's stability and security. The students, who did not have a clear view of what was happening within the party, hoped that a Dubček might appear to save Polish socialism. The young leadership failed to understand the centrality of Moczar's worldview to the regime's position. They perceived the "partisans" as illiterate and unintellectual, the antithesis to their

---

130. AIPN 01288/25, MSW Department II, *notatka*, Warszawa dnia 28 marca 1968 roku.

131. Document 52, in *Opozycja wobec rządów komunistycznych w Polsce 1956–1976: wybór dokumentów*, ed. Zygmunt Hemmerling and Marek Nadolski, 321–25. Drafted by Jakub Karpinski, Jadwiga Lewicka, and Andrzej Mencwel.

brand of enlightened socialism, and did not comprehend the depth of suspicion toward "foreign elements" and Jews within the party. The national cause of the national poet around which the students had hoped to rally the Poles did not prove urgent enough. Gomułka and Moczar, the champions of communist nationalism, managed to easily crush the budding revolt, leaving the reform movement in shambles.

6

"ZIONISM IS NOT A DANGER TO POLAND"

The Purge Erupts, Surges, and Ends

AFTER THE DUST OF THE MARCH PROTESTS SETTLED, the Polish communist regime escalated its attempts to purge the party and the state of "Zionists" and "revisionists." The party and the Ministry of Internal Affairs went on the attack, accusing Jews of betraying and backstabbing Poland. From newspaper editorials, party rallies, and party cell meetings, an urgent call came out to Jews to leave the country. The regime encouraged both anyone implicated in the March demonstrations and any Jews involved in Jewish organizations to emigrate. Although the party did not purge only Jews, Jews found themselves ousted even when they had no direct involvement in recent events. Many Jews and intellectuals quickly realized that they had no future in Poland and petitioned to emigrate. The regime did not charge most of the incarcerated students of Jewish descent; the party under Gomułka's leadership preferred to force them to leave the country. After all, the heads of the regime saw Jews as a threat to the stability of the socialist system and to Gomułka's government. Continuing the homogenization project, they wanted to finally rid themselves of this problematic minority, which they had never accepted as part of the socialist nation.

By May the campaign subdued, and Gomułka began to wind down the assault on Jews since he felt, as did others in the party, that the "partisan" faction had gone too far and turned from anti-Zionism to open antisemitism. By the end of the campaign, thousands of Jews had already left Poland. This chapter describes the last attempts of the students to protest the regime's behavior and the government's strong reaction. No longer fighting on the streets, the students printed pamphlets, presenting their truth to the Polish public. The official press reacted with an intensified attack on "world Zionism" and a purge of "Zionists" from the party and state apparatus. Next, the anti-Zionist campaign transformed into open antisemitism reminiscent of the 1930s and 1940s. Once the "Jewish problem" was allowed back into public discourse, the myth of the "Jewish commune" surfaced again. Leading party members found that when they opened the door to antisemitism, they brought in the demons of Polish chauvinism. Polish nationalists for many years accused the ruling communist party of being a "Jewish party," and after March 1968, they got their day in the sun. In late April, Gomułka expressed concerns about the direction of the anti-Zionist campaign, and by the summer of 1968, he had ordered the party members to stop seeking out Zionist enemies.

From March 7 to July 1968, the Ministry of Internal Affairs arrested 2,937 people, including 799 students and 943 workers, disproving the claim that the working class did not support the protests. Within forty-eight hours 1,987 were released, while the rest were either held without trial or prosecuted. Those defined as "hooligans" found themselves in punitive army units.[1] Families of arrested students also came under attack, fired from their jobs and persuaded to resign from the party. The press continued to name demonstrators of Jewish origins and their parents. In one instance, a piece in *Kurier Polski* from March 26 lashed out at medical student Andrzej Neumark and his father, Stanisław Neumark, a director at the Ministry of Arts and Culture. The article claimed that the father enjoyed a high standard of living and vacationed at a luxury country house owned by the government. The director's lifestyle influenced his son, who became part of the "banana youth," a group of spoiled and privileged students. Until his arrest, the son, Andrzej, participated in the protests and worked with Michnik and Szlajfer against the regime. The newspaper presented the Jewish father and his son as belonging to a socioeconomic class alienated from most Poles.[2] Shortly after the article's publication, Stanislaw Neumark lost his position and his party membership.[3]

In the first days of April, professors, public officials, and cultural officers suspected of Zionism, which now meant having Jewish origins or expressing support for the students, lost their jobs. An all-out purge of Zionists thus

---

1. AIPN 01288/24, 189.
2. "Bananowiec," *Kurier Polski*, March 26, 1968.
3. Mieczysław Rakowski, *Dzienniki polityczne 1967–1968* (Warsaw: Iskry, 1999), 180.

began. Warsaw University fired professors Kołakowski, Baczko, Morawski, Bauman, and Hirszowicz, in effect decimating the Philosophy Department, the bastion of intellectual unrest at the university.[4] The Ministry of Internal Affairs reported that the general public was "satisfied" with the cleansing of "Zionist elements" from the party and state and that many looked forward to a brighter future for Poland after the purge. Others expected the universities to be more willing to accept students from working-class or peasant origins. So great was the demand for purge that in the Łódź area, the Security Services claimed, the population was "unhappy" that "no one" had been removed from the party for "pro-Zionist" stances. According to the Security Services, by bringing an end to Zionist and Jewish influences that had plagued the party and academia, causing "economic difficulties," the regime acted in the service of the people, particularly the lower classes.[5]

In Gdańsk, on April 3, the Security Services arrested a group of six young men of Jewish origins, claiming that they had formed a clandestine organization to battle communism. The head of the alleged group was twenty-year-old Jakub Szadaj, a Jew holding an obviously Jewish name who was also active in the TSKŻ. The officers accused the group of making plans to accumulate "weapons and explosives" and take up arms against the communist regime. During the arrests, the police seized typewriters, pamphlets, a radio, and "military jackets," finally getting what they considered to be proof that Jews were scheming to destabilize the country. The Security Services maintained that one Bolesław Piwnica, also a Jew, inspired the young saboteurs. Piwnica admitted he had some knowledge of the group but said he was unaware of its goals. In December 1968, Jakub Szadaj received a ten-year sentence in prison, the longest given following the March events.[6]

In Warsaw, the prosecutor planned to take legal action against fifty-eight people. The Ministry of Internal Affairs officials prepared an internal report specifying the information that the prosecution required. The report brought together the various actors in recent events, tying together different threads and oppositional groups and creating a narrative of the March events. The ministry's report divided the oppositional leadership

---

4. AIPN 0296/240, t.1, 34.

5. AIPN 0296/240, T.3, 1–4, 9–14, 19–21, 25–27, 31–41.

6. AIPN 0296/240, T.3, 24–25; Marek Andrzejewski, *Marzec 1968 w trójmieście* (Warsaw: IPN, 2008), 184–86. In August 1969, it was reduced to six years and eight months. IPN Gd 78/3, accessed July 4, 2020, http://katalog.bip.ipn.gov.pl/informacje/63814. In 1993, the court cleared Szadaj of all charges. He went on to become an activist in the Jewish community in Gdańsk.

into groups: "instigators," "commandos," and demonstration participants who had "personal ties" to the regime. Composed by high-ranking officers, the report mentioned two more categories of importance to recent events: "external" and "internal" instigators, the masterminds behind the student protests. The list of external enemies was short and included mostly international Zionism that "works against socialist countries, among them Poland."[7] The officers of the Security Services argued that it was "a not unknown fact" that among the organizers of recent events there were "disproportionally many people of Jewish descent" who had close connections overseas, particularly in capitalist countries, where Zionism "enjoys a great degree of freedom." Zionists belonged to both categories of enemies, external and internal. They included the usual embittered former high-ranking party members—such as Zambrowski, Staszewski, and Morawski—who were "removed from positions of influence" and therefore were working against the current government, as well as the ultimate enemies from within, Polish Jewish Zionists. The latter's political activity in Poland consisted of running discussions, printing pamphlets, organizing protests, and collecting money for Israel. An additional category of "enemies" lumped together "various oppositional groups" of writers, lawyers, and academics. Again, the writers, including Kijowski, Jasienica, Kisielewski, and Słonimski, were described as frequently expressing their anti-party views during meetings of the Polish Writers' Union and as having close ties to the "commandos." Several lawyers also had contact with the "commandos" and regularly took cases of "anti-state" crimes. The professors from Warsaw University, Baczko, Brus, Bauman, and Kołakowski, "prepared the cadres" and shaped the ideology of the opposition. The Ministry of Internal Affairs memo added that all of these groupings "kept contact" with "foreign enemy elements," meaning Zionists and Trotskyists. The authors of the report admitted that more information was needed on the student committees formed across Poland after March 8, which were "headed and initiated mostly by people of Jewish descent." Such detailed information could provide the basis for the political and legal decisions the authorities in Poland were considering.[8]

During the last few days of March, the media returned to a familiar topic: *Wielka Encyklopedia Powszechna* and the concentration camp entry. As explained in chapter 3, in the 1966 edition of the encyclopedia, the

7. AIPN BU MSW II 4798,73–82, quote on page 73.
8. AIPN BU MSW II 4798,73–82.

concentration camp entry pointed out that the Nazis had created two kinds of camps, concentration camps and death camps, and that in the death camps 99 percent of the victims were Jews and the rest were "Gypsies and others." After the start of the anti-Zionist campaign in June 1967, Vice Minister of Arts and Culture Kazimierz Rusinek and other *partisans* launched an attack on the encyclopedia's editors. They accused the editors, most of whom were of Jewish descent, of purposefully omitting Polish victims. In the summer of 1967, the authorities purged the State Publishing House and launched a press campaign explaining the mistakes in the encyclopedia. In March 1968, the media picked up the issue once more. Newspapers reminded readers that the encyclopedia's "false representation of history" played a central role in a Zionist anti-Polish campaign, increasing the sense of threat from Jews. In April 1967, the Ministry of Internal Affairs reports had claimed that in return for West German economic aid, "World Zionism" had started a campaign to shift the blame for the Holocaust from Germany to Poland. In 1968, reports claimed that the Zionists were trying to weaken socialism in Poland from within and for that purpose had orchestrated the March events; Zionist attempts to "slander Poland" in the international arena were another proof of their ongoing effort to "undermine socialist Poland."[9] For many Poles, recognition of Polish suffering and sacrifice during World War II and Poland's good reputation in the international arena were far more important than the stability of the regime. As it is today, allegation of antisemitism and collaboration with the Nazis hurt them to a greater degree than any student unrest. An anti-Jewish plot against Poland only served to augment already-existing anxieties about Jews and the memory of World War II. Contemporary Polish politicians repeat the same slogans, stressing "Jewish influence" over Holocaust commemoration and an anti-Polish plot.

The press followed the themes laid out by the Ministry of Internal Affairs and printed articles describing "the anti-Polish campaigns" and repeating arguments presented in internal reports from April 1967. Caricatures played an important role in portraying Israel as working for Germany. For instance, in April, the satirical weekly *Karuzela* ran an elaborate caricature showing a death camp and a German officer with angel wings carrying a sign that says "Paid" and giving money to a man marked by a large Star of David, who is yelling, "The Poles are guilty."[10] The caricatures were

---

9. AIPN 0365/ 46, T.4, 30–37.

10. The caricatures are reprinted in Agnieszka Skalska, *Obraz wroga w antysemickich rysunkach prasowych marca '68* (Warsaw: Narodowe Centrum Kultury, 2007), 148, 179, 180.

visual expressions of the claim that a German-Israeli conspiracy blamed the Poles for the crimes of the Holocaust, a theory still sounded in contemporary right-wing Polish media. The youth magazine *Walka Młodych* published an article on the "anti-Polish campaign" by the director of the Central Commission for the Investigation of Hitlerite Crimes in Poland, Czesław Pilichowski; as mentioned in chapter 3, he was the author of several reports condemning the encyclopedia's editors. The article began with allegations that the "West German and Zionist international press" printed many "anti-Polish" articles describing Auschwitz as a camp where only Jews were massacred.[11] For nationalist Poles, communists or not, the presentation of Auschwitz as the site of the Nazi mass murder of Jews, without mention of Poles, was an insult and any discussion of Jewish suffering had to be accompanied by reference to Polish victimhood.

In April 1968, the Auschwitz museum opened a new pavilion dedicated to the extermination of the Jews. A year earlier the Polish authorities had unveiled a monument in memory of the victims of the camp; a representative of the Israeli government, the minister of welfare Yosef Burg, participated in that ceremony. Both memorials caused dissatisfaction in Jewish circles around the world. As mentioned in chapter 3, the change in Polish politics in 1967 and the growing influence of the veterans' organization (ZBoWiD) led to a complete modification of the Birkenau monument's design: the museum's directors replaced the figures representing families with a large triangle, symbolizing political prisoners who had a red triangle on their camp uniforms. There were almost no Jews among the political prisoners in Auschwitz.[12] In April 1968 the Auschwitz museum authorities opened the "Jewish pavilion" in Block 27. The pavilion was planned years in advance, at first with the collaboration of Jewish organizations, but eventually it became smaller than intended and its exhibits came to present Jews as one group of victims among many others and Poles as a group persecuted in the same manner. Jewish organizations in the West, previously in close contact with the Auschwitz museum, were outraged by the changes to the memorial and by what they considered a misrepresentation of the Holocaust. They withdrew their association with the International Auschwitz Committee, and the president of the committee, a

---

11. *Walka Młodych*, no. 16 (628) April 21, 1968.

12. Jonathan Huener, *Auschwitz, Poland and the Politics of Commemoration, 1945–1979* (Athens: Ohio University Press, 2003), 162–84.

well-known French Jewish Auschwitz survivor, Robert Waitz, resigned.[13] The Polish press pinned the blame on the Jews; an article in the daily *Walka Młodych* claimed that the encyclopedia entry on concentration camps was "a drop in the sea" of "anti-humanist and anti-Polish" slanders connected with the Auschwitz memorial. In the piece, Pilichowski quoted an article from a West German magazine claiming that the Auschwitz museum falsified history since it centered on Polish victims and thus contradicted the socialist Poland's own *Wielka Encyklopedia Powszechna* entry on concentration camps, which emphasized the Jewish victims. In this article, Pilichowski finally found proof that West German and Zionist forces intended from the outset to use the encyclopedia as a weapon in anti-Polish propaganda. As the director of the Central Commission for the Investigation of Hitlerite Crimes in Poland, he reassured readers that the commission had not approved the encyclopedia's entry and that responsibility for the mistakes lay with the encyclopedia's editors. The encyclopedia "omitted" many facts and figures about crimes against Poles and "gave a distorted picture of the Hitlerite occupation and Hitlerite crimes in Poland; a picture eagerly utilized by the Zionist and neo-Nazis in West Germany."[14] Pilichowski accused "Zionists and imperialist Israeli forces" of exploiting the memory of World War II for political gain. He listed in his article several books on the Holocaust; most of them had already appeared in his internal reports for the government, as detailed in chapter 3. Now, he added to the blacklist works by recent Jewish émigrés from Poland and accused Henryk Grynberg, Stanisław Wygodzki, and Józef Muszkat of further slandering Poland's name.[15] The article thus both explained to the public the necessity of the purge of the State Publishing House, the Jewish Historical Institute, and the TSKŻ and established that the events of March 1968 went hand in hand with a wide Zionist Jewish effort to harm Poland and unsettle the communist regime. Ironically, Pilichowski ignored the fact that the forced emigration of these writers had led to their bitterness and harmed Poland's precious good name to a much greater degree.

Security Services reports from late March and April marked as "Zionists" those who had supported demonstrating students or who had accused the Polish regime of being antisemitic. The allegation of antisemitism was

13. Huener, *Auschwitz, Poland.*
14. *Walka Młodych*, no. 16 (628) April 21, 1968.
15. *Walka Młodych*, no. 16 (628) April 21, 1968.

considered tantamount to slandering Poland's name: after the Holocaust, many believed that, at least in the arena of international politics, explicit antisemitism had become unacceptable and contemptible. Jews who charged Poles with antisemitism were in fact participating in an anti-Polish conspiracy. The Ministry of Internal Affairs considered as a traitor anyone who claimed that the current Polish government was afflicted by antisemitism or that it utilized antisemitism for political purposes. In interwar Poland, some Polish politicians proudly declared their antisemitism and sought a solution to the "Jewish problem," but in the People's Republic of Poland, open antisemitism stood with the enemies of the regime—reaction, extreme right-wing nationalism, and fascism. In essence, Polish communists become entangled in a web they would find difficult to untangle: attacks on Jews from within the socialist discourse in Poland, which rejected antisemitism as a main tenet of prewar right-wing ideology, could not be sustained for very long in the post-Stalinist reality. In a report summarizing events in Warsaw in the last weeks of March, the authors mentioned several "Zionist elements" that supported the students' cause. In the Polish Radio, a group of workers of Jewish descent expressed solidarity with "provocative elements" and "Michnik's group." "Lawyers of Jewish descent" questioned the legality of the Ministry of Education's decision to expel Michnik and Szlajfer. Jewish employees of the Central Film Distribution branch in Warsaw reportedly spoke against the regime's handling of recent demonstrations, calling it "a provocation." At the Physical Education Academy, Dr. Andrzej Whol "defended Zambrowski" and argued that recent attacks on Zionists were "a deviation in the party."[16] In April 1968, the Ministry of Internal Affairs reported that the director and two vice directors at the Jewish Historical Institute all spoke in support of Zionists and against Poland. The informants claimed that the director, Arthur Eisenbach, had accused the government of pursuing "antisemitic policies" and compared participation in the Warsaw Ghetto Uprising memorial service organized by ZBoWiD to a visit to a "bordello." His two vice directors were also heard saying that the Polish regime was antisemitic.[17] Another example of "people known for their Zionist outlook who support the students" came from the Historical Institute at Warsaw University. Security Services officers claimed that at a meeting of the history faculty, Professor Tadeusz Manteuffel, one of the

16. AIPN 01288/ 22, *Warszawa, dnia 30 marca 1968.*
17. AIPN BU MSW II 967, 1–3.

most important historians in the country and a central figure in the Polish underground during World War II, supported a resolution protesting the militia's "brutal behavior" and suggested that "lies appear in the press." Manteuffel also defended "historians of Jewish descent" suspected of Zionism.[18] In June, the very same renowned professor would interview for Życie Warszawy to commemorate, for the first time in communist Poland, the anniversary of the creation of the interwar republic and to discuss the positive legacy of Józef Piłsudski.[19] The new national communism allowed for the reappearance of previously shunned national heroes and holidays—Pilsudski had objected to Marxist socialism and had fought fiercely against communism and the Soviet Union.

On April 10, Department III of the Ministry of Internal Affairs circulated a top-secret memo detailing the ministry's plans to purge Zionists (i.e., Jews) from the "state and economical apparatus." The report first disclosed that 184 people had already been removed from their jobs; about half were from Warsaw, but "the purge was not progressing evenly in all counties."[20] In Łódź, Wrocław, Gdańsk, and Kraków, there was "a pressing need" to further cleanse state institutions. Those cities were centers of "Zionist" and "deviationist" activity and of mass protests in March. The Ministry of Internal Affairs officers complained that the Security Services in Gdańsk had been "too liberal" toward "problematic persons." The report also accused the governing body of the Gdańsk Polytechnic of being lenient and not taking strong enough steps against the protestors. More but not enough progress had been made in Łódź: eighteen people had been fired from "central positions," among them the director of the famous Łódź Film School, Jerzy Toeplitz, and the rector of Łódź University, Józef Piątowski. The report mentioned that 51 of the 184 people already dismissed throughout Poland had held ministerial and directorial positions and that 27 had worked on the "ideological front": in the media, in publishing, and in the censorship office. At the same time, the authors of the report reminded the party that one "must not look at the problem of purging Zionists only in terms of quantity." The Ministry of Internal Affairs warned that there was not enough cooperation between the state administration and the party. Some former party members purged for "anti-Polish activities" stayed

---

18. AIPN 01288/ 22, *Warszawa, dnia 30 marca 1968.*

19. Jonathan Randal, "Poland to Mark Her 1918 Re-emergence as Nation," *New York Times*, June 24, 1968, 4, ProQuest Historical Newspapers.

20. AIPN 01288/23, *Uwagi pod adresem jednostek terenowych, 10.4.1968.*

employed in their "central positions" after losing their party affiliation. It created a dangerous situation that had to be corrected.

In the last part of their memo, the officers of the Ministry of Internal Affairs complained that the student movement had not been completely crushed. As proof, they mentioned the "hunger strike" in Wrocław. The "hunger strike" was a student boycott of the dining halls, organized in the first days of April by "young Jews." In Łódź, the local branch of the Security Services charted a plan of action. First, the officers would keep an eye on Jews and regularly report to the party on the "actual views and actions of people of Jewish nationality."[21] Second, particular attention would be given to persons who had "expressed solidarity with anti-Socialist elements." Third, the Security Services would make sure that "teams of workers" were not "wrongly influenced" and induced to "act irresponsibly." This kind of language incorporated Polish ideas about Jews—the authorities sought them out specifically and saw them as "corrupting" Poles—with socialist discourse, which emphasized the natural inclination of the proletariat for solidarity with the communist party. The Department III report finally recommended strongly that other counties take steps similar to those of Łódź, since the Security Services had difficulties with "fully recognizing certain groups such as professors and academic youth" and with "identifying some central links that accelerated the events." Local officers and agents found it hard to penetrate "already formed groups," and the amount of information the Ministry of Internal Affairs collected on the students and academic circles was still "small in relation to what was needed." Although the Security Services had recently recruited thirty new "secret collaborators" (*tajny współpracownik*) among the "illegal student committees," it did not "control" all student activities. The director of Department III called for the intensification of efforts to stop the rebelling students and purge the state administration.[22]

In a typical purge scene, the workplace party cell would hold a so-called extraordinary meeting and unanimously decide to expel from the party "Zionists" and "revisionists," usually Jews holding executive positions. During the meetings, the expellee would be accused of supporting Israel in 1967 and sympathizing with the students in March 1968. In other, more sensitive cases, the party representatives would simply inform the

---

21. AIPN 01288/23, *Uwagi pod adresem jednostek terenowych, 10.4.1968.*
22. AIPN 01288/23, *Uwagi pod adresem jednostek terenowych, 10.4.1968.*

"Zionists" about the party's decision to expel them from its ranks. As in the purges of the Stalinist era, the actions and words of the accused in the past were reinterpreted in light of their now-exposed Zionism. The party saw none of the actions of "Zionists" as innocuous or as stemming from misunderstandings. Such purges occurred in Kraków, Białystók, Łódź, Kielce—in all of Poland. For instance, in Opole, one Marian Smigielski Zylbernberg was removed from the party because of "improper behavior, not taking into account the party's factory organization and wrong politics."[23] In Wrocław, the party ousted for "Zionist activities" newspaper editor Bronisław Winnicki, university employee Wacław Meibaum, director of the local co-op Wiktor Fiternik, and state employee Jerzy Runge, all of "Jewish nationality."[24] By June the local party cells were reporting that 228 people had been found to have "pro-Israeli" and "pro-Zionist" views.[25]

The Radio and Television Committee was a cultural institution the party purged extensively because it was in charge of programming. In early April, the party's Bureau for Broadcasting prepared a report on the committee's "managerial cadres." According to its analysis, the committee did not adhere to "political-ideological criteria" in the assessment and advancement of employees or in the choice of managerial cadres.[26] As an example, the report described the case of Artur Fischer, who "until recently" had been editor of the "music and news" show. Fischer, it was claimed, had reached his position without the right qualifications. After June 1967, the party uncovered Fischer's "Zionist outlook" and his "organizational ties to the Zionist movements." Also mentioned in the report was Michał Birbrarej, a worker at the radio's foreign desk, who had immigrated to Israel in 1957 and returned to Poland two years later. Somehow, he still managed to achieve "a responsible position" in the radio. Regina Lityńska, part of a team of women at the Department for Children's and School Radio Programs, created "not a very good political atmosphere" at the radio; her son, Jan Lityński, had been a prominent activist in the student movement. There was an urgent need for "principled, concerted, and swift" action to correct the ideological-political distortions in radio and television, argued the party's radio and TV bureau. All employees "lacking appropriate education" had to be fired. The report ended with a list of conclusions and recommendations. The Radio and

---

23. AIPN 01288/23, Szyfrogram nr. 2802.
24. AIPN 01288/23, Szyfrogram nr. 2861.
25. AIPN BU 0365/ 41, t.5, *Notatka Służbowa*, 25.VI.1968r.
26. AAN 237 XIX- 300, 178–91, quote on page 179.

Television Committee must "stop tolerating the presentation of foreign (i.e., Zionist) political standpoints by certain workers," and the workplace party cells had to stress the political moral obligations of party members.[27] Notably, the authors of the report did not explicitly use the word Jew in their narrative. They hinted to Jewish members by linking them to "foreign" and "antisocialist" ideologies such as Zionism and implying that they belonged to a certain "social circle." Unlike many bulletins from the Ministry of Internal Affairs that directly named and blamed Jews, the high-ranking party bureaucrats refrained from using nationalist and racial criteria in their reports. They adhered to more traditional socialist language when referring to the purge of the state apparatus, using expressions like "change of the cadres" and "lack of political qualifications." As a result of the report, the Radio and Television Committee fired 103 employees.[28] During the 1968 purge, publishing houses and the press in Poland lost 200 employees to emigration.[29]

No institution was exempt from the purge. The Ministry of Foreign Affairs underwent an extensive upheaval in April 1968. The Minister of Foreign Affairs, Adam Rapacki, was not one of Moczar's allies, and he objected to the anti-Zionist campaign. As a senior politician in office since 1956, Rapacki felt that he could hold ground, but intense party pressure and deteriorating health eventually led to his resignation. On April 8, Gomułka informed the Politburo that Rapacki wanted to quit his post and in the meantime was taking a "medical leave."[30] Rumors claimed that when Ministry of Internal Affairs officials handed him a list of Jews to be fired from his ministry, Rapacki had added his name to the top of the list and left the ministry.[31] One fascinating case to follow in the purge of the Ministry of Foreign Affairs is that of Vice Minister Marian Naszkowski, who was accused of Zionism and diversion and removed from the party. On March 21–22, the ministry's party cell held meetings to criticize and chastise vice ministers and senior officials, specifically pointing to Vice Minister Naszkowski, a veteran member of the Polish postwar diplomatic corpus.[32] A month later, in

---

27. AAN 237 XIX- 300, 178–91.

28. AIPN 01288/24, *Notatka, Lista osób zwolnionych z zajmowanych stanowisk w okresie od czerwca 1967 do maja 1969 r.,* June 23, 1969.

29. AIPN, 01288/24, *Wykaz osób zwolnioncych z zajmowanych stanowisk,* June 1969.

30. "Protokół nr. 52 z posiedzenia Biura Politycznego 8 VI 1968r.," in *Centrum władzy: protokoły posiedzeń kierownictwa PZPR, wybór z lat 1949–1970,* ed. Antoni Dudek, Aleksander Kochański, and Krzysztof Persak (Warsaw: ISP-PAN, 2000), 396–99.

31. According to John Darnton, the New York Times Warsaw Bureau chief. See John Darnton, "Waking Up, Getting Out," *New York Times,* March 30, 1968.

32. Józef Winiewicz, *Co pamiętam z długiej drogi życia* (Poznań: wyd. Poznańskie, 1985), 576.

late April, the party cell sent a letter to Gomułka outlining the allegations against Naszkowski: first, the vice minister accused "party activists" of anti-semitism in an attempt to limit the party cell's role in the ministry; second, Naszkowski failed to fulfill his part as senior party member in that he did not express correct views on "recent events"; third, he "cultivated" certain people who "differed" from what was required of the ministry's employees, such as Gelbert, Goldblat, Hellman, and Rogulski (all Jewish names). This letter was shortly followed by a second report, addressed directly to Comrade Gomułka and further detailing Naszkowski's sins. The party activists blamed Naszkowski of abusing his rank to "stigmatize as antisemites" new employees while recruiting to the ministry a group of "bourgeois and petty bourgeois" workers of "Jewish descent." They asked the first secretary to remove Naszkowski from his position and take disciplinary action against him.[33] Despite the letters' intimation that Naszkowski was a Zionist and a Jew, he probably was not Jewish.[34] Gomułka responded to the letters in a meeting of the Politburo on April 6, saying that the atmosphere at the Ministry of Foreign Affairs was "unhealthy" and that he could not conclude whether "all the accusations tossed at him [Naszkowski] were justified" since "such allegations could be made against any other worker in a mana-gerial post." Gomułka would not make a clear determination, but he did add that the tense situation at the Ministry of Foreign Affairs could not continue and therefore the Politburo had to consider removing Naszkowski anyway.[35]

The party cell at the Ministry of Foreign Affairs held another meeting a few days later, on April 10. The activists discussed Naszkowski's role in Edward Ochab's visit to Cairo in 1965. Ochab, who had been first secretary briefly in 1956, had served since 1964 as president of the Council of State and, during the very same days in April 1968, had resigned in protest of the anti-Zionist campaign. The former ambassador to Egypt, Kazimierz Sidor, testified on the visit to the Middle East, and he recollected that he had made extensive preparations for Ochab's meeting with Nasser but that in the end, and to the surprise of the Egyptian president, "the Polish delegation con-centrated on the problems of Jewish martyrdom in Poland."[36] The officials

33. Document 6, in *Marzec '68: między tragedia a podłością*, ed. Grzegorz Sołtysiak and Józef Stępień (Warsaw: Profi, 1998), 309–14.

34. Eisler, *Polski Rok 1968*, 579.

35. "Notatka z dyskusji na posiedzeniu Biura Politycznego z dn. 8.IV.68 r.," in *Z Tajnych Archi-wów*, ed. Andrzej Garlicki (Warsaw: Polska Oficyna Wyd. BGW, 1993), 339.

36. "Odpis wyciąg z protokołu posiedzenia Komitetu Zakładowego PZPR przy MSZ z dnia 10 Kwietnia 1968r.," in *Marzec '68: między tragedia a podłością*, ed. Grzegorz Sołtysiak and Józef Stępień, 316.

from Poland also told Nasser that they supported Israeli-American plans to divide the water of the Jordan River between Israel and its Arab neighbors. Because of disagreements between Egyptian officials and the Polish delegation, a joint communiqué on the meeting was not issued, a fact "seen as proof of political differences between Egypt and Poland." Sidor further claimed that before the official trip a ministry employee had informed him of Naszkowski's request to travel from Cairo to Tel Aviv and report to the Israelis on the meetings with Nasser. At the same time, Naszkowski allowed Israel to hold in Warsaw a meeting of Israeli ambassadors to Eastern Europe. It was a "Zionist" decision that the Arab ambassadors failed to understand and that caused employees at the Ministry of Foreign Affairs to no longer "trust comrade Naszkowski."[37]

On May 6 the Politburo discussed Naszkowski's case and resolved to end his tenure as vice minister. Yet the Politburo also decided to take disciplinary steps against Kazimierz Sidor for presenting the party cell "with unfounded charges against comrade Naszkowski."[38] Naszkowski, who was not a Jew, became a victim of the anti-Zionist purge: his political alliances trumped his ethnic identity, and he became an "honorary Jew." As a veteran diplomat, former Stalinist, and ally of Ochab, he fitted the profile of a "Zionist," a "bankrupt" official who cunningly survived upheavals in the party and state and who promoted Israeli interests over Polish ones. Still, probably because Naszkowski was not Jewish, the central organs of the party dismissed the harshest allegations against him and enabled him to get another job. He was not the only one fired from the ministry: three ambassadors were called back to Poland, and several department directors were dismissed.[39] Though the number of those forced to resign from the Ministry of Foreign Affairs was not high, the purge noticeably affected the highest ranks of the state apparatus, causing upheaval in government ministries and major institutions.

---

37. "Odpis wyciąg z protokołu posiedzenia Komitetu Zakładowego PZPR przy MSZ z dnia 10 Kwietnia 1968r.," in *Marzec '68: między tragedia a podłością,* ed. Grzegorz Sołtysiak and Józef Stępień, 315–20.

38. "Protokół nr. 53 z posiedzenia Biura Politycynego 6 V 1968r.," in *Centrum władzy: protokoły posiedzeń kierownictwa PZPR, wybór z lat 1949–1970,* ed. Antoni Dudek, Aleksander Kochański, and Krzysztof Persak (Warsaw: ISP-PAN, 2000), 400.

39. "Protokół nr. 53 z posiedzenia Biura Politycynego 6 V 1968r.," in *Centrum władzy: protokoły posiedzeń kierownictwa PZPR, wybór z lat 1949–1970,* ed. Antoni Dudek, Aleksander Kochański, and Krzysztof Persak (Warsaw: ISP-PAN, 2000), 400–402. It was not the end of Naszkowski's career, as he was appointed editor of the Marxist journal *Nowe Drogi.*

A May report from the Warsaw Committee to the Central Committee assured the Polish communist leadership that during the preceding two months "party and state organizations had been securitizing their cadres."[40] Since March, 483 people "in the rank of manager" were removed from their jobs. Those fired worked in government ministries, central state institutions, trade unions, academia, the press, and "cultural organizations." More than half of the employees purged were also affiliated with the Central Committee or with one of its departments. At the same time, the Warsaw party branch expelled from its ranks 316 members who did not follow the correct political line or who were categorized as "unsuitable."[41] In the whole of Poland, 750 employees were forced out, a tiny number in a country of 40 million citizens. Yet the purge greatly affected certain fields, and in particular high-ranking state jobs, it was a purge of socialist elites. Of these, 25 held ministerial-level positions, 245 held vice ministerial ones, and 228 were department directors. About half of the purged were academics, artists, journalists, and "cultural workers." None became officially unemployed since unemployment did not exist in a communist economy: some retired and received pensions, others received lesser jobs, and many emigrated. The Department III report on the purge mentioned that several of the emigrants, particularly the academics, became employed by "anticommunist Western circles."[42]

The purge arrived at the highest-ranking offices of the state, but there it took an unanticipated turn. At a Politburo meeting on April 8, it became clear that not everyone in the top echelons of the party agreed with Gomułka's line. The meeting began with Gomułka announcing personnel changes: as mentioned above, Edward Ochab, the chairman of the State Council (*Przewodniczący Rady Państwa*), was leaving his post. Gomułka denied rumors that Ochab had resigned in protest of the anti-Zionist campaign, and he proposed Marian Spychalski as Ochab's replacement. Spychalski, a former officer in the communist underground, the People's Army (*Armia Ludowad*) had been imprisoned during the Stalinist period for "nationalist deviation" and released in 1956. He served in the Polish

---

40. AKW PZPR 260, 158.

41. AKW PZPR 260, 158–171. Of those fired, 318 worked in government ministries and other central state institutions; 47 in trade unions; 49 held academic posts; 24 worked in the press and in "cultural organizations"; and 39 worked in factories and services.

42. AIPN 01288/24, Notatka, *ilość osób zwolnionych z zajmowanych stanowisk w okresie od czerwca 1967 do maja 1969 r.*, 23.06.69.

government as minister of defense and was a supporter of Moczar's "partisan" faction and an ally of the first secretary. For the post of minister of defense, Gomułka recommended General Wojciech Jaruzelski, chief of staff of the Polish Army. Since 1967, Jaruzelski had been carrying out a vast purge of the army, dismissing all "pro-Zionist" officers.[43]

Gomułka then complained at length about the minister of health, Jerzy Sztachelski: "[We] do not know who he is, neither a revisionist nor a communist with conviction." He also complained about the vice minister of health, Walenty Titkow. Gomułka told the Politburo that he had spoken with Titkow in the past—when the vice minister had been the secretary of the Warsaw Party Committee—and asked him to take strong action against Michnik's discussion club but that Titkow had "disregarded the matter."[44] Both Sztachelski and Titkow lost their positions.

Edward Ochab himself spoke at the meeting. He supported the first secretary, but he also believed that "reaction at large" was the regime's main enemy, while Zionism by itself was only "a small force among reactionary powers." He added that the infamous article in *Słowo Powszechne* naming Jewish students and their parents had caused "great unrest in the party," since all those mentioned in the article were "neither connected with West Germany nor Zionists." In a final jab at the party, Ochab wondered why "we could not defend Jewish comrades against unjust insinuations in television, the press, etc."[45]

Ochab was not the only one in the Politburo expressing unease about the development of the anti-Zionist campaign. The chairman of the Planning Committee and longtime member of the communist party Stefan Jędrychowski complained that in spite of Gomułka's "clear speech" on March 19, "in practice [the press] did not differentiate between Zionists and Jews" and it treated Zionism as "the greatest danger [to socialism]."[46] Jędrychowski felt that the propaganda disproportionally focused on Zionist enemies and neglected to inform the working class about "other reactionary

---

43. "Notatka z dyskusji na posiedzeniu Biura Politycznego z dn. 8.IV.68 r.," in *Z Tajnych Archiwów*, ed. Andrzej Garlicki, 338–39.

44. "Notatka z dyskusji na posiedzeniu Biura Politycznego z dn. 8.IV.68 r.," in *Z Tajnych Archiwów*, ed. Andrzej Garlicki, 340–41.

45. "Notatka z dyskusji na posiedzeniu Biura Politycznego z dn. 8.IV.68 r.," in *Z Tajnych Archiwów*, ed. Andrzej Garlicki, 341. Topolski, Grudzinski, Górecki, and Zambrowski were the students mentioned.

46. "Notatka z dyskusji na posiedzeniu Biura Politycznego z dn. 8.IV.68 r.," in *Z Tajnych Archiwów*, ed. Andrzej Garlicki, 342.

forces." He mentioned the case of Naszkowski, who was mistakenly identified as a Jew. After all, said Jędrychowski, the party did not want its members to bring their grandparents to party meetings to prove that they were not Jews, a practice reminiscent of Nazi times and certainly unseemly for a communist regime. It was inappropriate for communists to discuss origins (meaning race) in such a way. Despite of all his criticism, Jędrychowski agreed with the personnel changes proposed by the first secretary.[47]

Next to take the floor was Ignacy Loga-Sowiński, a known Moczar supporter. Loga-Sowiński objected to the previous speakers. "World Zionism," he argued, played a central and unique role in recent events. The fight against antisemitism, he said, crucially depended on the "attitudes of the Jews toward Zionism." Looking around, Loga-Sowiński could not find many *true* loyal communists among Polish Jews: "If in our factories Jewish fellow citizens would have worked as laborers together with us . . . things would look differently."[48] The first secretary of the Katowice region (and Gomułka's successor), Edward Gierek, concurred with Loga-Sowiński that there was a real need to purge Zionists from the highest ranks of the party.[49] Zenon Kliszko, another "partisan" and close ally of Gomułka, complained that the party was "terrorized" and that its members were accused of antisemitism for trying to purge Zionists. Citizens of Jewish descent, he noted, spoke out only on the issue of antisemitism. Kliszko denied that the Ministry of Internal Affairs was the driving force behind the anti-Zionist campaign. The ministry did not initiate the purge conducted at other ministries and did not order the article in *Słowo Powszechne*, Kliszko assured the Politburo. The students' behavior provoked the campaign, and "citizens of Jewish descent" pushed the students into hostile actions. Professors like Brus and Bauman chose Jewish assistants, making the personnel of some university departments "fifty percent Jewish." But, said Kliszko, the party could not prevent these developments for fear of being accused of antisemitism. He saw the party's moves against Zionists as necessary to preserve the communist regime.[50] Vice Prime Minister Franciszek Waniołka agreed

---

47. "Notatka z dyskusji na posiedzeniu Biura Politycznego z dn. 8.IV.68 r.," in *Z Tajnych Archiwów*, ed. Andrzej Garlicki, 341–43.
48. "Notatka z dyskusji na posiedzeniu Biura Politycznego z dn. 8.IV.68 r.," in *Z Tajnych Archiwów*, ed. Andrzej Garlicki, 343–44.
49. "Notatka z dyskusji na posiedzeniu Biura Politycznego z dn. 8.IV.68 r.," in *Z Tajnych Archiwów*, ed. Andrzej Garlicki, 344–47.
50. "Notatka z dyskusji na posiedzeniu Biura Politycznego z dn. 8.IV.68 r.," in *Z Tajnych Archiwów*, ed. Andrzej Garlicki, 347–50.

with Kliszko and added that "for the first time since the World War II the party can expose Zionism for what it is."[51] Both of these members sounded accusations against Jews that have a familiar ring: Jews were cast as conspirators who were overrepresented in universities, where they promoted their own, and as the ones to blame for Stalinism.

In contrast, the next Politburo member to speak at the meeting, Chairman of the Science and Technology Committee and Vice Prime Minister Eugeniusz Szyr, warned the party's leadership that many party members had had enough of the anti-Zionist propaganda; they had read sufficient articles exposing Zionists. "Not all must prove that they are not Zionist . . . that they are not guilty," explained Szyr. As a prewar Communist Party member who had participated in the Spanish Civil War, Szyr denied any allegations that he was ever a Zionist and complained that "today people do not know the struggle between Jewish communists and Zionist Jews before the war."[52] Another veteran communist, Władysław Wicha, agreed that the propaganda had overly focused on Zionists; he had heard the slogans "to cleanse the party and state of Zionists" and "Moses to Dayan" too many times.[53]

At the end of the Politburo meeting, Gomułka had the final words. He reiterated that Zionism was *not* the greatest danger to the regime. Revisionism was now a bigger problem: revisionist ideas had influenced not only Jews but every segment of Polish intelligentsia. The party criticized and purged whoever worked against it from inside, Jews and non-Jews alike, the first secretary assured the Politburo. However, he also pointed out that the members of Jewish descent in the highest ranks of the party—"Zambrowski, Morawski, and Werfel"—were revisionists. Over and over again, the first secretary stressed to the Politburo that Zionism was not the main threat to the regime and that not all revisionists were Zionists. "Zionists as such we did not have in the party, of course," Gomułka finally said, countering the claims of the Ministry of Internal Affairs that Jewish nationalism in itself threatened the party.[54] Thus, according to the secretary, the party had to be cleansed of revisionists, not just Zionists. This position probably reflected

51. "Notatka z dyskusji na posiedzeniu Biura Politycznego z dn. 8.IV.68 r.," in *Z Tajnych Archiwów*, ed. Andrzej Garlicki, 350–51.
52. "Notatka z dyskusji na posiedzeniu Biura Politycznego z dn. 8.IV.68 r.," in *Z Tajnych Archiwów*, ed. Andrzej Garlicki, 351.
53. "Notatka z dyskusji na posiedzeniu Biura Politycznego z dn. 8.IV.68 r.," in *Z Tajnych Archiwów*, ed. Andrzej Garlicki, 351–55.
54. "Notatka z dyskusji na posiedzeniu Biura Politycznego z dn. 8.IV.68 r.," in *Z Tajnych Archiwów*, ed. Andrzej Garlicki, 355–358.

the secretary's worry that the party would become even more associated, in the minds of Poles, with Zionism/Jews. Gomułka's statement contradicted most press articles and party slogans, indicating that already in early April he wanted to slow down and refocus the anti-Zionist campaign. He worried about "unhealthy tendencies to attack every Jew for being a Jew," a practice that in Poland evoked the German occupier and prewar nationalists, both enemies of communism. "In the working class could appear elements that would like to crush all Jews," warned Gomułka, and "this state of affairs could lead to violence," something that had already happened during the 1956 wave of anti-Jewish sentiments.[55] The Politburo discussion brought to light the objections many high-ranking party dignitaries had to the anti-Zionist policy Gomułka had pursued. In the past, the party's propaganda had emphasized its fight against antisemitism and "reactionary forces" in Polish society. Now it concentrated on destroying the feared "Zionist threat" by seeking Zionists and exposing Jewish conspiracies. Even Gomułka began to sense that things might have gone too far.

Certain publications that began arriving at the desk of the Censorship Department confirmed Gomułka's worries. The censors started limiting the anti-Zionist campaign, and not every anti-Jewish article or book could be published: they did not approve what they considered overtly racial language or articles that tried to prove the existence of the "Żydokomuna." In one instance, the department banned an article written for the weekly *Za Wolność i Lud* (For freedom and the people) entitled "Something about the Gestapo." The piece, by one J. Grenia, accused Jewish Stalinists of allowing Nazi criminals to escape punishment as part of a large-scale Jewish conspiracy. "The Bermans (referring to Jakub Berman)," claimed Grenia, released Nazi officers on death row from Polish jails while arresting "Polish patriots," former national underground fighters. In the late 1940s, Jews, "Różański, Fejgin, Światło, Berman, and his people," took over the country and "cleansed Poland": they captured true Polish "patriots" and silenced "the real socialist Poland." Grenia contended that "the Zionist mafia was in charge of the local judiciary . . . the state prosecution was in its hands." When de-Stalinization arrived in 1956, the same "mafia" sent the highest-ranking officers from the secret security apparatus, "the most compromised people," to Israel, where they would not have to pay for their crimes against

---

55. "Notatka z dyskusji na posiedzeniu Biura Politycznego z dn. 8.IV.68 r.," in *Z Tajnych Archiwów*, ed. Andrzej Garlicki, 355–358.

the Polish nation.[56] Even in the anti-Zionist atmosphere of 1968, the censors could not allow for the publication of an article that claimed that Jewish "gangsters" had once ruled communist Poland. This argument went far beyond the "partisan" vision of Polish postwar history, according to which Jewish Stalinists stirred the party in the wrong direction and were responsible for Stalinist deviations but did not impose communism on Poland and were not part and parcel of the communist regime.[57]

The censors disapproved another article that demarcated the boundaries of the anti-Zionist discourse from a different angle, a piece about kosher slaughter that was reminiscent of prewar antisemitic propaganda. Entitled "The Limits of Tolerance" and prepared for the daily *Słowo Polskie*, the article described Jewish traditional animal slaughter at length, found it particularly cruel, and called on the Polish government, still "overly liberal toward Jewish religious practices," to ban it. The article further claimed that Jewish butchers received more meat from the state distribution network. The censors rejected the publication of "The Limits of Tolerance" on the grounds that it represented old-style interwar antisemitism and had little to do with the anti-Zionist campaign.[58]

The April 1968 report of the Censorship Department for Film, Television, and Theater mentioned two amateur plays also banned for their antisemitic content. The censors stopped their production since "certainly, the battle against Zionism cannot be used to produce and popularize programs of an antisemitic nature. From Lublin and Białystok we were informed that there were attempts to bring back old plays that ridicule or simply vilify Jews as such."[59] The demons of prewar antisemitism were raising their ugly heads. An amateur troop of the Białystok Workers' Union intended to stage a Christmas-style play about Herod, the Roman ruler of Judea in the time of Jesus. The censorship argued that the play "caricatured" and belittled Jews. The second play, to be staged in Lublin, was *Flisacy* (Raftsmen), by the popular nineteenth-century Polish playwright Władysław Ludwik Anczyc. The censors maintained that the play presented Jews as "intrusive exploiters" of Poles and as responsible for Poland's economic woes avows. Jews were pathetic characters, speaking a mix of Yiddish and Polish and

56. AAN GUKPPiW 830, 19–30.

57. AAN GUKPPiW 830, 19–30.

58. AAN GUKPPiW 830, 31–33.

59. AAN GUKPPiW 847, 68–72. Quote on page 68.

obsessively discussing money issues. The censors expressed concern that the play was even approved for stage by the local department of arts and culture, and they demanded that the party authorities clarify to the locals that such work should not be staged as it was "politically harmful."[60] The communist party in Poland had spent the preceding decades building a new Polish society that rejected chauvinism and extreme right-wing politics; it could not allow the traditional Polish antisemitism to reappear on the public scene. It could not allow the suppressed to return.

The pinnacle of the anti-Zionist campaign gone awry came from Łódź, where the local party branch had printed two booklets about Zionism that the censors felt had crossed the line, and therefore the censors ordered the Łódź committee to cease distributing them. The pamphlets addressed the first years of the Polish People's Republic and the prominence of Jews in the Stalinist leadership. The authors, Zbigniew Faliński, Wiktor Malski, and Henryk Maciejewski, worked for the Łódź party's Propaganda Department. The first pamphlet, *Polityka partii i rządu i jej przeciwnicy* (The policy of the party and the government and its opponents), argued that Stalinists of Jewish origins always adhered to Zionism but had hidden it well so far. They had been "closet Zionists" ever since the establishment of the communist regime, and they constantly undermined the socialist state. The root of the problem was the "excessive concentration of Polish citizens of Jewish descent in decisive, highly sensitive departments," which resulted from the Polish intelligentsia's antagonism toward communism and the large percentage of Jews among Polish communists who had spent World War II in the Soviet Union.[61] The authors further hinted that the Jews had become NKVD agents during the war. Upon returning to Poland, "Polish communists of Jewish descent" created "units of people of single national origin" in key governmental departments, particularly the Ministry of Public Security (i.e., the security apparatus). The "foreign" Stalinist elements used their power to persecute former Polish Home Army fighters and establish a reign of (Jewish) terror in Poland.[62] The authors of *The Policy of the Party and Government and Its Opponents* presented the hard core of

---

60. AAN GUKPPiW 847, 68–72. For more on Raftsmen, see Magdalena Opalski and Yisrael Bartal, *Poles and Jews: A Failed Brotherhood* (Waltham, MA: Brandeis University Press, 1992), 24.

61. I could not find the original pamphlets mentioned in party reports. They are extensively quoted in a Radio Free Europe research report. A. Ross Johnson, *New Documents of the 1968 Purge*, April 11, 1968, Radio Free Europe Research, East Europe, 3–4.

62. A. Ross Johnson, *New Documents of the 1968 Purge*, April 11, 1968, Radio Free Europe Research, East Europe, 3–4.

"partisan" ideology. Stalinism in Poland was more than a deviation; it was a foreign ideology forced by the Jews: Jews victimized Polish socialists, used all means to destroy Polish patriots, and were fully to blame for Stalinist crimes. Even after the fall of Stalinism, Jewish Stalinists remained in positions of power because they had used the Jewish-controlled press to accuse their critics of antisemitism. Then they became "revisionists" and protected the "revisionist" intellectual elite. The authors reproached Gomułka's government for being overly tolerant and patient with the former Stalinists, allowing them to "make themselves at home in various lucrative administrative posts, ministerial positions, publishing houses, government offices, embassies, etc." Following the June 1967 War, the Jews in the party and state administration felt great attraction to Zionism and launched an attack. They planned to "reshuffle" key government and party posts and to gain ever greater influence on Poland. The pamphlet also charted a way forward. Lessons had to be derived from the March events: "cliques" should not be allowed; editorial boards had to be criticized; universities must undergo "intense political" examination; and student meetings had to adhere to the rules. The regime should remove the Stalinist/Reformist/Zionist Jews, establish greater "control" over public administration, and penetrate the cultural and academic intelligentsia so that those dangerous Jews would not return.[63]

The second banned pamphlet was entitled *Syjonizm, jego geneza, character polityczny i antipolskie oblicze* (Zionism, its origins, political character, and anti-Polish countenance). The author, Władysław Kmitowski, presented a far wider anti-Polish Zionist conspiracy than the first Łódź publication and diverged completely from the regime's mainstream propaganda campaign. The language Kmitowski used was much closer to prewar antisemitic discourse than to socialist jargon. According to the pamphlet, Jewish capitalists who had profiteered from World War II controlled the economy of Western countries; eight hundred of them, all billionaires, met in Jerusalem to pledge their support for Israel. However, the Jewish leadership did not want all Jews to immigrate to Israel since someone had "to watch over the Jews' financial domination of the world." Kmitowski clearly reiterated antisemitic allegations that a Jewish cabal ruled the world economy. Furthermore, to prove his point, the author of the pamphlet— which was printed and distributed by the communist party in communist

---

63. Johnson, *New Documents of the 1968 Purge*, 3–4.

Poland—quoted a passage about Jewish rule over gentiles from *The Proto-cols of the Elders of Zion* as if it were a historical document.

He thus completely diverged from the image the communist party had been trying to promote for decades, of an anti-reactionary, anti-racist party. Kmitowski even confronted Gomułka's division of Jews into Zionists, cosmopolitans, and loyal citizens, arguing that one could not trust any of the Polish citizens of Jewish nationality unless they publicly condemned the "anti-Polish campaign" in the West and expressed gratitude to Poles who risked their lives to save them during the Holocaust. For Kmitowski, Zionist was an ethnic, not political, category—and Zionist equaled Jew. He did not use socialist phrases or argumentation, and his views mirrored popular antisemitism.[64] The censors and party officials in Warsaw were outraged after reading the pamphlet, and they stopped its circulation immediately. The Łódź secretary of the local party committee wrote to Gomułka that both pamphlets, "in some way, falsified and distorted the many problems of the role of Zionism in Poland," and apologized for their publication.[65]

Władysław Gomułka was a communist leader, a true believer, and he could not allow the anti-Zionist campaign to go as far as to undermine the very legitimacy of the communist regime, as both Łódź pamphlets had done. One had insinuated that Jews imported communism to Poland, and the other had used crude antisemitic language that obviously contradicted the party's official anti-reactionary position. The first secretary must have begun to wonder if he had lost control over the campaign and opened the Pandora's box of Polish antisemitism, which frightened him no less than the Zionist menace. The Politburo meeting held at the beginning of April 1968 revealed that by then not everyone in the party followed the Ministry of Internal Affair's view of Zionists as the most dangerous and perfidious enemies of socialist Poland. At the time, the ruling Polish United Workers' Party (PUWP) was beginning preparations for its Fifth Congress, and it did not want the Zionist theme to dominate the debates. The in-depth reports of party committees and commissions in anticipation of the congress were not infused with anti-Zionist language but rather discussed in general terms the problems of ideology and revisionism. Its authors called on party members to be vigilant about attempts by "reactionaries, revisionists, and Zionists"—in that order—to undermine the socialist regime in Poland. A

---

64. Johnson, *New Documents of the 1968 Purge*, 8–12.
65. AAN KC PZPR 237.V - 745, 62–65, quote on page 62.

memo on "cultural institutions" reminded the party that the battle against "revisionism and anticommunism" was being waged in the cultural sphere. Other party reports argued that a major reorganization of academia was needed; "the latest events have shown us that in many of the important humanistic studies departments, especially in philosophy, sociology, and economics, the political and cadre situation is such that many academics are under the influence of the forces of revisionism."[66]

On April 22, the party's leadership met to discuss the reports and prepare for the upcoming congress. The discussants barely mentioned the issue of Zionism. Rather, they spoke of the dangers of revisionism and capitalist influences. One of the party's chief ideologues, Jerzy Putrament, talked about the "acceleration of the Cold War and the growing pressure on Poland from Western countries." Others mentioned the March events, the "problems with the youth," and the need for reform in academia, but little was said about the wave of anti-Zionism still sweeping Poland.[67]

First Secretary Gomułka authoritatively explained to party members that "there has been a great misunderstanding [duże nieporozumienie] that Zionism is the main danger to socialism. Dangerous are all the forces of reaction and particularly dangerous in our specific conditions are first of all the forces of Polish reaction and Polish revisionism. Zionist elements joined the alliance of these forces."[68] Gomułka not only wanted to lessen the importance of Zionism but also called on the party to curb verbal attacks on Jews. Despite his earlier support for the campaign, apparently it was a "great misunderstanding," an overreaction toward Jews. The first secretary complained about insinuations that the newly appointed minister of national defense, Wojciech Jaruzelski, had a Jewish wife (as Gomułka had). Gomułka was furious; such suggestions played into the hands of the enemy and should cease. Party members should immediately stop searching for clandestine Jews; that was a practice reminiscent of the enemies of socialism, who adhered to racial ideologies. Gomułka was unhappy with the growing public display of anti-Jewish sentiments, which often came hand in hand with anticommunist rhetoric. He wanted an "end to anarchy in the party" and insisted that the party cease criticizing the censors, who had been under scrutiny since June 1967. The Censorship Department, he

---

66. AAN PZPR XI A.147, 10–55, quote on page 41.

67. AAN PZPR XI A.147, 235–260.

68. AAN PZPR XI A.147, 235.

warned, could not function under constant pressure and ongoing allegations of collaboration with Zionism.[69],[70] The anti-Zionist campaign was getting out of hand.

Gomułka also calmed the personal fears of party heads: "Rotation should happen only when one can replace weak cadres with strong ones," he said. Fast and vast changes would only harm the party. With these words, the first secretary signaled to the party's decision-making bodies that he was still the man in charge. He was not blindly following the "partisans'" lead or fully aligning himself with Moczar, the minister of internal affairs. Finally, Gomułka complained that Central Committee members "write too little for the press, far too little," and thus allowed Moczar and his "partisans," obsessed with the struggle against Zionism, to dominate the mass media. Gomułka's words to party leaders were understood as a clear message to roll back the anti-Zionist campaign and to refocus on the struggle against revisionists.[71]

A few days later, the director of the party's Press Department, Stephan Olszewski, sent Gomułka the text of a speech made on April 6 by the head of PAX's Propaganda Department, Zygmunt Przetakiewicz. Olszewski titled his memo *Charakterystyka obozu przewrotu w Polsce* (The characteristics of the coup camp in Poland), thus indicating to the first secretary his disapproval of Przetakiewicz's remarks, which he found far too radical. Przetakiewicz, a prominent member of the prewar extreme right-wing organization RNR-Falanga, went back to his political roots. In his address to PAX activists in Bydgoszcz, a small town, Przetakiewicz portrayed Zionists as responsible for everything that went wrong in the communist bloc and, like the Łódź activists, chose antisemitic tropes over socialist discourse. Zionists were everywhere: to prevent socialist countries from sending aid to Egypt during the Suez Crisis in 1956, they instigated events in Hungary, which forced the Soviet Union to intervene. Zionists influenced the imperialist governments of West Germany and the United States and even controlled the Polish Catholic organization *Znak*, revealed Przetakiewicz. The chief propagandist of PAX told his audience that Zionists had created the recent crisis in Poland and Czechoslovakia to once more divert attention from the Middle East; actually, they had already taken over the Communist Party in Czechoslovakia (as well as in many countries in Western Europe).

---

69. AAN PZPR XI A.147, 247–60.
70. AAN PZPR XI A.147, 245–47.
71. AAN PZPR XI A.147, 247–60.

The Zionists had been responsible for the rehabilitation of Rudolf Slánský, the Jewish first secretary of the Czechoslovak Communist Party executed in 1952 after a show trial. Now, the Zionists plotted with the West German government to topple communism in Poland and install in the country a "second *Generalgouvernement* ruled by a group of liberal Jews."[72] In this narrative, the language of the perpetrators is turned on the victims: A Jewish cabal, in collaboration with Germans, aspired to create a Nazi-like regime in Poland. According to Przetakiewicz, the only way to save Poland was to create a new "patriotic socialism," along the lines PAX promoted. Such a regime would not tolerate Jews in powerful positions and would not reject Catholicism as communists did. In evoking an international Jewish conspiracy aimed at global domination, the PAX official clearly strayed from Polish socialist discourse and used anti-Jewish language taken from the lexicon of the interwar Polish fascist radical right, to which Przetakiewicz had belonged. It was a crass attempt to dress old tropes in socialist discourse, and it differed from the views and language used by either Gomułka or Moczar, both steeped in socialist ideology.[73]

The first secretary also began receiving letters from Jews and non-Jews complaining of the antisemitism of the regime. In one instance, a professor from Gliwice, Józef Lendwoń, wrote a letter to the editors of the weekly *Polityka* and sent a copy to Gomułka, telling them about his ten-year-old daughter. The little girl had come home crying: children at school refused to play with her because she was Jewish. Lendwoń explained to her that she was not Jewish, but he felt outraged. "Defending children of every descent must be the moral duty of every decent man,"[74] he forcefully argued in his letter. Helena Sznyterman wrote to Gomułka about her husband, whose only connection to Judaism was Yom Kippur; he observed Yom Kippur in memory of his family murdered in the Holocaust. Now her sons, in their early twenties, faced unexpected difficulties as Jews in socialist Poland. She did not want them "to suffer their whole lives" for having a Jewish father or to regret living in Poland, where "the ashes of my husband's family" lay. At the end of her letter, Sznyterman angrily asked Gomułka, "How do I explain to my sons that the Party that fights against oppression around the world divides its own citizens into two categories? Please tell me?"[75]

72. AAN 237/ XIX–353, 37–55, quote on page 45.
73. AAN 237/ XIX–353, 37–55.
74. ANN PZPR XI A.301, 29.
75. ANN PZPR XI A.301, 24–28.

Another particularly heartbreaking story brought to Gomułka's attention was that of Army Major Tadeusz Langer, a Holocaust survivor purged from the army in 1968. His aunt, Stanisława Langer, wrote Gomułka a letter about his plight, asking the first secretary to help Langer clear his name. During the anti-Zionist campaign it had been insinuated that he had behaved "wrongly" in a German concentration camp (Auschwitz). Rejecting the innuendos, the aunt pointed out that Langer was only seventeen when liberated from the camp. A friend of Langer's from Auschwitz also wrote to Gomułka and assured the first secretary that there was no truth in the accusations and that, in fact, Langer had helped the Polish underground fighters in the camp.[76] A few prewar Jewish communists also wrote to Gomułka expressing their indignation at the anti-Zionist campaign. Why had they been targeted by the very regime that they had fought for?[77]

At a Politburo meeting to discuss the upcoming party congress in late April, Gomułka stated that the party was moving in the wrong direction. The first secretary berated his own party apparatus for persecuting veteran Jewish party members, who had served communism for the last forty years:

> Until 1939 we sat in jails, many low-ranking KPP [Polish Communist Party] members sat in jails, of course among them were many Jewish comrades. We have to look at the facts—who did not know, didn't know—but I knew because I sat with them. And today what is going on? . . . People were lost, lost because of what? Because of *some mythical struggle against Zionism*, the devil knows what struggle. *The class compass is lost*, and comrades, if we lose our class compass, then we as a party, we are going blindly, and all sorts of *wrong ideas* will develop in the ranks of the party.[78] Now we are making new mistakes, *nationalistic mistakes*. . . . We simply must stop talking and writing on the topic of Zionism. . . . Who leads politics there, who? Who is against us? From where come the dangers to socialism? . . . From Zionists? . . . That is wrong. That is losing all sense of class [war].[79]

Remarkably, these were the words of the first secretary to the inner circle of trusted party leadership, pleading with them not to abandon class struggle in the name of nationalism and not to continue on an anti-Jewish path. It was an about-turn for Gomułka, who here removed himself from responsibility for the anti-Zionist campaign. Obviously, the allegation that the regime was essentially Jewish harmed, in his eyes, the legitimacy of its

76. ANN PZPR XI A.301, 23, 34.
77. ANN PZPR XI A.301.
78. AAN PZPR XI A.148, 304, 302.
79. AAN PZPR XI A.148, 306. Emphasis in the original.

rule over a Polish Catholic majority. Gomułka had indeed been a communist for decades, and now he feared not only for the reputation of the regime but also for its very foundations—racial principles could not openly dominate a socialist society. Gomułka had sought a homogenous nation-state, not a racially pure one; he distinguished between nation and race. Yet when speaking publicly, Gomułka employed once more the arsenal of the anti-Zionist campaign, as if nothing had changed. On May 1, the International Workers' Day, the first secretary gave a speech in Warsaw in which he condemned Israel, world Zionism, and the "Zionist campaign against Poland" at length. Gomułka accused "Western Zionist" leadership of doing nothing to help the Jews during the Holocaust, while Poles risked their lives to save their fellow citizens. These same circles "now accuse us of antisemitism," Gomułka lamented loudly. He also claimed that Zionists had such strong influence in the United States that they increased discrimination against American citizens of Polish descent. In Poland, in contrast to the United States, he assured the listeners, Jews enjoyed "full equality"; he objected to all forms of racism.[80] This speech was the last on the topic; in his subsequent public appearances, Gomułka did not return to the March 1968 anti-Zionist discourse. The first secretary was quick to abandon his own policy: the visible, public parts of the campaign lasted for only a few months.

The most conspicuous step Gomułka took to end the campaign was to remove Mieczysław Moczar from the Ministry of Internal Affairs, a move that emphasized his displeasure with partisan circles. Little is known about the decision, how and when it was reached and who exactly was involved. Some have claimed that Brezhnev had warned Gomułka that Moczar had gone too far and that, in any case, those in Moscow were not fans of the Polish nationalist. This claim reinforces the argument that Soviets had not orchestrated the anti-Zionist campaign and had not supported Polish national communists; Brezhnev certainly would not have wanted communism to be openly associated with Jews in a Soviet bloc country. Moczar's demotion was officially announced only in July 1968, when Moczar became a Politburo member, stepping down as minister of internal affairs. As his replacement Gomułka chose Kazimierz Świtała, a rather marginal figure in the party and not one of Moczar's protégés in the ministry. Świtała had only moved to the Ministry of Internal Affairs in June 1967, during the war, and he was probably not Moczar's own choice of a substitute. In any

---

80. AAN KC PZPR 237/V–904, 7–9.

case, Moczar's influence waned, and in 1971, along with others, he was also removed from the Politburo.[81]

After the May speech, Gomułka touched publicly on the themes of Zionism only when explaining to party members that Zionists were not the primary enemies of socialism in Poland and that therefore the time had come to end the campaign against them. Polish dailies published fewer and fewer articles about the Zionist threat. However, the campaign could not be stopped so quickly. The purge of Jews from workplaces continued late into the summer of 1968.[82] On September 14, Gomułka gave a significant public speech at a Warsaw factory and explained why Zionism was not a threat to Poland and why Jews did not control the Communist Party. He was retreating from the very positions he had expressed a few months earlier:

> We declared and we say again, *Zionism is not a danger to Poland.* Comrades, these Zionists, well, I don't how many there are, I don't have the statistics about how many Poles of Jewish decent there are. If there are twenty thousand or twenty-five thousand, I don't know how many. I know that lately, after March, about one thousand have gotten permissions and are leaving. And certainly, more will go; another two thousand thus will leave our country and go. And that is something normal. It is not dangerous. *There are some comrades who think that the entire government is in the hands of Zionists. I don't want to say in Jewish hands, but I will say in Zionist hands. Comrades, that is nonsense, absolute nonsense.*[83]

Clearly, Gomułka understood his mistake: once a public discussion on the role of Jews in the party had begun, the genie was out of the bottle and Poles began speaking of a Jewish-dominated Communist Party, a belief already well spread among the population. This development had to end; it risked the stability of the regime more than a Zionist plot would. Fear of Żydokomuna trumped the fear of the Żyd (the Jew). A month later, on October 15, Gomułka and the director of the party's Education Department, Andrzej Werblan, met with "educational workers" (i.e., teachers). Both Gomułka and Werblan stressed the importance of the fight against "revisionism" and against "reactionary forces." "Revisionists," not specifically Jews or Zionists, infiltrated academia and in March agitated against the socialist regime.[84] Zionism disappeared from public discourse; it was

---

81. Eisler, *Polski Rok 1968*, 610–11.
82. AIPN BU 0365/41, T.5.
83. AAN 237/V/906, 22. Emphasis mine.
84. AAN 237.XVI-539, 8–29, 30–49.

no longer on the agenda of the Polish United Workers' Party. Besides, by that time Jews had also gradually disappeared from the public landscape in Poland.

The Aftermath

Worries about public outbursts of anti-Jewish sentiment was probably one of the factors in the Polish government's decision not to hold large-scale open trials against those involved in the March events. Only the top leaders of protesting students were indicted and received prison sentences. Others were sentenced to time served or had to pay fines.[85] The government did not prosecute the academics or politicians that the Ministry of Internal Affairs and the press depicted as the masterminds behind the demonstrations. Prominent intellectuals or men like Jasienica, Kisielewski, Smolar, or Lipski, singled out as the leading enemies of socialist Poland and time and again condemned during the propaganda campaign, did not face any legal action. The regime preferred that they just leave Poland. Upon receiving their applications, the Polish passport offices willingly issued travel documents for professors, writers, journalists, managers, and most of the students involved in the March protests. The only condition: relinquishing their Polish citizenship.[86] Though Soviet policies varied and were inconsistent on Jewish immigration, Brezhnev had a similar approach toward "Jewish troublemakers" in the early 1970s.

Nevertheless, a small group of organizers of the March 1968 events was indicted, and the trials began in November 1968. The regime focused on the *commandos*, those behind the protests: Seweryn Blumsztajn, Teresa Bogucka, Józef Dajczgewand, Wiktor Górecki, Irena Grudzińska, Jacek Kuroń, Irena Lasota, Jan Lityński, Karol Modzelewski, Adam Michnik, Henryk Szlajfer, Barbara Toruńczyk, and Antoni Zambrowski. The prosecutors described Kuroń and Modzelewski as the ideological mentors of the rebelling students. The Zionist issue was all but abandoned; indictments dealt with "revisionist" activity and the events concerning "Forefathers' Eve."[87] On December 5, 1968, Lityński and Blumsztajn stood trial; the state charged them with membership in a secret organization, and both pleaded not guilty. When questioned by the prosecution, Lityński frequently answered

---

85. AIPN 0644/176, *spis zawartosci teczki*, 1–51.
86. AIPN 01288/24, *informacja, 5 VII 1972.*
87. AIPN BU MSW II 4798, 52–56.

that he did not remember details, and Blumsztajn told the judge that he believed his actions were legal, since all he did was "discuss different matters regarding politics with friends in private meetings."[88] Other prominent *commandos* were called to the stand during the trial, including Wiktor Górecki, Henryk Szlajfer, Antoni Zambrowski, Irena Grudzińska, Irena Lasota, Stanisław Gomułka, and Józef Dajczgewand. Szlajfer gave a "complex" and detailed testimony, naming Kuroń, Modzelewski, and Michnik as leaders of the *commandos*. On the other hand, Dajczgewand testified that the two accused were his close friends and that he did not think their activities were illegal. A report on the trial mentioned that Dajczgewand behaved "provocatively, exchanging greetings and smiling. He was called to order twice." Grudzińska and Lasota refused to answer questions or claimed not to recall events and people. All in all, the witnesses said and disclosed very little in their testimonies and refused to go along with the prosecution's attempts to present the *commandos* as an organized, almost military group that posed a clear danger to the socialist government. On the last day of the trial, the accused were given the floor. Lityński told the judge that he never participated in a conspiracy but that he still supported Kuroń and Modzelewski's political views. He condemned the prosecutor for using the word Zionism because it was "an expression of racism." Lityński and Blumsztajn both asked the court to acquit them.

On December 12, 1968, the court found both guilty and sentenced them to prison: Lityński received two and a half years and Blumsztajn two years.[89] They joined Dajczgewand, who was already serving a two-and-a-half-year prison verdict.[90] In January and February, the courts handed prison sentences to the rest: Kuroń and Modzelewski received three and a half years; Michnik, three years; Szlajfer, Toruńczyk, and Zambrowski, two years; Gorecki, twenty months; Bogucka, Grudzińska, and Lasota, eighteen months.[91] Despite the prison sentences, the regime underplayed the *commandos'* trials: testimonies were kept short, the accused could say little, and press coverage was minimal. In September 1969, as part of a general amnesty on the occasion of the twenty-fifth anniversary of the creation of People's Poland, the authorities released from prison almost all

88. AIPN BU MSW II 6657, 213.
89. AIPN BU MSW II 6657, 211–18; AIPN BU 02041/19, 142–59.
90. AIPN 0332/105, 87.
91. Jerzy Eisler, *Polski Rok 1968*, 458.

commandos, with the exception of Kuroń and Modzelewski, who remained behind bars until 1971.[92]

Though the regime sooner or later freed most of those arrested or jailed, the students could not return to their studies: the universities expelled most of them. Prominent professors had already been fired and had immigrated to the West. All in all, 230 "academic workers" lost their positions during the anti-Zionist purge and left Poland: 37 assistant professors, 25 full professors, and 10 heads of schools and departments. Another 200 employees were removed from research institutions, including 40 professors. Some of the most well-known academics were Zygmunt Bauman, who immigrated to Israel and then to Leeds; Leszek Kołakowski, who became a fellow at All Souls College in Oxford University; and Bronisław Baczko, who landed at the University of Geneva.[93] The 1968 purge was minuscule in relative terms, but it harmed elites and universities for decades, both because of the meaningful loss of faculty and because of the curbing of academic freedom. Polish academia changed its face: it no longer served as a breeding ground for new and exciting theories about socialism and the future of humanity. The vibrant spirit of the 1960s vanished.

The TSKŻ was the first to bear the brunt of the anti-Zionist campaign in June 1967, and it suffered another round of allegations after March 1968, though links between its members and recent events were quite weak. The regime tried to keep the Jewish association under its control, but most of its activists refused to support the official party positions laid out by Gomułka. Some, as discussed in chapter 4, believed that the storm would shortly pass and preferred to keep quiet for a while. But most were deeply disturbed and frustrated: from the outset of the March anti-Zionist campaign, the editors of the Yiddish newspaper *Folks Sztyme* declined to present the party line. The paper did not publish translations of either *Trybuna Ludu* editorials or official speeches against the protesting students. As the anti-Zionist propaganda intensified, turning anti-Jewish, the situation of TSKŻ members became unbearable. They could not and would not remain silent. On March 23, in reaction to Gomułka's famous speech ("nationalist Jews . . . identified not with Poland but with Israel"), the Yiddish daily ran an exceptional editorial protesting the accusations of the first secretary: "In the 24 years of

---

92. Jacek Kuroń, *Wiara i wina: do i od komunizmu* (Wrocław: Wydawnictwo Dolnośląskie,1995), 294–302.

93. AIPN 01288/24, Notatka, *ilość osób zwolnionych z zajmowanych stanowisk w okresie od czerwca 1967 do maja 1969 r.*, 23.06.69.

People's Poland's existence, we the Jews, loyal citizens of our *homeland*, our blood and later our labor and cultural work, our instructive work among the elderly and the young, our international socialism do not suggest any nationalist tendencies . . . that is why we are offended at any attempts to question the patriotism and the internationalist stance of our association and its institutes."[94] The TSKŻ rejected all allegations that it was somehow linked to Zionist organizations or was committed to undermining socialism in Poland, their homeland. Many members had been loyal to the Polish Communist Party since its inception, and they refused to accept the party's blatant anti-Jewish stance.

In the atmosphere of 1968, the Jewish comrades of TSKŻ could resist pressure from the regime only for so long, and in the end their choices were very limited: either cooperate with the new party line or leave Poland. It became clear that the socialist government of Poland pursued neither dialogue with the protesting students of Jewish descent nor the criminalization of the alleged Zionists. The party they proudly belonged to simply wanted them to leave their homeland and emigrate, in essence to disappear. They, the last faithful Jewish communists, were finally shown the door.

On April 26, in a meeting of the editorial board of *Folks Sztyme*, one member, who happened to be my mother's father, Józef Goldkorn, declared he would not write any more articles against Zionism, as "today they tell us to criticize Zionism, tomorrow they will call Smolar a Zionist ideologue and the day after tomorrow call Sfard a spy."[95] Shortly after, he resigned from the party and immigrated to Israel. Others followed suit: the editor in chief of *Folks Sztyme*, Smolar, and its technical director, Lichtensztein, were both fired and left Poland. As described in chapter 5, in late March the police arrested David Sfard's son, Leon, bringing the situation close to home and forcing the vice president of the TSKŻ to resign and subsequently to immigrate to Israel with his family, including Leon. Leopold Domb, David Sfard, and Hersh Smolar now all lay at rest in Israel, after years of being active in the Association for Yiddish Writers and Journalists in Israel. Every week, my grandfather would put on his tie and take the bus to Tel Aviv, to the associations' home, Beit Leyvik, where the "exiles" would meet to speak Yiddish and exchange ideas in their mother tongue. Samuel Tenenblat , the journalist and new editor of *Folks Sztyme*, remained

---

94. AIPN BU MSW II 7249, 77.
95. AIPN BU MSW II 1065, 2.

in Poland and continued to serve the communist regime. Within a short time, the entire apparatus of the TSKŻ collapsed. By July 1968, all but two members of the presidium left their positions.[96]

Secretaries of TSKŻ branches all over Poland also submitted their resignations. The ban on contact with the Joint meant the TSKŻ lost 80 percent of their funding and could no longer maintain various operations. The Central Jewish Commission for Social Assistance had no independent source of funds and was liquidated. ORT vocational schools shut down, and so did the four Jewish schools in Poland. The TSKŻ transferred to the Polish government ownership of its buildings around Poland, including a Jewish country hostel in the small village Śródborów where Jews often vacationed in the summer. Several of the directors of the Jewish Historical Association left Poland as well. The Jewish Theater lost a great deal of its budget, and several actors immigrated to Israel and other countries, including the director and legendary actress Ida Kaminska.[97] In September 1968, the daily *Folks Sztyme* became "a sociocultural, literary-artistic weekly magazine" no longer interested in political issues. Since every publication in Yiddish had to be translated into Polish—for the convenience of the trusted non-Jewish censors—the Yiddish publishing house *Idisz Buch* printed only four books during 1968.[98] The Jewish social-cultural association was reduced to a small, understaffed, and underfunded shadow of itself. In May 1968, the former president of TSKŻ, Domb, sent a letter to Gomułka warning him that the Communist Party's anti-Zionist campaign had led to the liquidation of "a thousand years of Jewish culture in Poland." Domb demanded that Gomułka, "in the name of our party's Leninist politics," do something to stop the campaign.[99]

Most Polish Jews neither belonged to the TSKŻ nor participated in Jewish activities. They identified themselves as "Polish citizens of Jewish descent" and felt that Poland was their only homeland. Some stayed in Poland after World War II because they wanted to participate in the building of socialism and belonged to the state and party apparatus. Some chose assimilation; others were married to non-Jews. But it made little difference: from March to May 1968, the communist regime distrusted, targeted, and attacked Jews living in Poland, regardless of their self-identification. Many

---

96. AIPN BU 0365/41, t.5, *Tezy dot. sytuacji w środowisku żydowskim, 7.4.1968.*
97. AIPN BU MSW II 6614, 260–67.
98. AIPN BU MSW II 6614, 260–67.
99. ANN PZPR XI A.301, 38–39.

"Polish citizens of Jewish descent," and especially those in "influential positions" (*na wpływowych stanowiskach*), were purged from the party, and they
subsequently lost their jobs. It happened mostly, but not entirely, in the big
cities. In Warsaw, Kraków, Wrocław, and Łódź, party cells at workplaces
denounced Jewish employees and ordered them to "go home." Students
released from jail rushed to leave the country with their parents. Anyone
whose family had somehow been involved in the demonstrations or suspected of Zionism was unable to get a professional job or enter (or reen-
ter) a university. The regime blocked Jews from any possibility of obtaining
key positions in the state. Young Jewish men and women quickly realized
it would be impossible for them, discredited as potential enemies of the
socialist state, to fulfill their personal aspirations in Poland; their future
would be one of menial or low-ranking employment, nothing resembling
their hopes and dreams. In the typical words of a "March emigrant": "We
didn't want to be second class citizens, so we left."[100]

As the anti-Zionist campaign intensified, some Polish Jews, particularly the older generation, even feared for their lives. Living among the
ghosts of the Holocaust, they believed that the possibility of a "second
genocide" always existed. Jews who survived the Nazis declared that "this
time" they were not going to wait and see what happened; they were leaving immediately. In their memoirs, the 1968 emigrants tell of "a sense of
urgency"; within a few months, "everyone" around them filed for a visa out
of Poland. One emigrant remembers "parents saying they can no longer
live in Poland now that everything reminds them of the horrible years of
the Holocaust. They cannot confront such fear again, they must leave."[101]
Yet quite a lot of the "non-Jewish Jews" stayed in Poland. According to the
Ministry of Internal Affairs' statistics, the majority (60%) of Jewish emigrants came from Warsaw.[102] Jews living in small cities and towns felt the
impact of March 1968 events to a much lesser extent. Either too old or too
attached to leave, married to Christians or just assimilated, a few thousand
Polish Jews living in the periphery decided to weather the storm and stay.
They were also probably less politically involved; the demonstrations and
denunciations in Warsaw meant less to them. A Jewish citizen from the
small town of Mysłowice remembered that he had no Jewish friends and

---

100. Teresa Torańska, *Jesteśmy: Rozstania '68* (Warsaw: Wyd.Świat Książki), 105.

101. Joanna Wiszniewicz, *Życie przecięte: opowieści pokolenia Marca* (Wołowiec: Wydawnictwo
Czarne, 2008), 320.

102. AIPN 01288/24, *informacja*, 5 VII 1972.

that the events in Warsaw did not influence his everyday life.[103] Some Polish citizens of Jewish descent fought the regime's decision to label them as traitors and remained in Poland for ideological reasons, working in menial jobs until they could return to their studies and positions. As a result of the anti-Zionist campaign, 13,500 to 15,000 Jews (more than half of the estimated 25,000 Jews living in Poland in the mid-1960s) emigrated from Poland from June 1967 till June 1972. Thirty percent immigrated to Israel, and the rest spread around the world, settling mostly in Scandinavia and North America.[104]

With the collapse of the TSKŻ and the shutting down of Jewish institutions, the hope for or the illusion of a resurrection of Jewish life in Poland vanished for the next few decades. Although the Jewish social-cultural organization failed to build a numerically significant Yiddish-speaking community in postwar Poland, its activities gave the older generation hope and a sense of continuity while keeping alive some form of Polish Jewish secular culture. The closing of the TSKŻ offices on Nowogrodzka Street in Warsaw symbolized the end of the efforts of the remnants of Polish Jewry to continue the legacy of the prewar Jewish leftist parties that promoted Jewish cultural autonomy. The vibrant Yiddish-speaking street of the 1930s Polish towns was never repaved.

Only when the purge of Zionists from the party and state apparatus reached its height and verged on hysteria did Gomułka and other political leaders understand its danger: an unrestricted attack on Jews in Poland would sooner or later lead to a popular attack on the communist party in Poland. In Polish nationalist discourse, the communist party had been seen as a Jewish party for decades, and for some Poles, "communists" were synonymous with "Jews." Since the 1950s, the ruling Polish United Workers' Party had tried to escape the association between Jews and communism and presented itself as a patriotic movement offering Poland a new beginning in new lands cleansed of Germans and other minorities.[105] But in 1967–68, in a series of actions that proved harmful to the regime, First Secretary Gomułka and Minister of Internal Affairs Moczar opened the door for a renewed examination of the old connections between Jews and the

---

103. Joanna Wiszniewicz, *Życie: opowieści pokolenia Marca*, 408, 476.

104. Numbers are contested; some claim it is closer to 13,500 and others to 15,000. AIPN 01288/12, 5.VII.1972.

105. Joanna B. Michlic, *Poland's Threatening Other: The Image of the Jew from 1880 to the Present* (Lincoln: University of Nebraska Press, 2006), 69–108.

communist party. What began as a hunt for Zionist Jews quickly became a hunt for communist Jews. That could not be allowed: "Żydokomuna," the Jewish-Communist nexus, would not reappear as a legitimate theme in People's Poland's public discourse. The result would be too harmful to the regime's claim to rule in the name of the Polish working class. The last official, government-induced anti-Jewish campaign in Europe thus came to a quiet end in late 1968. For most Polish Jews, it came too late. Their institutions had been destroyed, and they were forced to leave a country they loved and considered to be their homeland. For the communist regime, it had been a success mired by controversy in the party and by the awakening of latent demons. The Jews had left, but the opposition had not disappeared: in the 1970s it regrouped and realigned to form a united movement that would in the end contribute to the end of communism.

CONCLUSION

THE EXPULSION OF JEWS FROM COMMUNIST POLAND OFFERS a case study of a minority group that has been cast in the role of "security threat" and forced to leave its homeland. It is not the first time Jews have been accused of being a danger to society; since the rise of the modern nation-state, Jews in Europe have repeatedly been seen as foreign and alien, and at times threatening, to the dominant ethnic majority. During World War II, in Hungary and Romania, the right-wing regimes became increasingly suspicious of Jews, particularly in border regions, viewing them as colluding with the enemy. In Romania, the regime deported Jews to the Transnistria region, at the eastern border, where hundreds of thousands died as a result of murder, starvation, and disease. In Hungary, local authorities were eager to be rid of Jews living in newly acquired border territories, and they played a key role in the Nazi deportation of hundreds of thousands of Jews to their death in Auschwitz. In postwar Poland, the communist regime deported millions of Germans from border territories in the west and hundreds of thousands of Ukrainians from the eastern border regions while encouraging the emigration of Jews. Decades before these atrocities, during World War I, the Ottoman authorities committed genocide against the Armenian minority, whom they considered security threats and potential allies of the Russian Empire. During the period this study focuses on, Jews fared better: they were not deported, killed, or forced on trains, and they were able to pack and ship their belongings—our family still eats off plates sent from Poland in the 1960s. Nevertheless, they were made to leave, and they were stripped of citizenship. The June 1967 War, international politics, and rising nationalism had made them a security threat once more. In an ironic twist, this time Jews were not suspected communists but rather Jewish nationalists, cast as the agents of world Zionism. The communist regime shattered their dream of belonging.

The Expulsion of Jews from Communist Poland traces the origins, development, and consequences of the anti-Zionist campaign waged by the communist government of Poland in 1967 and 1968. As Polish Jews reacted with relief to the outcome of the Six-Day War, the Security Services and the ruling party apparatus viewed them with fear and suspicion. Anxiety about

Jewish influence then colored the regime's assessment of the March 1968 student protests. Rather than identify the protests as outbursts of a young and reformist opposition, a generational struggle, state leaders saw a Zionist assault on independent Poland. The first secretary, Władysław Gomułka, and those in his circle created an atmosphere of crisis around Poland's Jews, portraying them as treacherous enemies of socialism. They thus saw the anti-Zionist campaign as a means of self-defense against those who wished to harm the socialist nation. The decision-making process and the progression of the 1967–68 campaign challenge the notion that the communist regimes in Eastern Europe operated seamlessly, in a top-down structure in which the rank-and-file party bureaucrats and party members obeyed a party line dictated by orders of the heads of state. Rather, the discourse and terms employed by mid- and lower-level officials facilitated the atmosphere of fear and sense of crisis around Poland's Jews. Gomułka had not ordered the fabrication of evidence against Jews, but he interpreted certain reports on the behavior of Jews sent from the Ministry of Internal Affairs as proof of growing Jewish unrest. Indeed, officials in the Ministry of Internal Affairs created an atmosphere of fear and crisis around Poland's Jews well before the March 1968 demonstrations and student rebellion. The regime's reaction to the protests therefore stemmed from the mood of the previous summer, when Polish Jews appeared as Zionist traitors. Following the work of the feminist scholar Sarah Ahmed on emotions, *The Expulsion of Jews from Communist Poland* demonstrates how fear of Jews played a role in communist politics: it aligned bodies and minds against a Jewish menace to create a sense of crisis, separating Jews from other party members and from those perceived as the legitimate members of the Polish nation.

In the summer of 1967, events occurring thousands of kilometers away from Warsaw radically changed the lives of the tiny community of Polish Jews. On June 5, 1967, war broke out in the Middle East, and the region became a theater of the Cold War, with the Soviets supporting the Arab states and the United States backing Israel. Throughout the Soviet bloc, governments broke diplomatic ties with Israel. The communist press published articles attacking Israel and Zionism, portraying Israel as an aggressor working in the name of American imperialist interests. Immediately before the war, Jews around the world expressed anxiety about the fate of Israel and fear of disaster. Polish Jews, though mostly non-Zionists, had friends and families in Israel and voiced similar concerns. The Ministry of Internal Affairs saw these expressions, which Polish Jews considered legitimate, as manifestations of the questionable loyalty of Jews. State officials presented in their reports patterns of seditious behavior among Polish Jews who disregarded the anti-Israeli party line and celebrated Israel's victory. Jews went against the official stance, subverting the authority of the regime and harming its foundations. Israel was an ally of the United States and thus was Poland's enemy; supporting Israel therefore meant disloyalty to socialism. Though the Jews in Poland had various ways of defining themselves—as Jews, Polish Jews, or Poles of Jewish descent—the Security Services increasingly saw *all* Jews as threatening. In some cases, they imposed Jewish identity on Jews who no longer identified as such or on Poles who supported their Jewish colleagues. Once the Ministry of Internal Affairs' numerous reports on the "Jewish issue" reached First Secretary Gomułka, he became outraged and anxious. He wondered how Jews could turn their backs on the party that had rescued them from the Nazis and had given them equal rights. On June 19, 1967, Gomułka addressed the Polish nation, characterizing Polish Jews as a "fifth column" (i.e., a security threat) and calling on them to choose a homeland. The first secretary's words launched the anti-Zionist campaign. The Ministry of Internal Affairs and party officials sought out and purged Polish Jews working for party and state administration, accusing them of serving "international Zionism." The press printed articles condemning the conduct of Polish Jews. When student protests erupted in March 1968, the Ministry of Internal Affairs blamed the Jews once more. They believed that their warnings were proved correct: Jews were destabilizing the country. The minister and his advisers claimed that "world Zionism" conspired against People's Poland and that the demonstrations figured in the Zionist attempt to undermine communism. The attack on Jews in the media and their purge from the administration and academia intensified. The party leadership never contemplated negotiating with the protesters; reforms were not on the table. First Secretary Gomułka, in particular, refused to consider giving in to "Jewish troublemakers." Since the stability and durability of the government of People's Poland depended on Soviet support, without which communism in Poland could not survive, no "Polish Dubček" appeared: the battle for reforms was lost from the beginning. The regime reacted to student protests with brutal force, sending secret and uniformed police to crush the demonstrations.

Gomułka thereupon asked Polish Jews to leave their homeland after they had survived wartime genocide and postwar atrocities and had lived for two decades in communist Poland. Though Gomułka's government had been encouraging Jewish emigration since he came to power and had displayed growing nationalist tendencies, the anti-Zionist campaign surprised most Jews. Some had been loyal party members for years; others had tied their fortunes to People's Poland in other ways. Many never contemplated leaving before June 1967. They did not know that since the mid-1960s, high-ranking officials in the Ministry of Internal Affairs had been writing reports describing Polish Jews as a duplicitous minority working in the interests of "world Zionism," an imperialist and anticommunist movement. The officials saw Jews as a possible threat to the stability and success of socialism in Poland.

But the party heads eventually fell victims to their own panic: focusing on the Jewish menace, they failed to see how this would lead to a resurfacing of the myth of Żydokomuna power that they had sought to quash for twenty years. Removing Jews from the party and the state administration did little to weaken the myth in communist Poland. Once public discourse allowed for discussion of Jewish participation in the regime, nationalist and anti-Jewish voices began to reemerge. The belief that Jews had inflicted communism upon Poland had not disappeared after World War II but had become a taboo topic, something ordinary Poles might talk about only in private, with people they trusted. Now, with newspaper articles attacking Jewish party members and blaming them for the crimes of Stalinism, some seized the day, endeavoring to publish anti-Jewish and explicitly antisemitic articles and pamphlets. Their attempts went far beyond the party line, repeating antisemitic stereotypes from the interwar period about the connection of Jews and communism. This, clearly, was not an intended outcome of the anti-Zionist campaign. And so, rather hastily, Gomułka put an end to the campaign, reminding the party that its main enemy was the reactionary, not the Zionist. Overnight, the theme of the party's propaganda changed, refocusing on "reactionary elements."

From the point of view of its supporters, the anti-Zionist campaign had been a limited success. In the long term, it had failed to eliminate the opposition, since the young generation remained hostile to the regime, while older Poles had never really adopted communism. The anti-Zionist campaign had distracted party leaders from rising discontent on the ground, not among intellectuals of Jewish descent but among ordinary Poles. The leaders of the anti-Zionist campaign could nevertheless pride themselves on the success of the purge of Jews: they had managed to force hundreds out of party organs and government institutions. Prominent "citizens of

Jewish descent" no longer served in higher-ranking positions of the People's Republic, and new cadres of apparatchiki filled the Jews' positions. Academia also underwent significant transformation, as well-known professors left Poland and an entire generation of future scholars went with them. Most of the victimized Jews emigrated from Poland, while others of Jewish descent chose to assimilate completely, changing their names and never mentioning their origins. A third group also emerged: Jews who discovered their Jewish origins in 1968 and then began to explore new identities; they would be the future of the remaining tiny Jewish community in Poland. After 1968, the Jewish Social Cultural Association, the TSKŻ, became a rump organization, with little funding and a minuscule membership. Organized and open Jewish communal life all but ceased in Poland for almost two decades. Among the student leaders of Jewish descent, very few chose to stay in Poland and carry on the battle. *The Expulsion of Jews from Communist Poland* thus exposes the impossible position of Jews in People's Poland. The state interpreted the attempts of Jews to preserve Jewish identity as an integral part of the Polish socialist nation, as a threat to the nation.

There is no documentation in Polish sources that suggests the Soviets initiated the campaign. The Soviet leadership certainly did not preside over the campaign: after the Soviet invasion of Hungary in 1956, Moscow wanted public disturbances quietened and dissent suppressed, but cared less about the details. Soviet and Polish immigration policies at the time, furthermore, differed markedly, and Brezhnev may have supported the removal of Moczar from the Ministry of Internal Affairs because the Polish government allowed Jews to immigrate. Pushing Jews to leave Poland in 1968 figured within a broader context: Gomułka resumed the "Polish Road to Socialism" during the "Polish October" of 1956 and encouraged minority emigration, including that of Jews. Indeed, from 1960 to 1980, about half a million Polish citizens emigrated, many of them inhabitants of formerly German territories in western Poland.

Another broader context was the anti-Zionism and fear of "Jewish power" that emerged periodically in the countries of the communist bloc. During the Slánský trial in Czechoslovakia in 1952, for example, many party leaders of Jewish descent were accused of Zionism, among other things, and Israeli diplomats also stood trial in Prague as "Zionist spies." Ideas about Jews in communist discourse drew from anti-Jewish stereotypes prevalent in Europe and from a conspiratorial vision of politics typical to communism. Christian anti-Judaism painted Jews as traitors, killers of Christ, while political antisemitism imagined them as a greedy cabal conspiring to control humanity; Jews appear as inherently immoral in both cases. Communist anti-Jewish views echoed Catholic scholars of the prewar period who merged racism and anti-Judaism to question Jewish conversion to Christianity. According to historian John Connelly, "Technically, Jews were supposed to convert for the sake of salvation. Actually, the church in Central and Eastern Europe was extraordinarily suspicious of those who tried to enter it, never tiring of warnings."[1] Communists in Central and Eastern Europe similarly suspected that Jews had not truly converted to communism and continued to carry a treacherous potential through international networks to promote Jewish interests, chiefly the advancement of Zionism. Communists particularly feared Jewish nationalism, which they considered capitalist and aligned with the imperialist United States.[2] In 1960s Poland, certain sections of the regime saw Jews precisely through this prism, as a group that could turn on the party and operate as an enemy within. This was not old antisemitism in "new clothing," as some scholars have claimed, but rather a new phenomenon of national communism that drew from past perceptions of Jews common to the region and from communist ways of making sense of the world.[3]

The atmosphere of fear and crisis surrounding Polish Jews also reflected a culture of fear typical of the Cold War era and the late twentieth century. As Joanna Bourke has argued, fear is grounded in the discourse of a period: the words available and considered legitimate for expressing one's emotions. "To be understood, individuals communicating their fears need to conform to certain narrative structures, including genre, syntax, form, order and vocabulary."[4] Fear is a cultural as much as a physiological phenomenon. During the first decades of the Cold War, fear plagued public discourse on both sides of the "Iron Curtain," finding expression in fear of nuclear war and bomb drills and in a relentless search for spies and enemies. In early

---

1. John Connelly, *From Enemy to Brother* (Cambridge, MA: Harvard University Press, 2012), 34.

2. The fear of Jewish nationalism and its connections to US money is borne out in the transcripts of the interrogations and trials of the Soviet Anti-Fascist Committee. See Joshua Rubenstein and Vladimir P. Naumov, eds., *Stalin's Secret Pogrom: The Postwar Inquisition of the Jewish Anti-Fascist Committee* (New Haven, CT: Yale University Press, 2001).

3. For discussion of communist antisemitism as "old wine in new bottles," see Joanna Beata Michlic, *Poland's Threatening Other: The Image of the Jew from 1880 to the Present* (Lincoln: University of Nebraska Press, 2006).

4. Joanna Bourke, *Fear: A Cultural History* (Emeryville, CA: Shoemaker & Hoard, 2005), 287.

communist Poland, a significant culture of fear centered on West Germany. Fear of German rearmament played to Polish history, as German/Prussian troops had overrun Polish soil several times. The communist party presented itself as the only guarantor of peace, the only government that could keep the Germans at bay. Communist regimes fit well with Bourke's observation that "fear is manipulated by numerous organizations with a stake in creating fear while promising to eradicate it."[5] Defense against "German militarism" in Poland is one example, and the March 1968 events provide another. Fear of Jews also drew from the available cultural arsenal. The party explained that behind student protests stood Jewish traitors seeking to take over Poland, assuring Poles that the regime would protect them. Jewish conspiracies would be exposed and averted. That is not to say that the heads of the regime cynically orchestrated the anti-Zionist campaign, but rather that out of concern for the stability of the state, from the basis of ideas they actually believed, they created an atmosphere of crisis and panic. As a result, the party sought to find Zionists and suspicious Jewish members and remove them. This kind of culture of fear very much exists in public discourse around the world today. Political actors and various agencies addressing the "refugee problem," for example, tend to create and intensify a sense of threat and fear, bolstering the public's sense of insecurity in an age of social media and a time when threats, real and imagined, seem to lurk everywhere.

Much of the anti-Zionist campaign revolved around the memory of World War II and the Holocaust. Media outlets accused Jews of distorting the memory of the war by casting Poles in the roles of perpetrators instead of victims. According to these allegations, Jews acted in this way for money: reparation payments and military aid for Israel received from West Germany. Much as in the discourse in contemporary Poland, the instigators of the 1968 campaign saw Poles as the main victims of the war and, at the same time, as saviors of Jews; state authorities saw any attempt to discuss the complexities of the German occupation as anti-Polish libel or misrepresentation of the past. As in the statement issued by the Israeli and Polish prime ministers in 2018, antisemitism and anti-Polonism were considered equivalent phenomena. Officially, in 2018 as in 1968, the Polish government set out to fight both. Polish politicians today echo the voices of 1968 and share an obsession with the question of collaboration with the

---

5. Bourke, *Fear*, 385

German occupiers and "righteousness." In this narrative, a great number of Poles saved the lives of Jews under German occupation while themselves suffering from Nazi terror and persecution; collaborators were marginal figures, on the outskirts of society. Claiming otherwise was, and still is, part of an international conspiracy against Poland, a plot to slander Poles by making them appear antisemitic. This nationalist discourse on the Holocaust, collaboration, and anti-Polonism constitutes a central legacy of the anti-Zionist campaign. Indeed, March 1968 was a formative moment for national communism. Even if, for a brief moment, it had given the communist regime legitimacy to rule over Poland, it was no longer a "Jewish" regime, but a truly Polish one defending "Polish values."

Less than two years after March 1968, the Gomułka regime again faced a crisis. This time Gomułka paid the price. In December 1970, the government announced a substantial increase in the price of food, sparking worker protests. The focal point of the demonstrations was the Gdańsk shipyards, where thousands of workers protested and rioted against the regime and the "Red Bourgeoisie." Workers' slogans echoed those of the 1968 students, demanding not only an improvement in living condition but also greater civil rights. Violence ensued, as the Polish Army dispersed the demonstrations using bullets and tanks. In adjacent Gdynia, the army killed at least forty-four workers, and in Szczecin, near the German border, about sixteen. The protests brought dramatic change. The excessive violence sealed Gomułka's fate: within a couple of weeks, the Politburo dismissed him from the post of first secretary and from the Politburo. After almost fifteen years in power, Gomułka enjoyed little support from Brezhnev, who showed him the door. With him left Prime Minister Cyrankiewicz and the former minister of internal affairs, Moczar. Not long after the events of 1968, the "partisan" faction and Gomułka's allies lost much of their power and influence. A workers' uprising had ended their reign, emphasizing their failure in understanding the mood of Polish society; young workers had, after all, also participated in great numbers in the March 1968 events. A different cohort of pragmatic politicians stepped onto the stage, taking Polish communism in a new direction.

The dissidents of 1968 who stayed in Poland, the "class of '68," as Timothy Garton Ash named them, continued the struggle against the regime. In 1976, Jacek Kuroń, Adam Michnik, Jan Józef Lipski, Jerzy Andrzejewski, and others established the Workers' Defense Committee (Komitet Obrony Robotników, KOR), an organization devoted to supporting striking workers, specifically those indicted for participating in workers' strikes in Warsaw and Radom that year. As Lipski put it, their aim was "to stop the intelligentsia from sleeping while the workers were being beaten."[6] The intellectuals who had once belonged to leftist circles now created a group aimed at toppling the communist regime. No longer did they pursue adjustments to the system, but instead they sought its replacement through a partnership between the worker leadership and the dissidents. It the 1970s KOR established a clandestine publishing house and "flying universities," which offered an alternative education to communist-controlled academia. A few years later, KOR became the intellectual backbone of the independent trade union Solidarity (Solidarność), finally bridging the gap between intellectual and worker opposition.

In 1980, because of another episode of worker unrest and mass strikes, the regime allowed for the establishment of an alternative trade union, free from the party, and Solidarity was born. The organization explicitly acknowledged its debt to the events of March 1968: during the short time when the government permitted some free discussion, Warsaw University held the first conference on the March events. A Solidarity workers' committee at Warsaw University issued declarations on the topic, expressing regret over the 1968 events, stating that the dismissal of students and faculty had been illegal, and condemning "antisemitic and anti-Zionist" excesses and purges. Liberalization did not last long, though. In December 1981, Wojciech Jaruzelski, the recently appointed prime minister and first secretary, declared martial law, outlawing Solidarity and arresting many of its leaders. The regime detained around ten thousand men and women during martial law and killed dozens. The opposition went underground, continuing clandestine activities throughout the 1980s. The dissidents' efforts finally bore fruit in 1989, when, as a result of dramatic changes in Moscow and growing unrest in Poland, Jaruzelski agreed to negotiate on the future of Poland with the leaders of Solidarity, among them Michnik and Kuroń. The "Round Table Talks" led to the end of the communist regime in Poland. In the end, Jaruzelski, who had purged Zionists from the army in 1967–68, gave up his throne to the alumni of the "class of '68."

Once they had left Poland, the Jewish immigrants established a form of community, cultivating the memories of 1968. Every three years, a few hundred members of "Reunion '68" gather at the Dan Gardens Hotel in Ashkelon, a city in Israel, south of Tel Aviv, on the shores of the Mediterranean.

---

6. Interview with Lipski, http://www.webofstories.com/play/jj.lipski/121;jsessionid=BA23596537E 36F87ACC932D940CACF90.

The organizers of the reunions are former participants in TSKŻ summer camps, where they developed a "strong identification with their camp group, which increased their self-respect and created a special communal energy."[7] They reunited for the first time in 1989, together with families and friends from Europe, the United States, and Australia. These Polish Jews sense that they are a distinct social group who participated in and fell victim to a failed experiment to rebuild Jewish life in communist Poland. As the late scholar Joanna Wiszniewicz wrote in 2008, "that sense of identification with the community of campers has proven so meaningful that it has lasted for over thirty years and it survives in the lively social and organizational activity of the campers, now nearly sixty years old."[8]

In 2008, almost twenty years after the collapse of communism, the newspaper Adam Michnik founded with other dissidents in 1989, *Gazeta Wyborcza*, commemorated the fortieth anniversary of the student protests with dozens of articles. A website devoted to the topic was launched, featuring commentaries, recollections, photographs, and documentary films. By and large, the March 1968 events were presented as protests against communist cultural censorship. The anti-Zionist campaign and the purge of Jews received less attention, although the president of Poland, the late Lech Kaczyński, strongly condemned both in a public address. Speaking during a ceremony at Dworzec Gdański train station, the president asserted that the "antisemitic campaign" of March 1968 had hurt many Polish Jews, causing their emigration. Further, he lamented the loss of those who could have made substantial contributions to Poland. Kaczyński dubbed their departure "a loss for the entire Polish people" and called on the train station to become a place of memory so that events like those of March 1968 would not happen again.[9] The president spoke in front of a plaque unveiled in 1998 to commemorate the March events. It reads, "Dedicated to those who after March '68 left Poland with travel documents valid in one direction only: 'They left behind them more than they possessed.'"[10] A Polish Jewish activist speaking at the ceremony explained that it is a memorial of

7. Joanna Wiszniewicz, *Życie Przecięte: Opowieści Pokolenia Marca* (Wołowiec: Wydawnictwo Czarne, 2008), 8.
8. Joanna Wiszniewicz, *Życie Przecięte: Opowieści Pokolenia Marca*, 8.
9. "Prezydent RP wziął udział w uroczystościach z okazji 40. rocznicy wydarzeń Marca '68" in the official website of the Polish president, https://www.prezydent.pl/archiwum-lecha-kaczynskiego/aktualnosci/rok-2008/art,148,60,prezydent-rp-wzial-udzial-w-uroczystosciach-z-okazji-40-rocznicy-wydarzen-marca-68.html.
10. The monument cites the author Henryk Grynberg.

"pain, the unhealed pain of separation."[11] Addressing the crowd in another ceremony at Warsaw University, Kaczyński once more stressed the anti-semitic aspect of the March events, not only the repression of intellectual opposition, pointing out that the persecution of citizens of Jewish descent and their forced emigration was a tragic part of 1968.

Ten years later, in 2018, with the other Kaczyński twin, Jarosław, at the helm of the country (though not as president but as the chief of the ruling party), the March 1968 commemoration looked and sounded very different. Gone were the self-congratulation of dissidents and their sense of pride in Polish liberal democracy. These were replaced with anger and fear, fear that Poland was once more turning away from democracy and toward xenopho-bia and antisemitism. The Polish president, Andrzej Duda, apologized for the March events, but this time few listened to his words; the rally at Warsaw University quickly turned into an antigovernment protest. The anniversary had come at a time when the government was busy taking over the supreme court and battling free speech. *Polin*, the museum for Polish Jewish history, launched an exhibition and a series of events on March 1968, including plays, films, and performance art, which drew over a hundred thousand visitors. Entitled *Obcy w Domu* (Strangers at home), the exhibit showcased the mag-nitude of the hate campaign in 1967–68, forgotten by many Poles, as well as the voices of those forced to leave in March 1968. When it opened, certain politicians condemned it, claiming that it left out some of the "context" of Polish history and that it constituted a statement on contemporary political debates.[12] The director of *Polin* paid the price: Dariusz Stola, who had also written an important monograph on the anti-Zionist campaign, lost his job at the museum the following year. Visiting the exhibit thus became a form of protest, as it exposed the discursive similarities between national com-munists (the partisans) and contemporary right-wing Polish politicians. The obsession with Poland's good name, the conspiracy theories, the denial of anti-Jewish sentiments, and the centrality of the image of Poles as saviors—all rang familiar to Poles of all ages, including those unfamiliar with the story of 1968. Sadly, this is the legacy of March 1968: not a diverse and demo-cratic society, but an oppressive and exclusionary nation-state, then and now.

11. "Marzec '68: Z Dworca Gdańskiego z biletem w jedną stronę," 03.08.2008, https://www.rmf24.pl/fakty/polska/news-marzec-68-z-dworca-gdanskiego-z-biletem-w-jedna-strone,nId,208120#crp_state=1.
12. "Politycy atakują muzeum Żydów. Spór o wystawę 'Obcy w domu. Wokół Marca '68' Tomasz Urzykowski," *Wyborcza*, March 17, 2018, http://warszawa.wyborcza.pl/warszawa/7,54420,23153019,politycy-atakuja-muzeum-zydow-spor-o-wystawe-obcy-w-domu.html.

INDEX

Adam Mickiewicz University, 84
Adenauer, Konrad, 74
Ahmed, Sara, 5, 198
Aleichem, Sholem, 25
American Historical Review, 18
American Joint Distribution Committee (JDC), 33, 35, 42–43, 57, 63, 116
Anczyc, Władysław Ludwik, 179
Andrzejewski, Jerzy, 115, 135
Anielewicz, Mordechai, 67. See also Warsaw Ghetto Uprising
antisemitism, 11, 19, 31–32, 34, 73, 80, 130–131, 178–179, 185; and anti-Zionist campaign, 13–14, 120, 133, 136–137, 149, 160–161; and Communist Party, 22, 38, 178, 180; and Egzamin, 88; and international politics, 167; and June 1967 War, 50–51, 113, 133; and language, 117; and Marxism, 20; political, 20, 38, 202; popular, 182; and present-day Poland, 203, 207; and Simon Wiesenthal, 86; and Stalinism, 10, 181; and violence, 19–20, 30–32; and Władysław Gomułka, 61, 187; and World War II, 164
Armia Krajowa (AK, or Home Army), 69–71, 73, 75, 103, 107, 112, 180
Armia Ludowa (AL), 21, 69, 174
Ash, Timothy Garton, 204
Auschwitz, 41, 65, 71–72, 77, 86, 116, 165–166, 186, 197. See also Auschwitz museum; concentration camps; International Auschwitz Committee
Auschwitz museum, 165–166

Babel, Isaac, 49
Baczko, Bolesław, 132, 162, 191
Balicki, Stanisław Witold, 114
Barmor, Jacob, 30
Bauman, Janina, 17, 54, 107
Bauman, Zygmunt, 54, 94, 107, 132, 162–163, 176; and departure from Poland, 11, 17, 191

Bazyłow, Ludwik, 128, 130
Belzec, 71
Ben-Gurion, David, 47, 74, 81
Berman, Adolf, 23
Berman, Jakub, 23, 27, 39, 178
Białystok, 70, 135, 170, 179
Bierut, Bolesław, 23, 27, 69
Bikont, Anna, 100
Birenbaum, Halina, 70
Birkenau (Brzezinka), 65, 68, 77, 165
Blumsztajn, Seweryn, 99, 110, 120–121, 123, 189–190
Bocheński, Jacek, 113
Bogucka, Teresa, 120–121, 180, 189
Bourke, Joanna, 202–203
Brezhnev, Leonid, 187, 189, 201, 204
Britain, 69, 103, 149, 191
Bromberg, Adam, 76
Brus, Włodzimierz, 107, 147, 163, 176
Brzezinski, Zbigniew, 27
Budapest, 95. See also Hungary
Bundism, 23–24, 81
Bureau of Censorship, 88–89
Burg, Yosef, 165
Bydgoszcz, 184

Catholic Church, 53, 67, 158
Catholicism, 8, 62, 90, 95–96, 127, 131, 185, 187; and Jewish assimilation to, 9; and Jews, 135, 148; and "Polonization" of Communist Party, 39. See also PAX; Znak
Catholic Intelligentsia Club (Klub Inteligencji Katolickiej), 98
Catholic University, 129
censorship, 17, 83, 88, 94, 97–98, 116, 141, 168, 206; and Censorship Department, 178, 183; and Censorship Department for Film, Television, and Theater, 179; and Department of Press and Radio, 87; and Dziady, 109–115, 123, 130

Central Committee. *See* Polish Central
Committee
Central Committee of Jews in Poland
(Centralny Komitet Żydów w Polsce, or
CKŻP), 22–24
Central Control Committee (Centralna
Komisja Kontroli Partyjnej), 101
Citizens' Militia Reserves (Ochotnicza
Rezerwa Milicji Obywatelskiej, ORMO),
122, 124–131, 134, 137, 142–145, 148–150, 154,
157–158
Cold War, 36, 41, 183, 198, 202
collaboration, 1–2, 5, 67, 91, 164–165, 203–204
collectivization, 24
Central Commission for the Investigation of
Hitlerite Crimes in Poland, 65, 72, 78–80,
84, 91, 165–166
Central Jewish Commission for Social Assistance, 191
Commission for the Protection of Sites of
Suffering and Martyrdom (CPSSM), 70, 80
communism, 24, 32, 45, 94, 104, 125–126,
155–156, 199; in Eastern Europe, 5, 202;
and "enemies of," 101; end of, 196, 206;
and ethnonationalism, 38, 40; and Home
Army, 21; and Jews, 7, 15–16, 19–20, 30, 92,
116, 182, 185, 195, 200; language of, 148;
national, 4, 31, 34, 37, 39, 42, 168, 202, 204;
opposition to, 10, 12, 115, 180; reform of,
3, 10, 28, 43, 107; and Stalinism, 179; and
Władysław Gomułka, 178, 186; and World
Zionist Organization (WZO), 45. *See also*
Żydokomuna (Judeo-communism)
Communist Party of Poland (KPP), 19–20,
103, 186
concentration camps, 3, 21, 68, 89, 146, 180,
186; and *Wielka Encyklopedia Powszechna*
(The great general encyclopedia), 16, 65,
71, 76, 78–80, 82, 84, 163–164, 166. *See
also* Birkenau (Brzezinka); Auschwitz
(Oświęcim); Gusen; Holocaust; Mauthau-
sen; Stutthof
Confino, Alon, 67
Connelly, John, 91, 99, 202
Crimea, 25, 43
Crooked Circle Club (Klub Krzywego
Koła), 98

Cyrankiewicz, Józef, 29, 98, 131, 204
Czechoslovakia, 15, 41, 158; Communist
Party of, 104, 124, 184–185; and Jews, 7,
184, 201; and reform, 17, 94, 123, 150; and
students, 17, 128–129, 150; Warsaw Pact
invasion of, 9, 95. *See also* Prague Spring
Czytelnik, 56, 116

Dajczgewand, Józef, 108, 120, 128, 134, 136,
189–190
Dayan, Moshe, 53, 81, 136, 147, 177
Dejmek, Kazimierz, 109, 111–112, 114, 130, 153.
See also Dziady
de-Stalinization, 32, 69, 90, 124, 178
Diner, Dan, 91
dissidents, 10–12, 105, 116, 204–207
Dmowski, Roman, 93
Dobrowolski, Stanisław Ryszard, 114
Documentary Film Studio, 56
Domb, Leopold, 51–52, 60, 138, 152, 192–193
Dubček, Alexander, 17, 123, 158, 199
Duda, Andrzej, 207
Duszeńko, Franciszek, 71
Dziady, 94, 108–114, 117, 119–120, 123, 127,
129–130, 153

East Germany, 31, 78
Eastern bloc, 37–38. *See also* Soviet bloc
Eastern Europe, 5, 7, 9–11, 43, 99, 198, 202
Egypt, 40–41, 172–173, 184
Eichmann trial, 73–74
Eisenbach, Arthur, 137, 167
Eisler, Jerzy, 12
Endecja. See National Democratic Party
ethnonationalism, 4, 18, 38, 40, 57, 63
Etler, Edward, 89
European Union, 91

Faliński, Zbigniew, 180
fascism, 14, 80, 125, 134, 139, 156; before
World War II, 138, 185; and narrative of
World War II, 66; and People's Republic
of Poland, 167
Federal Republic of Germany (FRG), 64, 79,
90, 93, 136, 175, 203; and German minority
in Poland, 31; and the Holocaust, 66, 164;
and Israel, 44, 46–47, 74, 117–118, 134, 164,

203; and *Wielka Encyklopedia Powszechna* (The great general encyclopedia), 166; and Zionism, 43, 46, 184
Fidelis, Malgorzata, 32, 95
film, 89–90
Fischer, Artur, 170
Fiternik, Wiktor, 170
Folks Sztyme, 25, 50, 52, 63, 87, 191–193; editor of, 53, 127; and June 1967 War, 56–57, 60, 138
Friedlander, David, 81

Gdańsk, 65, 141–142, 144–145, 150, 162, 168, 204
Gdynia, 144, 204
genocide, 72, 74, 82, 88, 194, 197, 199
Germany. *See* East Germany; Federal Republic of Germany (FRG); Nazi Germany
ghettos, 51, 68, 70–71. *See also* Warsaw Ghetto Uprising
Gierek, Edward, 147–148, 150, 176
Gliwice, 185
Goldkorn, Józef, 192
Goldmann, Nahum, 44, 47
Gomułka, Władysław, 4, 35, 47–49, 101, 122, 137, 147–148, 175–178, 181–188, 198–201; and campaign against Polish Jews, 16–17, 38–39, 57–62, 65, 76, 120, 160–161, 182, 195; and Edward Ochab, 29, 174; and emigration policies, 33; end of reign of, 204; and Germany, 54–55, 134; and the Holocaust, 3, 58; and intellectuals, 17, 106, 108, 115, 153–156; and June 1967 War, 54, 61, 95, 154; and Marian Naszkowski, 171–172; as Minister of the Recovered Territories, 21, 29–30; and nationalism, 8, 23, 26–27, 40, 69, 159; opposition to, 16, 94–95, 100, 106, 119, 124, 136, 151–152, 155–156; and "Polish path to socialism," 19, 69, 94; and Polish United Workers Party (PUWP), 36; and Puławians, 28; purge of, 10, 23; and reform, 95–96, 98, 123, 155; and Soviet Union, 21, 26–27, 33, 95, 97, 109; speech by, 16, 58, 75, 77, 191; and Stalin, 23–24; and TSKŻ, 51, 60–61, 191, 193; and *Wielka Encyklopedia Powszechna* (The great general encyclopedia), 77, 83; and World War II, 21; and Zionism, 8

Gontarz, Ryszard, 2, 135–136
Górecki, Jan, 152
Górecki, Wiktor, 126, 128, 189–190
Grudzińska (Gross), Irena, 11, 104, 107, 110, 113, 128, 152, 189–190
Grudziński, Jan, 152
Grynberg, Henryk, 118, 166
Gumkowski, Janusz, 65–66, 71–72, 76, 79, 82–83
Gusen, 79

Halfin, Igal, 49
Hanebrink, Paul, 6
Haupt, Adam, 71
Hen, Józef, 137
Herzl, Theodor, 149
Himka, John-Paul, 91
Hitler, Adolf, 41, 53, 146
Holocaust, 3–5, 34–35, 67, 119, 166, 185, 187, 194; and antisemitism, 137, 167; and "blame" of Poland, 46, 66, 164; and censorship, 89; commemoration of, 5, 13, 67, 71, 164; and Eichman trial, 73–74; and Israel, 117, 165; and June 1967 War, 41; memory of, 203; narratives of, 73–75, 79, 85–87, 90–92, 164–165; and rescue, 3, 74–75, 91, 182; and Soviet Union, 68; survivors, 41, 70, 186; and Władysław Gomułka, 58
Home Army (AK). *See* Armia Krajowa
Hübner, Zygmunt, 110
Hungary, 33, 97, 104, 184, 197, 201. *See also* Budapest

industrialization, 24
intelligentsia/intellectuals, 18, 54, 100, 103, 113, 180–181, 189; academic, 99, 102, 106, 162, 181; and anti-Zionist campaign, 10, 13, 200; and censorship, 17, 97; in Czechoslovakia, 94; and emigration, 160; and Israel, 52; and Jerzy Eisler, 12; Jewish, 26, 55–56, 94, 109–110; and June 1967 War, 63; leftist, 15, 17, 106, 205; and reform movement, 9, 92, 94–99, 135; and Solidarity, 205; and Soviet Union, 15, 21, 25, 27, 56, 116; and students, 120, 131, 151; and Tadeusz Walichnowski , 107; traditional, 110; in Warsaw, 105, 108–110, 114, 116, 135; and

Władysław Gomułka, 17, 154, 177; and workers, 129, 140, 155, 205; and World War II, 76

International Auschwitz Committee, 86, 165. *See also* Auschwitz

International Women's Day, 121, 125

Israel, 2, 44–46, 47–57, 60, 62–63, 163, 166, 181; and antisemitism, 136; and anti-Zionist campaign, 16, 42, 58–69, 77, 132, 147, 149, 169–170, 173, 198–199; and citizenship, 3, 39; and de-Stalinization, 178; and Eichmann trial, 74; establishment of, 7, 10; and immigration from Poland, 23, 29–30, 32–33, 39–40, 70, 116, 149, 170, 191–193, 195, 205; and Federal Republic of Germany (FRG), 47, 74, 79, 107–108, 117–118, 134–135, 164–165, 201; and JDC, 33; and June 1967 War, 4, 36, 40–42, 47–51, 56–57, 61, 64, 107–108, 120, 122, 128, 154; and Israel Defense Forces, 22, 49; and Ministry of Foreign Affairs, 33, 45; Mossad, 73; in Polish press, 36, 41, 117–118; and reparations, 47, 201; and show trials, 7, 201; and TSKŻ, 8, 46, 51, 56, 60–61, 138, 192; and Władysław Gomułka, 75, 187

Jankowski, Witold, 134

Jaruzelski, Wojciech, 175, 183, 205

Jasienica, Paweł, 120, 123, 135–136, 148, 154, 189; and *Dziady*, 115, 153; and Polish Writers' Union, 113, 153, 163; as vice president of PEN (Poets, Essayists, and Novelists) Club, 111

Jedlicki, Jerzy, 106

Jędrychowski, Stefan, 175–176

Jewish Antifascist Committee (JAC), 25, 43

Jewish Cultural Society (Żydowskie Towarzystwo Kultury w Polsce, or ŻTK), 24–25

Jewish Historical Association, 193

Jewish Historical Institute, 46, 72, 137, 166

Jewish Society for the Encouragement of Fine Arts, 68

Jews; and Adam Michnik, 94, 134; Antoni Słonimski, 116, 154; and communism, 19–20, 22, 25, 108, 116, 182, 196, 200; and emigration, 19, 22, 24, 33, 45, 197, 200–201, 206–207; and Holocaust, 3, 34–35, 41, 67, 70, 73–74, 90–91, 137, 185, 187, 197; and Jewish Antifascist Committee (JAC), 43; and Ministry of Internal Affairs, 42, 47–48, 53, 56, 171, 194, 199–200; and Mieczysław Moczar, 16, 38–39, 75, 195; and purges, 4, 26, 38, 62–63, 122, 152, 156, 168, 177, 188, 194, 199–200, 206; and Security Services, 6, 8, 48, 131–132, 136–137, 199; and Soviet Union, 15, 25, 28, 39, 56, 59, 106, 116; and Stalinism, 25–26, 28, 30, 43, 52–53, 59, 68, 134, 177–181; terminology, 8–9; in the United States, 25, 73, 149; and Władysław Gomułka, 16–17, 38–39, 57–62, 65, 76, 120, 160–161, 182, 195; and World War II, 6, 9, 76–77, 85, 106, 110, 138, 193; and *Żydokomuna* (Judeo-communism). *See also* antisemitism; concentration camps; *Folks Sztyme*; Israel; Jewish Cultural Society (Żydowskie Towarzystwo Kultury w Polsce, or ŻTK); Jewish Historical Association; Jewish Historical Institute; June 1967 War; Polin, Museum of the History of Polish Jews; TSKŻ (Towarzystwo Społeczno-Kulturalne Żydów w Polsce); Yiddish; Zionism

Jordan, 40

June 1967 War, 4, 39–41, 106–108, 116, 120, 133, 138, 197–198; and Ministry of Internal Affairs, 38, 42, 44, 47–49, 56, 187; outbreak of, 36, 40; and Warsaw Pact, 52; and Władysław Gomułka, 54, 95, 154

Kaczyński, Jarosław, 207

Kaczyński, Lech, 206–207

Kajzer, Abram, 70

Kąkol, Kazimierz, 74

Kaminska, Ida, 119, 193

Kamiski, A. J., 89

Kasman, Leon, 103–104

Karst, Roman, 137

Katowice, 147–148, 150, 152, 176

Katyn Massacre, 73

Katz, Katriel, 33

Katzenelson, Yitzhak, 71

Kępa, Józef, 127, 136–137, 147

Khrushchev, Nikita, 26–29, 69, 93–95, 97

Kichelewski, Audrey, 35

Kielce, 170
Kijowski, Andrzej, 113–114, 116, 135, 163
Kisielewski, Stefan, 115, 135–136, 148, 154, 163, 189
Klafkowski, Alfons, 84–85
Klimaszewski, Mieczysław, 129
Kliszko, Zenon, 101, 109, 176–177
Kmitowski, Władysław, 181–182
Kołakowski, Leszek, 105, 113, 115, 132, 135, 147, 162–163, 191; and expulsion from party, 101–102, 106; and Marxism, 94; and reform, 97–98, 106
Kole, Ryszarad, 105
Kończewicz , Colonel S., 78
Konrad, Gustaw, 109
Konwicki, Tadeusz, 120
Korman, Jozef, 87
Kosinski, Jerzy, 46
Kotarbinski, Janina, 106
Kotarbinski, Tadeusz, 106
Kraków, 89, 129, 142, 145–146, 150–151, 168, 170, 194; Academy of Fine Arts, 56; and Jagiellonian University, 56, 122, 129, 143; students, 143, 151, 156; TSKŻ club, 56
Kraśko, Wincenty, 112, 114
Krasnowiecki, Władysław, 112
Książka i Wiedza, 56
Kuroń, Jacek, 102, 106, 121 123, 153, 189, 204–205; and Adam Michnik, 120, 204–205; and *Dziady*, 110; and Leszek Kołakowski, 101; open letter by, 99–100, 128; and prison sentence, 100, 108, 126, 190–191; and socialism, 97, 99–100; and Warsaw University, 100; and ZMS (the Socialist Youth Union), 99. *See also* Karol Modzelewski
Kuryluk, Ewa, 81
Kuryluk, Karol, 76, 80–81

Langer, Stanisława, 186
Langer, Tadeusz, 186
Łastik, Salomon, 54
Lasota, Irena, 121, 126–127, 129, 190
Latvia, 1
Law and Justice. *See* PiS, Prawo i Sprawiedliwość
Lederman, Ernest, 137

Lendvai, Paul, 11
Lendwoń, Józef, 185
Lipski, Jan Józef, 100, 189, 204–205
Lithuania, 1
Lityński, Jan, 110, 121, 123, 126, 170, 189–190
Łódź, 139, 156–157, 162, 169–170, 180–182, 184, 194; ghetto, 70; Film School, 141, 168, University of, 122
Loga-Sowiński, Ignacy, 176
Łubieński, Konstanty, 131
Lublin, 71, 129, 179

Maciejewski, Henryk, 180
Majdanek, 65, 71
Majewska, Barbara, 113
Majewski, Janusz, 89
Malski, Wiktor, 180
Manteuffel, Tadeusz, 167–168
Mark, Bernard, 72
Markowa, 1
Marszałek, Leon, 76, 80, 82–83
Marxism-Leninism, 28, 34, 93–94, 102
Mauthausen, 79, 85
Mazowiecki, Tadeusz, 131
Meibaum, Wacław, 170
Melman, Michał, 119
Mendelssohn, Moses, 81
Michnik, Adam, 11, 99–101, 119–121, 126, 161, 175, 204, 206; as a "commando" of protests, 189–190; and *Dziady*, 110–111, 119; and Jews, 94, 134; and prison sentence, 190; and revisionism, 96–97; and Solidarity, 205; supporters of, 105–108, 120, 124, 133, 135, 154; and TSKŻ, 152; and Warsaw University, 104, 111, 120, 122, 137, 161, 167. *See also* Szlajfer, Henryk
Mickiewicz, Adam, 113–115, 148; and *Dziady*, 94, 108–109, 111, 113–115, 157; monuments, 11, 129, 141, 143, 145; as national poet, 108; and nationalism, 110; and Władysław Gomułka, 153
Międzyrzecki, Artur, 113
Miłosz, Czesław, 115
Ministry of Internal Affairs, 31, 44, 100, 107, 116–117, 160–164, 168–169, 176–177; and antisemitism, 133, 167; and definitions of "Jew," 8; "ethnic turn" of, 62; and Federal

Republic of Germany (FRG), 46; and historians' views of, 12–13; and JDC, 43; and Jews, 42, 47–48, 53, 56, 171, 194, 199–200; and June 1967 War, 38, 42, 44, 47, 52; and Mieczysław Moczar, 38, 77, 79, 106, 134, 184, 195, 201, 204; and nationalization of communism, 42, 34, 64; and protests, 98l 104, 127, 129, 145, 189; and TSKŻ, 48, 51, 56, 60–61, 63, 139; and Władysław Gomułka, 49, 57, 59–60, 96, 119, 171, 195; and the *Wielka Encyklopedia Powszechna* (The great general encyclopedia), 16

Moczar, Mieczysław, 79, 81, 93, 106, 142, 158, 171, 175–176; and Jews, 16, 38–39, 75, 195; and nationalism, 42, 159; removal of, 188, 201; and socialism, 42; and TSKŻ, 60; and *Wielka Encyklopedia Powszechna* (The great general encyclopedia), 77; and Władysław Gomułka, 184–185, 187, 195, 204

Modzelewski, Karol, 106, 120–121, 123, 126, 189–191; and *Dziady*, 110; and Leszek Kołakowski, 101; open letter by, 99–100, 128; and prison sentence, 100, 108; and socialism, 97, 99; and Warsaw University, 99–100, 102; and ZMS (the Socialist Youth Union), 99. *See also* Jacek Kuroń

Molotov-Ribbentrop Pact, 20, 73

Morawiecki, Mateusz, 1–3

Morawski, Jerzy, 119

Morawski, Stefan, 132, 162–163, 177

Moscow, 21, 32–33, 109, 132, 153, 201, 205; and Bolesław Bierut, 23, 69; and emigration to Israel, 52; and Great Purge, 20; and Twentieth Congress of the Communist Party, 27; and Władysław Gomułka, 21, 29, 69, 97, 187. *See also* Russia; Soviet Union

Motyka, Lucjan, 109, 112

museums. *See* Auschwitz Museum; Polin, Museum of the History of Polish Jews; Ulma Family Museum of Poles Saving Jews in World War II

Muszkat, Józef, 166

Mysłowice, 194

Nagorski, Wiktor, 126

Nasser, Gamal Abdel, 41, 51, 53, 172–173

Naszkowski, Marian, 171–173, 176

national communism, 4, 16, 31, 39, 42, 168, 202, 204

National Democratic Party (*Endecja*), 38, 93

Natolin group, 27

Nazi Germany, 46–47, 54–55, 76, 86, 89; and occupation of Poland, 1, 21, 42, 60, 70, 82, 88, 90–91, 153, 166, 204; and Operation Reinhard, 65

Netanyahu, Benjamin, 2

Neumark, Andrzej, 161

Nomberg-Przytyk, Sara, 70

Nuremberg trials, 84

O'Bretenny, Zofia, 111

Obóz Narodowo-Radykalny (ONR), 138–139

Obóz Zjednoczenia Narodowego (OZN), 138

Obozy Koncentracyjne Hitlerowskie, 84–85

Ochab, Edward, 27–29, 132, 172–175

Olszewski, Stephan, 184

Opole, 170

Organization for Rehabilitation through Training (ORT), 35, 193

Osęka, Piotr, 13

Ostoja, Adam, 70

Oświęcim, 65, 68, 155

Ottoman Empire, 197

Państwowe Wydawnictwo Naukowe (PWN, National Scientific Publishers), 76, 81, 83

Parandowski, Jan, 112

PAX, 84, 112, 134, 184–185

PEN (Poets, Essayists, and Novelists) Club, 111–112, 137

People's Republic of Poland, 57, 68, 94, 98, 100, 111, 114, 156; and antisemitism, 167; and Jews, 180, 201

Peretz, Y. L., 25

Piętek, Henryk, 60

Piasecki, Bolesław, 134, 139

Piątowski, Józef, 168

Pilichowski, Czesław, 78–79, 165–166

Piłsudski, Józef, 103, 168

PiS, Prawo i Sprawiedliwość (Law and Justice), 2

Piwnica, Bolesław, 162

pogrom, 20, 31, 137–138. *See also* antisemitism

Poland, army of, 23, 28, 31, 135, 175, 186, 204–205; anticommunism in, 5, 2–21, 116, 135, 183; and collaboration, 1–2, 5, 67, 91, 164, 204;Committee for Public Security, 26, 96; Constitution of, 130, 142, 158; and de-Stalinization, 32, 69, 90, 124, 178; and emigration of Jews from, 3, 19, 22, 24, 33, 45, 59, 166, 171, 197, 200, 201, 206–207; and expulsion of Germans from, 21, 23, 29–30, 50, 64; and expulsion of Ukrainians from, 21, 23; and government-in-exile, 21, 69–70; and Ministry for Arts and Culture, 62, 79, 85, 112, 114, 161, 164; and Ministry for Chemical Industry, 62; and Ministry of Foreign Affairs, 45, 56, 81, 142, 171–173; and Ministry of Health, 56, 105, 175; and Ministry of the Interior, 16, 66, 75–76, 78–79; and Ministry of Justice, 78, 83–84, 105; and Ministry of Public Security, 26, 96, 180; Politburo of, 27, 171–178, 182, 186–188, 204; pre-partition, 109, 140; and Recovered Territories, 21, 30; and State Publishing House, 49, 164, 166. *See also* Ministry of Internal Affairs; People's Republic of Poland; Security Services
Polin, Museum of the History of Polish Jews, 18, 207
Polish Central Committee, 48, 103, 109, 132, 139, 174; Academic Department, 99; building, 126; Educational Department, 104; groups/debates within, 27, 104; and Stalinism, 26, 97, 103; and Władysław Gomułka, 29, 95, 101, 124, 184
Polish Communist Youth Union, 105
Polish National Theater, 108, 111
Polish News Agency (PAP), 50, 56
Polish Radio, 167
Polish-Soviet War, 20
Polish United Workers' Party (Polska Zjednoczona Partia Robotnicza, or PUWP), 11, 27, 156, 189, 195; and antisemitism, 18; Department of Education, 80; Fifth Congress, 82; and hard-liners of, 79; history of, 23; and nationalization of communism, 31; and protests, 4; and *Wielka Encyklopedia Powszechna* (The great general encyclopedia), 65–66, 78; and Władysław Gomułka, 36

Polish Writers' Union, 111, 113–117, 123, 135, 153, 163
Polska Kasa Opieki (PeKaO), 53
Polska Partia Socjalistyczna (PPS, Polish Socialist Party), 104
Pomerania, 29
Pomian, Krzystof, 132
Porter-Szűcs, Brian, 3
Poznań, 28, 84, 141, 143, 145–146
Poznański, Jakub, 70
Prague, 7, 9, 95, 140, 150, 201
Prague Spring, 9, 95
propaganda, 11–14, 43–46, 103–104, 109, 136, 200; and antisemitism, 115, 178–179; anti-Jewish, 117; anti-Zionist, 14, 74, 175, 177; campaign, 122, 145, 189; department, 180, 184; and Federal Republic of Germany (FRG), 79, 135; and June 1967 War, 36; Nazi, 7; and rescue, 2; Soviet, 25; and Władysław Gomułka, 55
The Protocols of the Elders of Zion, 182. *See also* antisemitism
Przetakiewicz, Zygmunt, 184–185
purges, 13, 90, 107, 158, 160–162, 168–171, 174, 205; and Adam Michnik, 104; of army, 175, 186; anti-Zionist, 17, 173, 177, 191, 195; and Jews, 4, 26, 38, 62–63, 122, 152, 156, 168, 177, 188, 194, 199–200, 206; of PWN, 83; of Radio and Television Committee, 170; and Stalinism, 20, 170; of State Publishing House, 164, 166; and Władysław Gomułka, 4, 23, 76, 156
Putrament, Jerzy, 93, 103, 114–115, 183

radio, 3, 29, 103, 117, 147, 162, 167, 170–171; and censorship, 97; and Department of Press and Radio, 87; and speech by Władysław Gomułka, 59. *See also* Radio Free Europe
Radio Free Europe, 26, 52, 98, 103, 118, 141
Rakowski, Mieczysław, 49, 103
Rapacki, Adam, 142, 171
reparations, 47, 74, 117
Righteous among the Nations, 2. *See also* Holocaust
RNR-Falanga, 184
Rokossovsky, Konstantin, 23
Romania, 33, 41, 197

Różewicz, Tadeusz, 90
Runge, Jerzy, 170
Rusinek, Kazimierz, 79–83, 85–86, 164
Russia, 3, 20, 29, 40, 125; and Adam Mick-
  iewicz, 157; and *Dziady*, 108–109, 121; and
  Jewish intellectuals, 116; and October
  Revolution, 20; and World War I, 93, 197.
  See also Soviet Union
Rutkiewicz, Jan Wojciech, 105
Rutkowski, Adam, 71, 137
Rybicki, Marcin, 105
Rybicki, Zygmunt, 124
Rzeszów, 147

Satat, Dov, 41, 54
schools, 94–95, 129, 133, 140, 145, 170, 185, 193;
  and anti-Jewish violence, 30; and high
  school students, 135, 144, 150, 155; and
  the Holocaust, 66, 73; Jewish, 9, 25, 139,
  191; and Łódź Film School, 141, 168; and
  Organization for Rehabilitation through
  Training (ORT), 35, 191; and TSKŻ, 60
Security Services (Urząd Bezpieczeństwa),
  121, 127, 135, 145, 157, 162–163, 166–169;
  and Adolf Berman, 23; and antisemitism,
  118, 120; and "commandos," 120; and
  defections from, 26; and *Dziady*, 117, 119,
  123; and Jews, 6, 8, 48, 131–132, 136–137,
  199; and June 1967 War, 107, 133, 197; and
  open letter by Kuroń and Modzelewski,
  99–100; and Polish Writers' Union, 111,
  113, 123; and students, 99, 119–120, 124–125,
  130, 136, 141–142, 144, 150; and TSKŻ, 51;
  and Władysław Gomułka, 96; and World
  Zionist Organization (WZO), 44
Sejm (Polish Parliament), 95, 102, 111, 131,
  139–140, 158
Sfard, David, 11, 17, 25, 51–54, 60–61, 118, 192
Sfard, Leon, 157–158, 192
Sfard, Regina, 17
Sforim, Mendele Mojcher, 25
show trials, 7, 43, 185, 201
Sidor, Kazimierz, 172–173
Sierakowiak, Dawid, 70
Silber, Marcos, 33, 39
Silesia, 29–31, 141, 147
Slánský, Rudolf, 185, 201

Śląsk, 56, 147
Slezkine, Yuri, 15, 116
Słonimski, Antoni, 106, 113, 115, 120, 135, 148,
  163; and *Dziady*, 112; and Jews, 116, 154
Słupecki, Tadeusz, 88
Smolar, Aleksander, 121, 127–128, 132, 152,
  189, 192
Smolar, Hirsch, 53, 127, 152, 192
Snyder, Timothy, 10
Social Cultural Association of Jews in Po-
  land (Towarzystwo Społeczno-Kulturalne
  Żydów w Polsce). *See* TSKŻ
Solidarity (Solidarność), 5, 121, 150, 205
Soviet bloc, 10, 24, 26, 33, 93, 121, 187, 198
Soviet Communist Party, 26–27, 29, 39, 44
Soviet Union, 15, 19–30, 50, 93, 109, 148–149,
  187; Army of, 7, 153; and "doctors' plot," 7;
  and the Holocaust, 68, 73; and Hungary,
  95, 97, 184, 201; and Israel, 47, 49, 53; and
  Jewish Antifascist Committee (JAC), 43;
  and Jewish immigration policies, 33, 59,
  189, 201; and Jews, 15, 25, 28, 39, 56, 59,
  106, 116; and Józef Piłsudski, 168; and
  June 1967 War, 36, 40–41, 47, 49, 52–53,
  95, 122, 198; and Nikita Khrushchev, 69;
  and NKVD (People's Commissariat of
  Internal Affairs), 43; and Polish Jews
  during World War II, 21–22, 30, 32, 180;
  and Polish Ministry of Internal Affairs,
  42, 53; press, 47, 56–57; and relations
  with Poland, 19, 153, 156, 199; satellites
  states of, 26, 121; Security Services of, 43;
  and Stalinism, 68; and *Wielka Encyklopedia Powszechna* (The great general
  encyclopedia), 73, 78; and Władysław
  Gomułka, 54, 58; and women, 32, 96;
  and *Żydokomuna* (Judeo-communism),
  7. *See also* Soviet bloc; Stalin; Stalinism;
  Warsaw Pact
Spanish Civil War, 177
Spychalski, Marian, 174
Śródborów, 193
Stalin, Josef, 25, 27, 96, 103; and antisemitism, 10; death of, 7, 26, 69; and denunciation by Khrushchev, 93; and Poland, 20;
  purges, 20; and Władysław Gomułka,
  23–24

Stalinism, 8–9, 29, 37, 97, 100, 136, 140, 173–174; and antisemitism, 10, 167; and cosmopolitans, 155; crimes of, 7, 27–28, 39, 200; and *Dziady*, 109; establishment of in Poland, 23; as Jewish, 177, 181; and Jews, 25–26, 28, 30, 43, 52–53, 59, 68, 134, 177–181; and Marxism, 94; in Poland, 31–34, 51, 59, 68, 97, 100, 104–105, 125–126; and Polish Writers' Union, 115; and Puławian reformist faction, 28; and purges, 170; and Roman Werfel, 132; and Roman Zambrowski, 56, 132; and socialist realism, 96; and terror, 26; and Władysław Gomułka, 95, 106, 153. *See also* de-Stalinization

Staszewski, Stefan, 53, 77, 163

Staszewski, Stanisław, 148

State Yiddish Theater Troupe, 118

Stola, Dariusz, 12, 31, 207

Stomma, Stanisław, 131

Stutthof, 65, 82, 85. *See also* concentration camps

Suez crisis, 184

Suzin, L. M., 68

Swiatło, Józef, 26, 178

Świtała, Kazimierz, 62–63, 79, 187

Syria, 40, 54

Szadaj, Jakub, 162

Szczecin, 41, 144–145, 204

Szechter, Ozjasz, 110

Szlajfer, Henryk, 108, 119–124, 126, 133–134, 136–137, 154, 161, 189–190; and Warsaw University, 111, 122, 124, 133, 137. *See also* Adam Michnik

Sznek, Zygfryd, 51

Sztachelski, Jerzy, 104, 175

Szyr, Eugeniusz, 177

Szyr, Joanna, 104

TASS (Telegraph Agency of the Soviet Union), 56

Tenenbaum, Natan, 50, 137

Tenenblat Samuel, 192

Titkow, Walenty, 175

Toeplitz, Jerzy, 168

Topolski, Fryderyk, 152

Toruń, 145

Toruńczyk, Barbara, 94, 105, 120, 126, 189–190

Toruńczyk, Romana, 105

Treblinka, 68, 71. *See also* concentration camps

TSKŻ (Towarzystwo Społeczno-Kulturalne Żydów w Polsce), 9, 46, 52–53, 56–57, 138–139, 151–152, 162, 166; after 1968, 201; as antinationalist, 34; and anti-Zionist campaign, 60–61, 63, 88, 191–193; budget of, 42; and charter of, 24; and Club Babel, 49–51, 128, 135–137; collapse of, 195; and David Sfard, 11, 25, 51; and foreign funding, 35; and Leon Sfard, 157; and Leopold Domb, 51, 60, 138, 152; and magazine *Nasz Głos*, 50; membership of, 34, 42; and Ministry of Internal Affairs, 48, 51, 56; and "Reunion '68," 206; and World War II, 25

Turski, Stanisław, 120

Twentieth Congress of the Communist Party of the Soviet Union, 27, 69

Ukraine/Ukranians, 1, 21, 23, 32, 64, 197

Ulma Family Museum of Poles Saving Jews in World War II, 1

Union of Polish Theater Artists, 112

United States, 44–46, 90, 105, 119, 151, 202, 206; and anti-Zionist campaign, 184, 187; Army, 85; and Israel, 41, 198–199; and June 1967 War, 198; and State Yiddish Theater, 118; and TSKŻ, 60; Uris, Leon, 46

Vienna, 86

Volksdeutsche, 135–136

Waitz, Robert, 166

Wałbrzych, 30–31

Walczak, Krystyna, 118

Walczak, Stanisław, 78, 80

Walichnowski, Tadeusz, 43–45, 47, 108, 117

Waniołka, Franciszek, 176

Warsaw, 119–120, 123, 147, 154, 162, 167–168, 194–195, 198, 205; Academy of Fine Arts, 126; and Communist Party, 48, 55, 174, 182; intellectuals, 55, 105, 108–110, 114, 116–117, 135; interwar, 30; and Israel, 30, 33, 173; and Jewish emigration, 194; and June 1967 War, 48, 52, 56; and Natolin group, 27; and Nikita Khrushchev, 27, 29; police, 53, 158;

and Polin, 18; and protests, 81, 111, 125–129, 144–145, 149, 157; and Security Services, 50; students, 49–50, 122, 134, 136–138, 141–145, 148–152, 156–157; synagogue, 53; Umschlagplatz, 68; and Władysław Gomułka, 187–188; Writers' Union, 111, 114, 116, 135, 153

Warsaw Committee (Komitet Warszawski), 101–102, 104–105, 174

Warsaw Ghetto Uprising, 67–69, 71, 138–139, 167

Warsaw Pact, 9, 29, 41, 52, 95

Warsaw Polytechnic, 122, 127–128, 139–140, 142, 157

Warsaw University, 99, 101–104, 130, 136, 147, 162; and Adam Michnik, 100, 106–107, 111, 120, 122; and Antoni Zambrowski, 133; and *Dziady*, 109, 123; and Leszek Kołakowski, 101–102, 162; Philosophy Department, 49, 131; and protests, 121–122, 124–132, 134, 145, 157–158; rector of, 120, 130; senate, 131, 142–143; and Tadeusz Walichnowski, 44

Warsaw Uprising, 21, 71

Ważyk, Adam, 120

Web, Marek, 137

Weber, Kurt, 90

Werblan, Andrzej, 99, 103–104, 188

Werfel, Katarzyna, 132, 134

Werfel, Roman, 132, 134, 177

West Germany. *See* Federal Republic of Germany (FRG)

Whol, Andrzej, 167

Wicha, Władysław, 177

Wieczorek, Paweł, 31

Wielka Encyklopedia Powszechna (The great general encyclopedia), 16, 66–67, 77–85, 87, 89–90, 113, 119, 165; entry on concentration camps, 65, 71, 78, 163, 163–164, 166

Wiernik, Bronisław, 90

Wiesenthal, Simon, 85–86

Winnicki, Bronisław, 170

women, 19, 32, 96, 105, 121

Workers' Defense Committee (Komitet Obrony Robotników, KOR), 204–205

World Jewish Congress, 35

World War I, 7, 93, 197

World War II, 7, 51, 94, 104, 109, 125, 128, 134, 156, 181; and the Central Commission for the Investigation of Hitlerite Crimes in Poland, 72; and censorship, 88–89; commemoration of, 67, 73, 75; and de-Stalinization, 69; and expulsion of Germans from Poland, 30, 64; and Federal Republic of Germany (FRG), 46; and June 1967 War, 41; and legislation, 1, 47; memorialization of, 16, 203; narratives of, 3–5, 66, 81–82, 92, 164; and Polish Jews, 6, 9, 76–77, 85, 106, 110, 138, 193; and Polish nationalism, 2; and Polish "partisans," 42; and Polish underground, 168; and Soviet Union, 7, 43, 69, 180; and veterans, 76, 91; and Warsaw Ghetto Uprising, 68; and *Wielka Encyklopedia Powszechna* (The great general encyclopedia), 65–66, 76, 81, 87, 90, 163; and Władysław Gomułka, 58, 60; and women, 105, 121; and Zionism, 166, 177; and *Żydokomuna* (Judeo-communism), 6–7, 200. *See also* concentration camps; Armia Krajowa (AK, or Home Army), Holocaust; Jewish Antifascist Committee (JAC)

World Rabbinical Assembly, 140

World Zionist Congress, 71

World Zionist Organization (WZO), 43–47

Woroszylski, Wiktor, 113

Wróblewski, 83

Wrocław, 30, 121, 143–144, 149, 151, 157, 168–170, 194; Jewish school, 139; and June 1967 War, 41–42, 54; Polytechnic, 141; TSKŻ, 56; University of, 122, 141

Wygodzki, Stanisław, 89, 116–117, 166

Wyszyński, Cardinal, 53, 95

Yalta Conference, 46, 73

Yiddish, 25, 35, 67–68, 70, 118–119, 139, 179, 192–193; and 1930s Poland, 195; and *Folks Styme*, 25, 50, 87, 138, 191; and Polish Jewry, 9; press, 26; and TSKŻ, 25, 139, 195. *See also Folks Sztyme*; State Yiddish Theater; TSKŻ

Zabłocki, Janusz, 131

Załuski, Zbigniew, 113

Zambrowski, Antoni, 56, 119, 132–134, 167, 189–190
Zambrowski, Roman, 29, 134, 148, 163, 177; and Nikita Khrushchev, 27; removal from the party, 152; and Stalinism, 56, 132; and Władysław Gomułka, 119
Zawadzki, Aleksander, 27, 29
Zawadzki, Kazimierz, 79–80, 82–83
Zawieyski, Jerzy, 131
Żegota (Rada Pomocy Żydom), 75
Zimand, Roman, 132
Zionism, 47, 116, 152, 161, 163, 170–171, 175–184, 190; and antisemitism, 145; and anti-Zionism, 9, 139, 151, 160, 183, 201; and Federal Republic of Germany (FRG), 46; and *Folks Sztyme*, 192; and Ministry of Internal Affairs, 43; as Jewish nationalism, 6–7, 34, 44, 63, 202; and Polish press, 149, 198; and show trials, 7, 201; and students, 95, 139–140, 146, 194; and Theodor Herzl, 149; and TSKŻ, 8, 34, 138; and *Wielka*

Encyklopedia Powszechna (The great general encyclopedia), 16, 66; and Władysław Gomułka, 8, 154, 182, 184, 186, 188; and "World Zionism," 42, 108, 164, 187, 197, 199–200; and Yiddish press, 26
Znak, 131, 184
ZRWM (Związek Religijny Wyznania Mojżeszowego, Religious Union of the Jewish Faith), 34–35, 53, 63
Zubrzycki, Geneviève, 66
Związek Bojowników o Wolność i Demokrację (Society of Fighters for Freedom and Democracy, or ZBoWiD), 76, 79–82, 91, 139, 146, 165, 167
Związek Młodzieży Socjalistycznej (ZMS, the Socialist Youth Union), 99, 106, 126, 145
Żydokomuna (Judeo-communism), 110, 116, 196; and anti-Zionist campaign, 15, 17, 178, 188; emergence of, 7; and fascist right, 138; resurfacing of, 200

ANAT PLOCKER (PhD, Stanford) is Adjunct Faculty specializing in Modern European History at Stockton University's program in Holocaust and Genocide Studies. Her work on 1968 Poland has appeared in edited volumes and journals.

Lightning Source UK Ltd.
Milton Keynes UK
UKHW011818070622
404079UK00001B/78